THE TRUE CHRISTIAN

J. C. Ryle

THE TRUE CHRISTIAN

BAKER BOOK HOUSE
Grand Rapids, Michigan

BAKER BOOK HOUSE

P.O. Box 2453, Grand Rapids, Michigan 49501, USA

Originally published as "The Christian Race" in 1900
Reprinted 1978

ISBN   0-8010-7688-9

Printed in Great Britain by Billing & Sons Limited,
Guildford, London and Worcester

FOREWORD

John Charles Ryle (1816–1900) hardly needs an introduction
as his best-known works have been re-issued and widely
read over the last twenty years. The fine qualities of his
writing have ensured that his books are still popular and
useful. The present volume, however, has been virtually
unknown, but it displays all the virtues of his more famous
writings. These sermons were originally published under the
title of *The Christian Race*, the subject of one of them, but the
present title of *The True Christian* gives a better summary of
the central thrust of these fine addresses.

Bishop Ryle, as he is still affectionately known even by
many who would not share his love of the Church of
England, was essentially a lover and teacher of biblical
truth. His uncompromising stand for evangelical doctrine
and scriptural holiness often made him unpopular with
those who favoured new ideas and superficial practices.
Those same virtues, however, make his *Holiness** and its
companion volume *Practical Religion* as relevant today as
ever they were, and they are equally evident in these
sermons.

Ryle is rightly noted for the marvellous simplicity of his
style and many have tried, so far in vain, to emulate his
writing. To be simple, plain and direct without being
superficial, trite and offensive is not as easy as some would
think, yet Ryle achieved this consistently and effectively,
not least in his *Expository Thoughts on the Gospels.** His
sermons, reflecting the directness of the spoken word, are

* Published by Evangelical Press

fine examples to all who would like to communicate more effectively with the man in the pew or the street.

While he called no man master, Ryle loved and honoured the Reformers, Puritans and eighteenth-century evangelical leaders whose lives, teaching and influence he commemorated in *Light from Old Times* and *The Christian Leaders of the Last Century*. These men were all zealous evangelists and Ryle followed them in this. Both in his many published tracts and in these sermons the salvation of sinners was his constant concern. His practical wisdom and scriptural discernment are never more evident than in this varied selection of his sermons.

In days when evangelical preachers are accused of being either superficial or dull, we have here a great example from one who was neither of these things. As Bishop Ryle explains and applies his texts with his customary simplicity and directness, the reader will find his conscience pricked and his soul examined. This volume is well worthy of a place alongside his other great works and we send it forth with the prayer that it may be equally useful.

The Publishers, 1978

CONTENTS

1 A BAD HEART (Jeremiah 17:9, 10)   1

2 REGENERATION (1) (John 3:3)   15

3 REGENERATION (2) (John 3:3)   28

4 REGENERATION (3) (John 3:3)   42

5 SAVING FAITH (John 3:16)   57

6 "COME UNTO ME" (Matthew 11:28)   67

7 THE LORD OUR RIGHTEOUSNESS (Jeremiah 23:17)   79

8 SELF-RIGHTEOUSNESS (Luke 18:9)   97

9 THE CHARACTER OF THE TRUE CHRISTIAN
   (John 10:27, 28)   111

10 THE PRIVILEGES OF THE TRUE CHRISTIAN
   (John 10:27, 28)   126

11 THE GRACE OF GOD IN VAIN (2 Corinthians 6:1)   139

12 THE CHRISTIAN RACE (Hebrews 12:1, 2)   154

13 "WHAT THINK YE OF CHRIST?" (Matthew 22:42)   168

14 THE UNCHANGING CHRIST (Hebrews 13:8)   179

15 THE SECOND ADVENT (THE TEN VIRGINS)
   (Matthew 25:1–13)   195

16 PROFIT AND LOSS (Mark 8:36)   219

17 ENOCH WALKING WITH GOD (Genesis 5:24)   231

18 DANIEL FOUND FAITHFUL (Daniel 6:5)   246

19 THE BLOOD OF THE LAMB (Revelation 7:14–17)   257

20 HEAVEN (Revelation 21:27)   273

21 READY TO BE OFFERED (2 Timothy 4:6–8)   286

I

A BAD HEART

"The heart is deceitful above all things, and desperately wicked : who can know it? I the Lord search the heart, I try the reins, even to give every man according to his ways, and according to the fruit of his doings."—JEREMIAH xvii. 9, 10.

THE first of these two verses contains a very strong saying, and one which the world in general is not at all disposed to believe. "The heart is deceitful above all things," says our text. "I deny it," says the unconverted man. "To be sure, my heart is very careless and very thoughtless, but it is an honest heart after all." "The heart is desperately wicked," says the text. "Nothing of the sort," replies the sinner. "I know that I neglect the means of grace very much, and perhaps I do not live as I ought to do, but I am sure I have a good heart at the bottom." "Who can know it?" asks the text. "Know it!" we are told: "why, we do not pretend to be such saints as you want men to be, but at any rate we do know our own hearts, we do know what our faults are."

And so, beloved, it appears there are two statements, and one of them must be false. The everlasting Bible is on one side, and flesh and blood on the other; God says one thing, and man says another. Now, I shall endeavour to persuade you this morning that the Scripture account of the heart is strictly and literally true and correct; it is a faithful likeness, a lively picture, and it must not be softened down and called figurative and extravagant, because it sounds rough and plain, and leaves you no room for boasting. O that the Holy Ghost may bring many of you to a right understanding of your own hearts! It is almost impossible to say how immensely important it is to have a clear view of their natural state: "with the heart man believeth unto righteousness," "out of the heart are the issues of life"; "man looketh on the outward appearance, but the Lord looketh on the heart"; in short, unless you really know the character of your own heart, you will never value the Gospel as you ought, you will never love the Lord Jesus Christ in sincerity, you will never see how absolutely necessary it was that He should suffer death upon the cross, in order to deliver our souls from hell and bring us unto God. I wish therefore, *firstly*, to prove to you the truth of the words "the heart is deceitful above all things, and desperately wicked"; *secondly*, I shall say a few words to remind you that God knows what is within you,—"I the Lord search the heart"; and, *thirdly*, I shall point out shortly the only remedy that can do you any good, if you would be saved. It is my earnest desire and prayer that you may all come unto Christ and be delivered from the wrath to come; but this will never be until you are convinced of sin, and you will never be thoroughly convinced until you know that the root and source and fountain of it all is within you, even in your own hearts.

I. Now, as to the natural deceit and wickedness of every man, woman, and child that is born into the world, first and foremost what says the Scripture? How is it written? What do we read? Hear the book of Genesis: "God saw that the wickedness of man was great in the earth, and that *every* imagination

of the thoughts of his heart was *only evil continually*" ;
" The imagination of man's heart is evil from his
youth." The first book of Kings : " There is no
man that sinneth not." The book of Psalms : " The
Lord looked down from heaven upon the children
of men, to see if there were any that did understand
and seek God. They are all gone aside, they are
altogether become filthy : there is none that doeth
good, no, not one." " The fool hath said in his heart,
There is no God. Corrupt are they, they have done
abominable iniquity, there is none that doeth good."
The book of Job : " How can he be clean that is born
of a woman ? " " Who can bring a clean thing out of
an unclean ? not one." The book of Proverbs : " Who
can say, I have made my heart clean, I am pure from
my sin ? " The book of Ecclesiastes : " There is not
a just man upon earth, that doeth good, and sinneth
not." " The heart of the sons of men is fully set in
them to do evil." " The heart of the sons of men is full
of evil, and madness is in their heart while they live.
The book of Isaiah : " All we like sheep have gone
astray, we have turned every one to his own way
" We are all as an unclean thing, and all our righteousnesses are as filthy rags." The words of the Lord
Jesus in the Gospel of St. Matthew : " Out of the heart
proceed evil thoughts, murders, adulteries, fornications
thefts, false witness, blasphemies : these are the things
which defile a man." The same words more fully in
St. Mark : " From within, out of the heart of men,
proceed evil thoughts, adulteries, fornications, murders,
thefts, covetousness, wickedness, deceit, lasciviousness,
an evil eye, blasphemy, pride, foolishness : all these evil
things come from within, and defile a man." O this
pure heart, this good heart which people speak of !—
these are not texts which describe the character of the

wicked only ; they are written generally of all mankind,
of you and me and the whole world, and they ought
to be sufficient proof of that which Solomon declares,
" He that trusteth his own heart is a fool."

But perhaps you would like to know what Bible
history teaches us upon this point : it is possible you
may flatter yourselves these are all single texts, and
probably do not mean something quite so strong as
I have made them appear. Be not deceived ; you
will find nothing to encourage you to think well of
yourself ; man's natural character is everywhere described in the same colours,—it is all black, very black.
Perhaps you sometimes try to think that the Bible is
a book which contains the history of many good
men, and an account of God's lovingkindness to us,
and a great store of good advice. No doubt it does
contain all this, but it contains something more too :
it contains the true description of man's heart, it strips
off the flimsy coverings which pride and self-conceit
throw over our natural dispositions, and it shows us
man as he really is ; it furnishes continual proof from
first to last of the inbred wickedness of our hearts, it
supplies us with countless examples of our inclination
towards sin, unless we are restrained and bent back
by the grace of God.

O beloved, that you would only search the Scripture
for yourselves on this matter ! I am not preaching my
own doctrine ; I am telling you that plain, humbling
truth which the Holy Ghost endeavours in every possible way to drive into our hearts, in that blessed
volume which was written for our warning.

You can hardly turn to a single part of Bible history
in which this doctrine does not come uppermost. Look
at the men before the flood ! who would have thought,
with Paradise as a witness before their eyes (for. until

the flood Paradise was on earth), who would have
thought they could have turned their backs on God,
and given themselves up to all manner of lusts and
sin ? And yet they did so, in spite of every warning,
and God was obliged to drown the whole world, excepting eight persons. Look at men after the flood !
Doubtless you would expect that every one would flee
from sin as if it were a serpent, remembering God's
wrath against iniquity ; and yet, behold, the first thing
that we meet with is the calling of Abraham and his
family to preserve the remembrance of God upon the
earth ; the whole world had become so sinful and
idolatrous, that the Lord Jehovah was obliged to interfere, as it were, in a special manner, and choose out
one man's home, that he might not be entirely forgotten.
And lest you should imagine things were not so very
bad, and this calling of Abraham not so very necessary,
the next event we meet with is the destruction of
Sodom and Gomorrah, because of their abominable
wickedness. Look at the history of Israel, the chosen
family itself. They went down into Egypt and dwelt
there, and two hundred years after they had gone back
so far in spiritual things that they had forgotten the
name of the God of their fathers. They were brought
out by miracles with a mighty hand, and yet they had
hardly got into the wilderness when they murmured
and desired to return to Egypt. They were taken
into the land of Canaan, and had the purest and the
best of laws given to them, and yet Joshua was scarcely
buried when they fell away after idols. Time after
time you read of their being in hard captivity for their
sins, time after time you read of God delivering them ;
and yet a few short years and it seems to have been
all forgotten. The Lord gave them judges and kings,
and priests and prophets and ministers, and preachings

and warnings ; and yet their history, with a few exceptions, is a history of unbelief; and backsliding and
transgression and crime down to the very day when
they crucified the Lord Jesus Christ Himself.   What
can you say to these things ?   If ever there was a
nation free from outward temptation and inducement
to sin, it was the Jews; they were hedged in and
fenced in on every side by the strictest rules, which
prevented them mixing with other nations, and never-
theless you see what they were.   You can only account
for it by taking the Bible reason : they had the root
of all the evil within them, they were men like ourselves, and as such they had hearts deceitful above all
things and desperately wicked ; and like too many among
ourselves they would not believe it, and so they fell.

   But I shall not leave the Bible here.   I say further
that you can hardly turn to a single family, even of
the best of God's servants, in which the natural corruption of our hearts does not appear more or less in
some one of the branches.   The firstborn in Adam's
house was Cain, a murderer.   The family of Noah,
that just man, contained Ham, the wicked father of
Canaan, the accursed race.   Abraham was the father of
Midian, an idolatrous people who deceived Israel in the
wilderness, as well as of Isaac.   Isaac was the father of
Esau, that " profane person," as well as of Jacob.   Jacob
was the father of Reuben, who defiled his father's bed,
as well as of Joseph.   Eli, the priest of the Lord, was the
father of Hophni and Phinehas, who made people abhor
the offering of God.   David was the father of Absalom
and Amnon as well as of Solomon.   Hezekiah, that
good man, was the father of Manasseh, the most
wicked of the kings of Judah.   Why am I telling you
these things ?   I tell you them to show you that good
education and good example cannot alone make the

children of the saints good, without the grace of God, to show you how deeply rooted is the corruption of our natural dispositions.

But I shall go even further. I say that you can hardly turn to a single character, among the holy men described in the Bible, who did not, to his own horror and dismay, fall at one time or another. Noah planted a vineyard, and was one day found drunken. David committed adultery with the wife of Uriah. Peter denied his Lord thrice. What does this prove? It proves beyond a question that the most excellent of the earth have found that the root of all their sinfulness is within them; they never boasted of the purity or goodness of their hearts, they have all placed upon record the truth that, although Satan does much and the world does much, still after all the great enemy is always within us; it is a heart deceitful above all things and desperately wicked. Pause, beloved, for an instant, and think of that: the men who were the friends of God, who lived most closely to Him, were those whom we find grieving and mourning over their sinful hearts most bitterly. Surely the heart must be more treacherous than you supposed.

Well, perhaps you will say, all this may be very true; the men we read of in the Bible certainly sinned very much; but things are altered now we live under the light of the Gospel. Things may be altered certainly in some respects; but the heart is just the same. I cannot see the smallest proof of any change there. So long as every newspaper contains accounts of crime in one shape or another of all descriptions; so long as gaols and prisons are full and new ones are continually building; so long as hundreds and thousands are every year tried and punished, and yet next year there are as many more committed; so long as men

make a god and an idol of money, and swear and pray
God to damn their souls, and break the Sabbath day
in every possible manner, and show an utter want of
affection and kindness to their own relations, and are
angry and passionate on the slightest occasion, and
think very lightly about fornication, and think it clever
and fair to deceive their neighbours, and do not hesitate
to say what is not true if it serves their interest, and
covet each other's money and house and land and
property from morning till night, and get drunk, as if
they gloried in ruining soul and body at once,—so long,
I say, as such things go on in England, which professes
to be a Christian country,—and you know they do go
on,—so long as such things go on in the face of God
who sees it all, and the Bible which condemns it all,
and the Church which witnesses against it all ; so long
shall I declare that the only possible reason which can
be given for it is the plain account of my text: "The
natural heart of every man is deceitful above all things
and desperately wicked." There must be some hidden
cause and fountain within us, or men would never be
guilty of such enormous folly.

But I will not detain you with proofs of this nature,
which you must all know. I would rather lay before
you a few questions which perhaps many of you have
not considered.

What, then, is the reason that men are so active
and industrious in their business and so careless about
their souls ? They give up their whole heart and soul
and mind to their labouring and planting and building
and gardening ; they rise early and go to bed late ;
they bestir themselves ; they are in earnest ; they think
it wrong not to be diligent and hardworking ; but as
for serving God, they seem to think it their duty to sit
still and do nothing.

What is the reason |that men have always so many
excuses to make in the service of God?—the most
ridiculous, the most trifling seem to satisfy them, and
yet they know that if they gave such excuses to an
earthly master, they would be dismissed at once from
his employment.

What is the reason that men pay such respect to
those above them upon earth?—their landlord, their
master, the rich and the noble, are always treated with
a proper reverence and deference ; and yet the Lord
God Almighty, the Maker and the Judge of all things,
is honoured when it is convenient, as if it was rather
a favour to attend His house and hear His ministers.

What is the reason that men can give smooth names
and soften down practices which God detests, and talk
of an adulterer as a gay man, and a drunkard as a
merry, cheerful man, and a riotous reveller as a wild
man ; while one who is striving to lay hold on Christ
is called mad, and one who has a tender conscience is
called narrow-minded, and one who thirsts after holiness
righteous overmuch ?

What is the reason that many can talk much and
show much knowledge about this world's matters, but
are grave and silent and ignorant about their souls—
can remember everything bad which they meet with, but
forget the good—can hear of others dying, and never
look at their own state—can see death coming near
their own doors, and yet neglect to make preparations
to receive him ?

Beloved, these things are wonderful, but are they not
true ? Man, so wise, so prudent, so thoughtful as he
is about the life that now is, seems a fool in the matter of
the world to come. And why ? " He has within him a
heart deceitful above all things, and desperately wicked."

And what is the reason that men who profess and

call themselves Christians do often find fault with the
doctrines they hear preached, and say they must be
wrong, they cannot be the truth of God, they are too
humbling, too strict: and yet they will not take the
trouble of looking at their Bibles, to see whether these
things be really so.

What is the reason that so many go on saying they
know all these things, and yet they never do them?
They are almost ready to take offence if we doubt their
acquaintance with the Gospel; but there they stop,
their knowledge does not seem to make the slightest
difference in their lives.

What is the reason that so many use the outward
forms of religion but never pray in secret,—I know that
certain of you did not pray last night nor yet this
morning,—that so many hear the Gospel preached week
after week and never apply it to themselves, and go
away from church as cold and unmoved as if they
had gone to be witnesses of instruction given to their
neighbours, but not meant for themselves?

What is the reason that so many encourage themselves with the idea it will be all right at the last, and
yet they cannot say why; and so many make a great
profession, and try to deceive ministers, as if God did
not see it all; and so many desire to have the name
of spiritual Christians on earth, who clearly are not
bearing the Cross nor showing the mind that was in
Christ Jesus?

Verily, beloved, there is but one reason to be given,
and that is the Bible reason. Conduct such as I have
described,—and you know I have mentioned matters
of everyday occurrence,—such conduct is so utterly
unlike the way in which men act about the care of their
bodies and the things of this world, that there must
be some hidden reason, some secret fountain of evil

within us. I say it is impossible to observe how
differently men generally live from the plain precepts
of the Bible; it is impossible to consider the number
and the variety of the ways in which God's law is
continually broken, and not to see the most decided
proof that man's natural heart is indeed deceitful above
all things and desperately wicked. Truly indeed were
the words added, "Who can know it?" Who can ever
understand how men can shut their eyes against such
light, and live after such a fashion as too many do?
Job thought he knew his heart, but affliction came and
he found he did not. David thought he knew his heart,
but he learned by bitter experience how wofully he was
mistaken. Peter thought he knew his heart, and in
a short time he was repenting in tears. Oh, pray,
beloved, if you love your souls, for some insight into
your own corruption; the veriest saints of God do never
quite discover the exceeding sinfulness of that old man
which is in them.

II. I promised to say a few words about the second
part of my text, but I shall not detain you long over
it. We read, "I the Lord search the heart, I try the
reins, even to give every man according to his ways,
and according to the fruit of his doings." There are
two things written here: one is that, although you do
not know your own hearts, the Lord God Almighty
does, and keeps a close watch over them; the other
is that He will one day call you to account, and
judge you accordingly. And do you not observe here
what the mind of the Spirit points to? Some men
might say, God will not be extreme to mark what is
amiss, I shall have peace though I walk in the
imagination of mine heart; but the prophet sweeps
away these refuges of lies by warning us of searching
and of judgment immediately after he has declared to

us the deceitfulness of man's heart. Remember, now, O unconverted man, that God has set your secret sins in the light of His countenance ; the vilest imaginations of your wicked heart, the deeds you have so carefully concealed from the sight of men, the abominable thoughts which you would not have your dearest friends suspect,—all have been seen through and through by that Pure and Holy One who will one day be your Judge. Remember that the wrath of God is revealed against all ungodliness and unrighteousness of men, who hold the truth in unrighteousness ; that the wicked shall be turned into hell, and all the people, too, who forget God, and neglect so great salvation ; that hell is everlasting woe : ten thousand times ten thousand years shall pass away, and the worm and the fire shall be just the same, and this is the place to which you are going. You do not like to believe the account we have given of your natural heart ; but look back over your life and tell us of one single day in which you have done all that God required and left nothing undone : you cannot find it ; and what will you do when each of the three hundred and sixty-five days in each of the twenty, forty, sixty years you may have lived shall come to light, when thousands of little things you now forget shall all appear, and God shall ask you, " What hast thou got to say, why these things should not condemn thee ? " Oh, be not deceived, but bear in mind that St. James has said one single offence will make you guilty, that Jesus teaches that in God's account a thought or a feeling is as bad as an outward act, that one wanton look is adultery, and that hatred is murder. Better be humble now and confess you did not know your own vileness, than flatter your vanity and self-conceit, and perish everlastingly.

III. Beloved, you are feeling disposed to say, "At this rate, who can be saved?" and I shall endeavour to give you very shortly the Bible answer ; I shall try to point out the way. Truly on any earthly plan salvation would be impossible, but with God all things are possible, and God has laid before us a path by which the vilest may get to heaven. You are thinking that I have gone too far, that I have spoken too strongly ; but you cannot say that I have gone beyond the Bible, nor yet beyond the Prayer-book, which you have used to-day and called yourselves miserable sinners.

I say, then, O ye miserable sinners, although your hearts are deceitful above all things, and desperately wicked, although there is no health in you, I say that God loves you exceedingly. He has given His only-begotten Son to suffer for your sins ; and now whosoever believeth in Him shall not perish, shall not be condemned, shall have everlasting life. "Who can be saved?" All, I answer, who give up their iniquities, and grieve over them, and put their whole trust in Jesus Christ. But these deceitful hearts? Repent and believe, and God shall wash them in the blood of the cross, shall make them as it were new, shall create them again in righteousness and true holiness ; shall fill them with the Holy Ghost, shall put love where there was hatred or indifference, shall put peace where there was doubt and anxiety, shall put strength where there was wickedness. Verily your sin does indeed abound, but you shall find, if you will only try it, that grace does abound far more. O ye miserable sinners, who are just now thinking well of your own state, and not alarmed about your souls, and rather offended at the picture I have drawn of your hearts—I ought to say our hearts, for my heart is naturally just as

abominable as your own—O ye miserable sinners, I
do beseech you to pray God that you may see clearly
the corruption of your nature ! I tell the young among
you, your hearts are desperately wicked, and so long
as you put off repentance and calling upon God you
are like an infant trifling with a razor—you are like a
fool playing with a tiger. I tell those among you
who are getting on in life, your hearts are desperately
wicked, and so long as you hold back and talk of a
more convenient season for coming unto Christ, you
are adding stone to stone and brick to brick to that
great wall which you have built up between yourselves
and the Kingdom of Heaven.

Your hearts are deceitful above all things, and except
they be changed, the Bible says you will most surely
perish. But in the name of my most loving Master
I offer to you a complete remedy ; I proclaim to you
the freest salvation. I entreat you not to reject it.
Come unto Jesus : He came not to save the wise in
their own eyes, but to seek that which was lost. Come
unto the Lamb of God : He taketh away the sins of the
world ; and though your hearts be full of iniquity they
shall be changed, "though your sins be as scarlet,
they shall be made white as snow ; though they be red
like crimson, they shall become as wool." But mark
my words : God hath witnessed that except ye choose
this way, the way of repentance and of faith, ye shall
have no salvation, and the more free and gracious are
the offers which ye reject, so much the more heavily
shall ye be judged in the last day. "O seek ye the
Lord while He may be found, call upon Him while
He is near : Let the wicked forsake his way, and the
unrighteous man his thoughts : and let him return unto
the Lord, and He will have mercy. upon him ; and to
our God, for He will abundantly pardon."

II

REGENERATION

"Verily, verily I say unto thee, Except a man be born again, he cannot see the Kingdom of God."—JOHN iii. 3.

IF the Bible be false, as some proud men have dared to say, there is no occasion for keeping one day in the week holy, there is no use in honouring church and making a profession of religion; we are no better than the beasts that perish, and the best thing a man can do is to eat and drink and live as he pleases. If the Bible be only half true, as some unhappy people strive to make out, there is no certainty about our everlasting souls: Christianity is all doubt and dimness and guesswork, we can never know what we are to believe as necessary to salvation, we can never be sure that we have got hold of the words of eternal life. Give up your Bible, and you have not a square inch of certainty and confidence to stand on: you may think and you may fancy and you may have your own opinion, but you cannot show me any satisfactory proof or authority that you are right; you are building merely on your own judgment; you have put out your own eyes, as it were, and, like one in the dark, you do not really know where you are going.

But if, beloved, the Bible be indeed the Word of God Himself and altogether true, and that it is so can be proved by witnesses without number; if the Bible be indeed true and our only guide to heaven, and this I

trust you are all ready to allow, it surely must be the
duty of every wise and thinking man to lay to heart
each doctrine which it contains, and while he adds
nothing to it, to be careful that he takes nothing
from it.

Now, I say that on the face of the Bible, when fairly
read, there stands out this grand doctrine, that we must
each of us between the cradle and grave go through
a spiritual change, a change of heart, or in other words
be born again ; and in the text you have heard read the
Lord Jesus declares positively, without it no man shall
see the kingdom of God.

Sinner, man or woman, mark that ! no salvation without this new birth! Christ hath done everything for
thee ; He paid the price of our redemption, lived for
us, died for us, rose again for us ; but all shall avail us
nothing, if there be not this work in us : *we must be
born again.*

Now, beloved, I desire to speak to you freely and
plainly about this new birth, in two or three sermons,
as a thing absolutely necessary to salvation ; and to-day,
at least, I shall try to show you from my text two
things : *first,* the reason why we must all be born
again, and *secondly,* what the expression to be born
again means ; and the Lord grant that the subject to
which I am going to call your attention for two or three
Sunday mornings may not be listened to and soon
forgotten, as a light and indifferent matter—but carried
home and thought over, and blessed to the conversion
of many souls !

I. Why, then, is this change of heart so necessary?
The answer is short and simple.   Because of the natural
sinfulness of every man's disposition.   We are not born
into the world with spotless, innocent minds, but corrupt
and wicked, and with a will to the thing which is evil

as soon as we have the power ; and the Scriptural
account is true to the letter—we are all conceived in
sin and shapen in iniquity. I need not stop now to
tell you how all this came to pass ; I need only remind
you that in the beginning it was not so. Our first
parents, Adam and Eve, were created holy, harmless,
undefiled, without spot or stain or blemish about them ;
and when God rested from His labour on the seventh
day, He pronounced them, like all His other works,
to be very good. But, alas for us ! Adam, by transgression, fell, and lost his first estate ; he forfeited the
likeness of God in which he had been made ; and
hence all we, who are his children, come into being
with a defiled and sinful nature. We are fallen, and we
must needs be raised ; we have about us the marks of
the old Adam—Adam the first, earthly and carnal—
and we must needs be marked with the marks of the
Second Adam, the Lord Jesus, which are heavenly
and spiritual. Do any of you feel a doubt of this ?
Consider only what we are by nature.

By nature we do not see Christ's spiritual kingdom
upon earth ; it is all hid from our eyes. Men may
be sharp and knowing in worldly matters, they may
be wise in the things of time ; but when they come
to religion, their understandings seem blind, there is a
thick veil over their hearts, and they see nothing as
they ought to see.

So long as they are in this natural state it is in vain
they are told of God's holiness and God's unchangeable justice, His spiritual law and His judgment to
come, their own enormous deficiencies, their own peril
of destruction—it matters not ; it all falls flat and dull
upon their ears ; they neither feel it nor care for it
nor consider it, and in a few hours they are as though
they had never heard it. It is to no purpose, while

in this condition, that Christ crucified and His precious
atonement are set before us ; we can see no form nor
beauty nor comeliness about Him ; we cannot value
what He has done, and, as far as we are concerned,
the wisdom and the excellence of the Cross, which
Apostles gloried in, seems all thrown away.   And
why is this ?   Our hearts want changing.   " The natural
man receiveth not the things of the Spirit of God ; for
they are foolishness unto him ; neither can he know
them, for they are spiritually discerned."   This is the
true account of all that weariness and lifelessness and
carelessness which we so often see in the worshippers
of God's house ; this is the secret of that awful indifference about spiritual things which prevails so widely
both among rich and poor, and makes the Gospel
appear a sealed book.   It comes from the heart.   Some
always fancy they want learning, some they have no
time, some they have very peculiar difficulties which
no one else in the world has ; but the truth lies far
deeper.   They all want new hearts.   Once give them
new natures, and you would hear no more about
learning, or time, or difficulty.   Every mountain would
be levelled and every valley filled up, that the way of
God might be prepared.

But again.   By nature we do not love the laws
of Christ's spiritual kingdom.   We do not openly
refuse to obey them, we should be angry with any
one who said we had thrown them aside, but we have
no love to them and delight in them ; it is not our
meat and drink to do our Father's will.   Oh no ! by
nature we love our own way and our own inclinations, and that is our only law.   We bring forth fruit
unto ourselves, but not unto God.   Our own pleasure
and our own profit take up all our attention, and
as for Him who made us and redeemed us, too many

do not give Him the very leavings of their time.
By nature we do not measure ourselves by God's
standard : who ever takes the Sermon on the Mount
as his rule of character? who ever admires the poor
in spirit, the mourners, the meek, the hungerers and
thirsters after righteousness, the merciful, the pure in
heart, the peacemakers, the men who are persecuted
for righteousness' sake? These are all people whom the
world despises, they are as nothing by the side of the
jovial and light-hearted, the men who love strong drink
and are held to sing good songs ; and yet these are
the persons whom Jesus calls blessed. What natural
man judges of sin as Jesus teaches us to judge? how
few look on drunkenness and fornication as damnable
sins !—yet the Bible says they are. How few consider
anger without cause as bad as murder, and wanton looks
as bad as adultery!—yet Jesus says they are. Where
are the men who strive to love their enemies, who
bless those that hate them, and pray for those who
despitefully use them ?—yet this is the rule that Jesus
has laid down. And why is all this? You see there
must be something radically wrong. By nature we
do not lay ourselves out to glorify God with our
bodies and spirits, we take no pleasure in speaking
to each other about Him, the concerns of this world
have a hundred times more of our thoughts ; and few
indeed are the parties where the mention of Christ
and heaven would not stop many mouths, and make
nearly all look as if the subject was very uncomfortable. And why is all this? Some talk of bad
example having done them harm, and some say they
have had a bad education, but the evil is far more
deeply seated ; that which is born of the flesh is
flesh, it comes from the carnal unrenewed mind, and
the remedy wanted is change of nature. A corrupt

tree can only bring forth corrupt fruit ; the root of the mischief is the natural heart.

Once more. By nature we are altogether unfit for Christ's kingdom in glory. The lives which we are in the habit of leading, and the practices we are fond of indulging, and the tastes we are always seeking to please, and the opinions we hold, are all such as prove we have no natural meetness for the inheritance of the saints in light. They do not follow after holiness in all their walk and conversation. Then what place can they occupy in that blessed abode where there shall enter in nothing that defileth, nor whatsoever worketh abomination?—how shall they stand in His presence, who chargeth even His angels with folly, and in whose sight the very heavens are not pure! They do not take pleasure in the exercise of prayer and praise on earth ; and how could they enjoy the employments of that glorious habitation, where they rest not day nor night worshipping and crying " Holy, holy, holy, Lord God Almighty, which was, and is, and is to come." They do not count it a privilege to draw nigh to God through Jesus Christ, to walk with Him, to seek close acquaintance with Him ; and where would be the comfort to them of dwelling for ever in the presence of the Lord God and the Lamb? They do not strive to walk in the steps of holy men of old, they do not take example from the faith and patience of the saints ; and with what face then would they join the society of just men made perfect ?—with what salutation, after a life spent in pleasing the devil and the world, would they greet Abraham and David and the Apostles and all that blessed company who have fought the good fight ? Alas ! beloved, a natural man in heaven would be a miserable creature,—there would be something in the air he could not breathe,

the joys, the affections, the employments would be all wearisome to him, he would find himself unfitted for the company of the saints, as a beast is unfitted on earth for the company of man ; he would be carnally minded, they would be spiritually minded, there would be nothing in common. I know there are vain dreamers who fancy death will work an alteration, that they may die sinners and rise again saints ; but it is all a delusion, there is no work nor device nor knowledge in the grave ; if we die spiritual we shall rise spiritual, if we die carnal we shall rise carnal, and if we are to be made fit for heaven our natural hearts must be changed now on earth.

In short, beloved, the plain truth is, that by nature men are all dead in trespasses and sins, aliens from the commonwealth of Israel, strangers to the covenant of promise, having no hope and without God in the world, prisoners in the hand of Satan, in a state of miserable condemnation, spiritually dark, blind, and sleeping ; and, worst of all, they neither know nor feel it. The cold corpse in the grave does not feel the worms that crawl over it ; the sleeping wretch who has unawares drunk poison does not know that he shall wake no more ; and so also the unhappy man who is still unconverted cannot understand that he is in need of anything. But still, every natural man in the sight of God is dead while he liveth ; his body, soul, and mind are all turned aside from their proper use, which is to glorify God, and so he is looked upon as dead. And this either is the state of every single soul among us at this minute, or else it used to be. There is no middle state ; we cannot be half-way, neither dead nor alive ; we were dead and have been brought to life, or we are now dead, and the work is yet to be done. Nor yet is this doctrine for publicans and

harlots only : it is for all without exception ; it touches
high and low, rich and poor, learned and unlearned, old
and young, gentle and simple ; all are by nature sinful
and corrupt, and because they are so Jesus tells us
solemnly not one shall enter into the heavenly rest
without being born again.

Beloved, this sounds strong ; it seems a hard saying,
perhaps. That is not my affair ; I am set to preach
Christ's Gospel and not my own. Search the Scriptures,
and you will see it is true.

II. The second thing for your consideration is the
exact signification and force of that peculiar expression
" to be born again." It is a change by which we once
more recover something of the divine nature, and are
renewed after the image of God. It is a complete
transforming and altering of all the inner man ; and
nothing can more fully show its completeness and
importance than the strong figure under which Jesus
describes it : He calls it a NEW BIRTH. We have all
been born once as men, but we must see to it we are
born again as true Christians. We have been born once
of the seed of Adam ; woe to us if we are not born the
second time of the seed of God ! We have been born
of the flesh, we must also be born of the Spirit. We
are born earthly, we must also be born heavenly ; we
are born corruptible, we must also be born incorruptible,
for our natural birth is not a whit more necessary to
the life of the body than is our spiritual birth necessary
to the life of the soul.

To be born again is as it were to enter upon a new
existence, to have a new mind and a new heart, new views,
new principles, new tastes, new affections, new likings
and new dislikings, new fears, new joys, new sorrows,
new love to things once hated, new hatred to things
once loved, new thoughts of God and ourselves and the

world and the life to come and the means whereby that life is attained. And it is indeed a true saying that he who has gone through it is a new man, a new creature, for old things are passed away,—behold, he can say, all things are become new! It is not so much that our natural powers and faculties are taken away and destroyed; I would rather say that they receive an utterly new bias and direction. It is not that the old metal is cast aside, but it is melted down and refined and remoulded, and has a new stamp impressed upon it, and thus, so to speak, becomes a new coin.

This is no outward change, like that of Herod, who did many things and then stopped, or of Ahab, who humbled himself and went in sackcloth and walked softly; nor is it a change which can neither be seen nor felt. It is not merely a new name and a new notion, but the implanting of a new principle which will surely bear good fruit. It is opening the eyes of the blind and unstopping the ears of the deaf; it is loosing the tongue of the dumb, and giving hands and feet to the maimed and lame,—for he that is born again no longer allows his members to be instruments and servants of unrighteousness, but he gives them unto God, and then only are they properly employed.

To be born again is to become a member of a new family by adoption, even the family of God; it is to feel that God is indeed our Father, and that we are made the very sons and daughters of the Almighty; it is to become the citizen of a new state, to cast aside the bondage of Satan and live as free men in the glorious liberty of Christ's kingdom, giving our King the tribute of our best affection, and believing that He will keep us from all evil. To be born again is a spiritual resurrection, a faint likeness indeed of the great change at last, but still a likeness; for

the new birth of a man is a passage from death to
life ; it is a passage from ignorance of God to a full
knowledge of Him, from slavish fear to childlike love,
from sleepy carelessness about Him to fervent desire
to please Him, from lazy indifference about salvation
to burning, earnest zeal ; it is a passage from strangeness towards God to heartfelt confidence, from a state
of enmity to a state of peace, from worldliness to
holiness, from an earthly, sensual, man-pleasing state
of mind to the single-eyed mind that is in Christ Jesus.
And this it is to be born of the Spirit.

Beloved, time will not allow me to go further with
this subject to-day. I have endeavoured to show you
generally why we must all be born again, and what the
new birth means ; and on Sunday next, if the Lord will,
I purpose to show you the manner and means by which
this new birth usually comes.

It only remains for me now to commend this matter
most solemnly to your consciences. Were it a doctrine
of only second-rate importance,—were it a point a man
might leave uncertain and yet be saved, like Church
government or election,—I would not press it on you
so strongly ; but it is one of the two great pillars of the
gospel. On the one hand stands salvation by free grace
for Christ's sake ; but on the other stands renewal of
the carnal heart by the Spirit. We must be changed
as well as forgiven ; we must be renewed as well as
redeemed.

And I commend this to you all the more because
of the times you live in. Men swallow down sermons
about Christ's willingness and Christ's power to save,
and yet continue in their sins : they seem to forget
there must be the Spirit's work within us, as well as
Christ's work for us—there must be something written
on the table of our hearts. The strong man, Satan,

must be cast out of our house, and Jesus must take possession ; and we must begin to know the saints' character experimentally on earth, or we shall never be numbered with them in heaven. Christ is indeed a full and sufficient title to heaven ; but we must have about us some meetness and fitness for that blessed abode.

I will not shrink from telling you that this doctrine cuts every congregation in two ; it is the line of separation between the good fish and the bad, the wheat and the tares. There is a natural part in every congregation, and there is a spiritual part ; and few indeed are the churches where we should not be constrained to cry, Lord, here are many called, but very few chosen. The kingdom of God is no mere matter of lips and knees and outward service—it must be within a man, seated in the best place of heart ; and I will not hesitate to tell you I fear there are many living members of churches who are exceedingly dead Christians.

Examine yourselves, then, I pray you, whether you are born again. Have you good solid reasons for thinking that ye have put off the old man which is corrupt, and put on the new man which is created after God in holiness? Are ye renewed in the spirit of your minds? Are ye bringing forth the fruits of the flesh or the fruits of the Spirit? Are ye carnally minded or heavenly minded? Are your affections with the world or with God? Are ye natural men or are ye spiritual men? Oh! but it were no charity in me to keep back this weighty truth ; and it will be no wisdom in you to put off and delay considering it.

Are ye born again? Without it no salvation! It is not written that you may not, or yet that you will have some difficulty, but it is written that you cannot

without it see the kingdom of God. Consider with
yourselves how fearful it will be to be shut out; to see
God's kingdom afar off, like the rich man in the parable,
and a great gulf between ; how terrible to go down to
the pit from under the very pulpit, well satisfied with
your own condition, but still not born again.   There are
truly many roads to perdition, but none so melancholy
as that which is travelled on by professing Christians—
by men and women who have light and knowledge
and warning and means and opportunity and yet go
smiling on as if sermons and religion were not meant
for them, or as if hell was a bed of roses, or as if
God was a liar and would not keep His word.

Are ye born again ?   I do not want to fill your heads,
but to move your hearts ; it is not a matter of course
that all who go to church shall be saved ; churches
and ministers are meant to rouse you to self-inquiry,
to awaken you to a sense of your condition ; and next
to that grand question, " Have you taken Christ for
your Saviour ? " there comes the second point, " Are
you born again ? "

Beloved, if you love life, search and see what is your
condition.   What though you find no tokens for good :
better a thousand times to know it now and live, than
to know it too late and die eternally !

Praised be God, it is a doctrine bound round with
gracious promises : no heart so hard but the Holy
Ghost can move it ; many a one could set his seal to
that, and tell you that he was darkness, darkness that
could be felt, but is now light in the Lord.   Many of
the Corinthians were bad as the worst among you,
but they were washed, they were sanctified, they were
justified, in the name of the Lord Jesus and by the
Spirit of our God.   Many of the Ephesians were as
completely dead in sins as any of you, but God

quickened them, and raised them up, and created them anew unto good works. Examine yourselves and draw nigh to God with prayer, and He shall draw nigh to you ; but if ye ask not, ye shall not have.

As for me, I make my supplication unto God, who can make all things new, that His Spirit may touch your hearts with a deep sense of this truth, for withont it my preaching is vain ; that there may be a mighty shaking and revival among the dry bones ; that you may never rest until you are indeed new men and can say, Verily we *were* dead but we are now alive, we *were* lost but we are now found.

III

REGENERATION (II)

"Verily, verily, I say unto thee, Except a man be born again, he cannot see the kingdom of God."—JOHN iii. 3.

ABOUT this new birth—without which no man or woman can be saved! You may remember I began to speak of it last Sunday morning, and I endeavoured to establish in your minds two main points, which it may be well to recall to your recollection now. First, then, I showed you the reason why this new birth is so absolutely necessary to salvation: it is because of our sinful hearts, our inbred corruption ; we are born from the very first with a disposition towards that which is bad ; we have no natural readiness to serve God,— it is all against the grain ; we have no natural insight into the excellence of Christ's spiritual kingdom, no natural love towards His holy laws or desire to obey them, no natural fitness for heaven; an unrenewed man would be miserable in the company of Jesus and the saints. In short, I said, it is not enough that we are born of the flesh once, natural men ; we must needs be born the second time of God and become spiritual men, or else we shall never taste eternal life. I then reminded you of the awful carelessness and indifference and deadness and lukewarmness and coldness and slothfulness about religion which doth so widely prevail ; and I observed that people were always ingenious in

28

framing reasons and making excuses for their own particular neglect of God, always supposing they had some special difficulty to contend with, which none else had—business, or poverty, trouble, or family, or want of time, or want of learning, and the like—always fancying if these difficulties were taken out of the way they should be such good Christians ; and I then told you to mark that the root of all these difficulties is the natural old heart, and the thing wanted is not leisure and ease and money and learning, but a new heart and a new principle within. Secondly, I went on to set before you the nature and character of this new birth. I showed that it was a change not outward only, but inward,—not in name only, but in spirit and in truth,—a change so thorough, so searching, so radical, so complete, that he who has gone through it may be called born again, for he is to all intents and purposes a new man : he was darkness, but he is now light ; he was blind, but he can now see ; he was sleeping, but he is now awake ; he was dead, but he now lives ; he was earthly-minded, but he is now heavenly-minded ; he was carnal, but he is now spiritual ; he was worldly, but he is now godly ; he once loved most the things corruptible, he now loves the things incorruptible ; he did set his chief affections on that which is mortal, he now sets them on immortality.

Lastly, I pressed upon you all the immense, the sur-passing importance of this doctrine, and I do so now again. I urged you, every one, to remember,—and I repeat it now,—it shall avail us nothing that Christ Jesus has brought in righteousness for us, if there be not also the work of the Holy Ghost within us ; that it shall profit us nothing to say we are redeemed, if there is not also good evidence that we have been indeed renewed.

I shall now go on, according to my promise, to set before you the first great cause of this new birth, and the means and the manner in which it comes ; and I once more pray God that the subject may not be carelessly put aside, but thought over and made useful to all your souls.

I. This new birth, then, this great spiritual change, whence comes it, and how does it begin ? Can any man give it to himself when he pleases ? Can any change his own heart ? No ! the thing is impossible. We can no more quicken and impart life to our souls than we can to our bodies ; we can no more rise and become new men in our own strength than wash away sins by our own performances. It is impossible ! The natural man is as helpless as Lazarus was when he lay still and cold and motionless in the tomb. We may remove the stone, as it were, and expose the sad work of death, but we can do no more. There must be a power far mightier than any power of earth in exercise before the natural man can awake and arise and come forth as a new creature. And to do all this is the special office of the Spirit of Christ, the Holy Ghost, whom Jesus promised to send. It is He that quickeneth ; it is He that giveth life. The Spirit alone can make the seed we scatter bear fruit ; the Spirit alone can lay the first foundation of that holy kingdom we want to see established in your hearts. It is the Spirit must move over these waste and barren souls before they can become the garden of the Lord ; it is the Spirit must open the darkened windows of our conscience before the true light can shine in upon those chambers within us. And so, he that is born again is born, not of blood, nor of the will of the flesh, nor of the will of man, but of God ; for the Spirit is very God.

Beloved, this is a very humbling and awful truth. The conversion of a sinner can never be that light, off-hand affair that some do seem to think it. This great change which must come over us can never be a thing so entirely within our reach and grasp that we may put off the old Adam like a cloak, and put on the new man, just when and where we please. Oh, but it is a work that cannot possibly be done without the hand of God! The same Power which first created heaven and earth, and called the fair world around us into being,—the same Power alone can create in us new hearts, and renew in us right minds—the same Power alone can convert the natural man into the spiritual.

Yes! you may dream of death-bed repentance, and say, By-and-by we will turn and become Christians ; but you know not what you are saying : the softening of the hard heart, and the entrance upon new ways, and the taking up of new principles, is no such easy matter as you seem to fancy—it is work that can only be begun by power divine, and who shall say you may not put it off too long ?

It is not the plainest and clearest preaching, however lovely it may sound, which can cause men to be born again, without the Spirit : you may set Paul to plant and Apollos to water, but the Spirit alone can give the increase ; we may raise up congregations fair and formal, and sinews and flesh and skin may cover the dry bones,—but until the Spirit breathes upon them they are no better than dead. Not all the wisdom of Solomon, not all the faith of Abraham, not all the prophecies of Isaiah, not all the eloquence of Apostles, could avail to convert one single soul without the operation of the Holy Ghost. " Not by might, nor by power, but by my Spirit, saith the Lord of hosts." And there-

fore I call this an awful truth. I know the Spirit is
promised to all who ask it; but I tremble lest men
should loiter and put off their souls' concerns so long
that the Spirit may be grieved and leave them in
their sins.

And still, beloved, awful as this truth may be to
sinners, it is full of consolation to believers; it is full
of sweet and unspeakable comfort to all who feel in
themselves the holy workings of a new and spiritual
nature. These can say with rejoicing, "It is not our
right hand nor our arm which hath brought us on
the way towards Zion; the Lord Himself was on
our side; it was He who raised us from the death of
sin to the life of righteousness, and surely He will
never let us go. Once we were sleeping and dead in
trespasses, but the Spirit awakened us and opened our
eyes. We caught a sight of the punishment prepared
for the ungodly; we heard a voice saying, 'Come unto
Me, and I will give you rest,' and we could sleep
no longer. And surely we may hope that He, who
graciously began the work of grace, will also carry it
forward; He laid the foundation, and He will not let
it decay; He began, and He will bring His handiwork
to perfection."

So much for the great Cause and Giver of the New
Birth—the Holy Spirit. It only remains for us to
consider the means through which it is ordinarily
conveyed, and comes, and the different ways and
manners in which it generally shows itself and produces
its wonderful effects.

Now, with respect to the means which the Holy
Spirit doth ordinarily use, I would not have you for
one minute suppose that I wish to limit or set bounds
to the Holy One of Israel. I do not for an instant
deny that some have been born again without any

outward visible machinery having been used—by a sort
of secret impulse which cannot be well explained ; but
I do say that, generally speaking, the Holy Ghost, in
giving to a man that blessed thing the new birth, is
pleased to work upon his heart more or less by means
which our eyes can see and which our minds can
understand. I would not, then, have you ignorant that
a man is seldom born again of the Spirit, without the
preaching of the Gospel having something to do in
the change. This is a special instrument for turning
men from darkness to light, and many a one can testify
that it was through sermons he was first touched, and
brought to the knowledge of the truth. It was Peter's
preaching which first touched the men of Jerusalem
after our Lord's death, insomuch that they were pricked
to the heart and said, " Men and brethren, what shall
we do ? " It was the command which Jesus gave to
the apostles before his ascension, they were " to preach
unto the people and to testify." It was a cause of joy
to Paul that Christ was preached at Rome : " I therein
rejoice," he says, " and will rejoice." It was his own
declaration about himself, " Christ Jesus sent me not
to baptise, but to preach the Gospel." No means is so
blessed in all the experience of Christ's Church as the
plain preaching of the Gospel ; no sign so sure of
decay and rottenness in a Church as the neglect
of preaching ; for there is no ordinance in which the
Holy Spirit is so particularly present, none by which
sinners are so often converted and brought back to
God. Faith cometh by hearing ; and how shall men
believe except they hear ? Therefore it is that we press
upon you so continually to be diligent in hearing Christ
preached ; for none are so unlikely to be born again
as those who will not listen to the truth.

And seldom too is a man born of the Spirit without

the *Bible* having something to do in the work. The Bible was written by men who spake as they were moved by the Holy Ghost, and he who reads it seriously and attentively, or hears it read, is seeking acquaintance with God in God's own way. You would find few indeed among the Lord's true people who would not tell you that the starting-point in their spiritual life was some saying or doctrine in Scripture ; some part or portion, pressed home upon their consciences by an unseen, secret power, was among the first things which stirred them up to think and examine their ways ; some plain declaration flashed across their minds and made them say, "If this be true I shall certainly be lost." Therefore it is we tell you over and over again, Search the Scriptures, search the Scriptures ; they are the sword of the Spirit, they are the weapon by which the devil is often driven out ; and he who leaves his Bible unread doth plainly not wish to be born again.

Once more. Never are men born of the Spirit without *Prayer.* I believe there would not be found a single case of a person who had been quickened and made a new creature without God having been entreated of and inquired of before. Either he has prayed for himself, or some one has prayed for him : so Stephen died praying for his murderers, and by-and-by Saul was converted. The Lord loves to be sought after by His guilty creatures ; and they who will not ask for the Holy Spirit to come down upon them have no right to expect in themselves any real change.

Such, then, beloved, are the means through which this new birth is generally given. I say generally, because it is not for me to set bounds to the operations of God ; I know men may be startled by sicknesses and accidents and the like, but still I repeat that preach-

ing, the Bible and prayer are the channels through
which the Spirit ordinarily works. And I say further
that in all my life and reading I never heard of a
man who diligently, humbly, heartily and earnestly
made use of these means, who did not sooner or later
find within himself new habits and principles ; I never
heard of a man steadily persevering in their use who
did not sooner or later feel that sin and he must part
company—who did not, in short, become a real child
of God, a new creature.

III. So much for the means through which the
Spirit generally conveys this new birth. There is yet
one point to be considered this morning ; and that
is the *particular manner* in which this mighty spiritual
change doth first touch a person and begin.

Now, on this point I remark, there are great diversities
of operations ; there is a vast variety in the methods
by which the Spirit works, and hence it is that we
can never say He is tied down to show himself in one
particular way ; we must never condemn a person and
tell him he is a graceless unconverted sinner because
his experience may happen to differ widely from our
own.

I would have you note, then, there is great diversity
in the time and age at which this change begins. Some
few have the grace of God in them from their very
infancy ; they are, as it were, sanctified and filled with
the Holy Ghost from their mother's womb ; they
cannot so much as remember the time when they were
without a deep sense of their natural corruption and
a lively faith in Christ, and an earnest desire and
endeavour to live close to God : such were Isaac and
Samuel and Josiah and Jeremiah, and John the Baptist
and Timothy. Blessed and happy are these souls ;
their memories are not saddened by the recollection

of years wasted in carelessness and sin ; their imaginations are not defiled and stained with the remembrance
of youthful wickedness.   But few indeed are to be
found of this sort.   There would be far more, I am
persuaded, if infant baptism were not so inconsiderately
and lightly regarded (as it too often is)—so scrambled
over ; but we have no reason to expect the children
of unbelieving parents can turn out anything else but
unclean and unholy ; and when children are brought
to the font without real faith and real prayer we
have no warrant for supposing the baptism of water
is accompanied by the baptism of the Holy Ghost.
And let me also add that much depends on the education which parents give ; and many a one could
tell you he got his first impressions of religion from
the teaching and example of a father and mother
who really feared God.

But again.   Many, perhaps the greater part of true
Christians in our day, are never born of the Spirit
till they come to age and have reached years of
maturity.   These were once walking after the course of
this world, perhaps serving divers lusts and pleasures,
perhaps decent outwardly and yet only regarding
religion as a thing for Sundays, not as a concern of
the hearts.   But by some means or other God stops
them in their career and turns their hearts back again,
and they take up the cross.   And bitter indeed is their
repentance, and great is their wonder that they could
have lived so long in such a fashion, and warm is the
love they feel towards Him who has so graciously forgiven them all iniquity.

Once more.   Some few, some very few, are first
brought unto God and born again in the advance and
in the decline of life.   Oh ! but it is fearful to see how
few.   There are not many who ever arrive at what is

called old age ; and of these I believe a very insignificant part indeed are ever brought to a saving change,
if they have not been changed. And little wonder
if we consider how deeply rooted a thing is habit,
how hard it is for those who are accustomed to do
evil to learn to do good. O brethren beloved, youth
is the time to seek the Lord ! I know that with God
nothing is impossible ; I know that He can touch the
rock that has long been unmoved, if He pleases, and
make the water flow; but still we very seldom hear
of old men or women being converted : grey hairs are
the time for burning the oil of grace and not for
buying it, and therefore I say, pray ye that your
flight be not in the winter of life.

IV. The next thing I would have you note is the
great diversity in the ways by which the Spirit, so to
speak, doth strike the first blow in producing this
new birth.

Some are awakened suddenly, by mighty providences
and interpositions of God ; they despise other warnings,
and then the Lord comes in and violently shakes them
out of sleep, and plucks them like brands from the
burning. And this is often done by unexpected
mercies,—by extraordinary afflictions and troubles, by
sicknesses, by accidents, by placing a man in some great
danger and peril ; and thousands, I am certain, will tell
us in heaven, " It is good for us that we were tried
and distressed ; ' before I was afflicted I went astray,
but now have I kept Thy word.' " This was the case
with Paul : he was struck to the earth blinded, while
going to Damascus to persecute, and he rose up an
humbled and a wiser man. This was the case with
Jonah : when he fled from the Lord's command, he
was awakened by a storm while sleeping on board
the ship. This was the case with Manasseh, king of

Judah: he was taken prisoner and laid in chains at
Babylon, and in his affliction he sought the Lord.
This was the case with the jailer at Philippi: he was
roused by the earthquake, and came and fell down saying, "What shall I do to be saved?" This is the case
spoken of by Elihu in the thirty-third of Job. And
here is the reason why we ought to feel so anxious
about a man, when God has laid His hand upon him
and afflicted him. I always feel about such a person,
"There is one whom the Lord is trying to convert: will
it or will it not be all in vain?"

Again. Some are awakened suddenly, by very little
and trifling things. God often raises up Christ's
kingdom in a man's heart by a seed so small and
insignificant, that all who see it are obliged to confess,
"This is the Lord's doing, and it is marvellous in our
eyes." A single text of Scripture sometimes; a few
lines in a book taken up by accident; a chance expression or word dropped in conversation, and never
perhaps meant by him who spoke it to do so much:
each of these seeming trifles has been known to pierce
men's hearts like an arrow, after sermons and ordinances
have been used without appearing to avail. I have
heard of one who could trace up the beginning of his
conversion to the saying of a perfect stranger: he was
profanely asking God to damn his soul, when the
stranger stopped him and said it were better to pray
that it might be blessed than damned; and that little
word found its way to his heart. Oh, how careful
should we be over our lips! Who knows what good
might be done if we only strove more to speak a word
in season?

Once more. Some are born of the Spirit gradually
and insensibly. They hardly know at the period what
is going on within them; they can hardly recollect

any particular circumstances attending their conversion, or fix any particular time ; but they do know
this, that somehow or other they have gone through
a great change, they do know that once they were
careless about religion, and now they hold it chiefest
in their affections : once they were blind and now they
see. This seems to have been the case with Lydia at
Philippi ; the Lord gently opened her heart, so that she
attended to the things spoken by Paul. This is what
Elijah saw in the wilderness ; there was the whirlwind
and the earthquake and the fire, and after all there was
something else—a still small voice. And here is one
reason why we sometimes hope and trust that many
amongst the hearers in our congregations may still
prove children of God. We try to think that some of
you feel more than you seem to do, and that the time
is near when you will indeed come out and be separate,
and not be ashamed to confess Christ before men.

There is one more diversity I would very shortly
notice. Remember there is diversity in the feelings
which the Spirit first excites : each feeling is moved
sooner or later, but they are not moved always in the
same order. The new birth shows itself in some by
causing exceeding fear—they are filled with a strong
sense of God's holiness, and they tremble because they
have broken His law continually ; others begin with
sorrow—they can never mourn enough over their past
wickedness and ingratitude ; others begin with love—
they are full of affection towards Him who died for
them, and no sacrifice seems too great to make for His
sake. But all these worketh one and the same Spirit ;
in this man He touches one string, and in that another ;
but sooner or later all are blended in harmony together,
and when the new creation has fully taken place, fear
and sorrow and love may all be found at once.

Beloved, time will not allow me to go further with this subject to-day. I have endeavoured to show you this morning who is the Worker, the Cause of the new birth : it is not man, but God the Holy Ghost. What are the means through which He generally conveys it : preaching, the Bible, and prayer. And lastly I have shown you there are many diversities in His operations : with some He begins in infancy, with some in full years, with some few in old age. On some He comes down suddenly and on some gradually, in some He first moves one sort of feelings and in some another ; but whatever be His operation, without the Spirit none can be born again.

And now, in conclusion, tell me not you mean to wait lazily and idly, and if the Lord gives you this blessed change, well, and if not you cannot help it. God does not deal with you as if you were machines or stones ; He deals with you as those who can read and hear and pray, and this is the way in which He would have you wait upon Him. Never was doctrine so surrounded with promises and encouragements and invitations as this. Hear what Jeremiah says : " I will put my law in their inward parts, and write it in their hearts ; and will be their God, and they shall be my people." Again : " They shall be my people, and I will be their God : and I will give them one heart, and one way, that they may fear me for ever, for the good of them, and of their children after them." Then what Ezekiel says : " A new heart also will I give you, and a new spirit will I put within you : and I will take away the stony heart out of your flesh, and I will give you an heart of flesh. And I will put my Spirit within you, and cause you to walk in my statutes." Then lastly what the Lord Jesus says : " Ask, and ye shall receive ; seek, and ye shall find : every one that asketh receiveth :

your Heavenly Father shall give the Holy Spirit to them that ask Him." And this is what we want you to do : until you pray for yourselves in earnest, we know there will be little good done ; and if any prayerless man shall say in the day of judgment " I could not come to Christ," the answer will be, " You did not try."

Then quench not the Spirit, grieve not the Spirit, resist not the Spirit ; His grace has been purchased for you : strive and labour and pray that you may indeed receive it. And then God has covenanted and engaged that He shall come down like rain on the dry ground— like water to wash away your soul's defilement, like fire to burn away the dross and filth of sin, and the hardest heart among you shall become soft and willing as a weaned child.

IV

REGENERATION (III)

"Verily, verily I say unto thee, Except a man be born again, he cannot see the kingdom of God."—JOHN iii. 3.

WE have reached the last point in our inquiry about the new Birth—I mean the *marks* and *evidence* by which it may be known ; the notes by which a man may find out whether he has himself been born again or no. To set before you the character of those who are indeed new creatures,—to warn you against certain common mistakes respecting this doctrine,—to wind up the whole subject by appealing to your consciences,—this is the work which I propose to take in hand this morning.

Now this point may be last in order, but it certainly is not least in importance. It is the touchstone of our condition ; it decides whether we are natural men or spiritual men, whether we are yet dead in trespasses, or have been quickened and brought to see the kingdom of God.

Many there are who take it for granted they have been born again,—they do not exactly know why, but it is a sort of thing they never doubted ; others there are who despise all such sifting inquiry,—they are sure they are in the right way, they are confident they shall be saved, and as for marks, it is low and legal to talk about them, it is bringing men into bondage. But, beloved, whatever men may say, you may be certain

Christ's people are a peculiar people, not only peculiar in their talk but peculiar in their life and conduct, and they may be distinguished from the unconverted around them ; you may be certain there are stamps and marks and characters about God's handiwork by which it may always be known ; and he who has got no evidences to show may well suspect that he is not in the right way.

Now, about these marks I can of course only speak very shortly and very generally, for time will not allow me to do more ; but I would first say one word by way of caution. Remember, then, I would not have you suppose that all children of God do feel alike, or that these marks should be equally strong and plain in every case. The work of grace on man's heart is gradual : first the blade, then the ear, then the full corn in the ear. It is like leaven : the whole lump is not leavened at once. It is as in the birth of an infant into the world : first it feels, then moves and cries, and sees and hears and knows, and thinks and loves, and walks and talks and acts for itself. Each of these things comes gradually, and in order ; but we do not wait for all before we say this is a living soul. And just so is every one that is born of the Spirit. He may not, at first, find in himself all the marks of God, but he has the seed of them all about him ; and some he knows by experience, and all, in the course of time, shall be known distinctly. But this at least you may be sure of : wherever there is no fruit of the Spirit, there is no work of the Spirit ; and if any man have not the Spirit of Christ, he is none of His. O that this question might stir up every one of you to search and try his ways ! God is not a man that he should lie ; He would not have given you the Bible if you could be saved without it ; and here is a doctrine on

which eternal life depends : " No salvation without the
new birth."

I. First, then, and foremost, I would have you write
down in your memories a mark which St. John mentions
in his first epistle : " Whosoever is born of God, doth
not commit sin " ; " whosoever is born of God, sinneth
not " ; " whosoever abideth in Him sinneth not : whosoever sinneth hath not seen Him, neither known Him."

Observe, I would not for one minute have you
suppose that God's children are perfect, and without
spot or stain or defilement in themselves. Do not go
away and say I told you they were pure as angels
and never made a slip or stumble. The same St. John
in the same Epistle declares : " If we say that we have
no sin, we deceive ourselves, and the truth is not in
us. . . . If we say that we have not sinned, we make
Him a liar, and His word is not in us."

But I do say that in the matter of breaking God's
commandments, every one that is born again is quite
a new man. He no longer takes a light and cool
and easy view of sin ; he no longer judges of it with
the world's judgment ; he no longer thinks a little
swearing, or a little Sabbath-breaking, or a little fornication, or a little drinking, or a little covetousness,
small and trifling matters ; but he looks on every sort
of sin against God or man as exceeding abominable
and damnable in the Lord's sight, and, as far as in
him lies, he hates it and abhors it, and desires to be
quit of it root and branch, with his whole heart and
mind and soul and strength.

He that is born again has had the eyes of his understanding opened, and the Ten Commandments appear
to him in an entirely new light. He feels amazed that
he can have lived so long careless and indifferent about
transgressions, and he looks back on the days gone

by with shame and sorrow and grief. As for his daily conduct, he allows himself in no known sin ; he makes no compromise with his old habits and his old principles ; he gives them up unsparingly, though it cost him pain, though the world think him over-precise and a fool ; but he is a new man, and will have nothing more to do with the accursed thing. I do not say but that he comes short, and finds his old nature continually opposing him—and this, too, when no eye can see it but his own ; but then he mourns and repents bitterly over his own weakness. And this at least he has about him : he is at war, in reality, with the devil and all his works, and strives constantly to be free.

And do you call that no change ? Look abroad on this world, this evildoing world : mark how little men generally think about sin ; how seldom they judge of it as the Bible does ; how easy they suppose the way to heaven,—and judge ye whether this mark be not exceeding rare. But for all this God will not be mocked, and men may rest assured that until they are convinced of the awful guilt and the awful power and the awful consequences of sin, and, being convinced, flee from it and give it up, they are most certainly not born again.

II. The second mark I would have you note is " faith in Christ," and here again I speak in the words of St. John in his first epistle : " Whosoever believeth that Jesus is the Christ is born of God."

I do not mean by this a general vague sort of belief that Jesus Christ once lived on earth and died—a sort of faith which the very devils possess ; I mean, rather, that feeling which comes over a man when he is really convinced of his own guilt and unworthiness, and sees that Christ alone can be his Saviour ; when he becomes convinced he is in a way to be lost, and must have some righteousness better than his own, and joyfully embraces that righteousness which Jesus holds out to all who will believe. He that has got this faith discovers a fitness and suitableness and comfort in the doctrine of Christ crucified for sinners which once he never knew ; he is no longer ashamed to confess himself by nature poor and blind and naked, and to take Christ for his only hope of salvation.

Before a man is born of the Spirit there seems no particular form nor comeliness about the Redeemer, but after that blessed change has taken place He appears the very chiefest in ten thousand : no honour so great but Jesus is worthy of it ; no love so strong but on Jesus it is well bestowed ; no spiritual necessity so great but Jesus can relieve it ; no sin so black but Jesus' blood can wash it away. Before the new birth a man can bow at Christ's name, and sometimes wonder at Christ's miracles, but that is all ; once born again, a man sees a fulness and a completeness and a sufficiency in Christ of things necessary to salvation, so that he feels as if he could never think upon Him enough. To cast the burden of sin on Jesus, to glory in the cross on which He died, to keep continually in sight His blood, His righteousness, His intercession, His mediation ; to go continually to Him for peace and forgiveness, to rest entirely on Him for full and free salvation, to make Jesus, in short, all in all in their hopes of heaven—this is the most notable mark of all true children of God—they live by faith in Christ, in Christ their happiness is bound up.

It is the spiritual law of God which brings them to this : time was when they were ready to think well of themselves ; the law strips off their miserable garments of self-righteousness, exposes their exceeding guilt and rottenness, cuts down to the ground their fancied notions of justification by their own works, and so leads them to Christ as their only wisdom and redemption ; and then, when they have laid hold on Christ and taken Him for their Saviour, they begin to find that rest which before they had sought in vain.

Such are two first marks of the Spirit's work—a deep conviction of sin and forsaking of it, and a lively faith in Christ crucified as the only hope of forgiveness—marks which the world perhaps may not see, but marks without which no man or woman was ever yet made a new creature. These are the two foundations of the Christian's character, the pillars, as it were, of the kingdom of God ; they are hidden roots which others can only judge of by the fruit; but they who have them do generally know it, and can feel the witness in themselves.

III. The third mark of the new birth is " holiness." What says the apostle John again ?—" Every one that doeth righteousness is born of God " ; " he that is begotten of God keepeth himself."

The true children of God delight in making the law their rule of life ; it dwells in their minds, and is written upon their hearts, and it is their meat and drink to do their Father's will. They know nothing of that spirit of bondage which false Christians complain of ; it is their pleasure to glorify God with their bodies and souls, which are His ; they hunger and thirst after tempers and dispositions like their Lord's. They do not rest content with sleepy wishing and hoping, but they strive to be holy in all manner of conversation— in thought, in word, and in deed ; it is their daily heart's prayer, " Lord what wilt Thou have us to do ? " and it is their daily grief and lamentation that they come so short and are such unprofitable servants. Beloved, remember where there is no holiness of life there cannot be much work of the Holy Ghost.

IV. The fourth mark of the new birth is spiritual-mindedness. We learn this from St. Paul's words to the Colossians : " If ye then be risen with Christ, seek those things which are above . . . . set your affection on things above, not on things on the earth."

He that is born again thinks first about the things which are eternal ; he no longer gives up the best of his heart to this perishable world's concerns : he looks on earth as a place of pilgrimage, he looks on heaven as his home ; and even as a child remembers with delight its absent parents, and hopes to be one day with them, so does the Christian think of his God and long for that day when he shall stand in His presence and go no more out. He cares not for the pleasures and amusements of the world around him ; he minds not the things of the flesh, but the things of the Spirit ; he feels that he has a house not made with hands eternal in the heavens, and he earnestly desires to be there. " Lord," he says, " whom have I in heaven but Thee ? and there is none on earth that I desire beside thee."

V. The fifth mark of the new birth is victory over the world. Hear what St. John says : " Whosoever is born of God overcometh the world : and this is the victory that overcometh the world, even our faith."

What is the natural man ?—a wretched slave to the opinion of this world. What the world says is right he follows and approves ; what the world says is wrong he renounces and condemns also. How shall I do what my neighbours do not do ? What will men say of me if I become more strict than they ? This is the natural man's argument. But from all this he that is born again is free. He no longer is led by the praise or the blame, the laughter or the frown, of

children of Adam like himself. He no longer thinks
that the sort of religion which everybody about him
professes must necessarily be right. He no longer
considers " What will the world say? " but " What
does God command? " Oh, it is a glorious change
when a man thinks nothing of the difficulty of confessing Christ before men, in the hope that Christ will
confess him and own him before the holy angels! That
fear of the world is a terrible snare ; with many
thousands it far outweighs the fear of God. There
are men who would care more for the laughter of a
company of friends than they would for the testimony
of half the Bible. From all this the spiritual man is
free. He is no longer like a dead fish floating with
the stream of earthly opinion ; he is ever pressing
upwards, looking unto Jesus in spite of all opposition
He has overcome the world.

VI. The sixth mark of the new birth is " meekness.'
This is what David meant when he said, in Psalm
cxxxi.: " My soul is even as a weaned child." This
is what our Lord has in view when He tells us we
" must be converted and become as little children."

Pride is the besetting sin of all natural men, and it
comes out in a hundred different fashions. It was
pride by which the angels fell and became devils. It
is pride which brings many a sinner to the pit,—he
knows he is in the wrong about religion, but he is too
proud to bend his neck and act up to what he knows.
It is pride which may always be seen about false
professors : they are always saying, We are the men,
and we are alone in the right, and ours is the sure
way to heaven ; and by-and-by they fall and go to
their own place and are heard no more of. But he
that is born again is clothed with humility ; he has a
very child-like and contrite and broken spirit ; he has

a deep sense of his own weakness and sinfulness, and great fear of a fall. You never hear him professing confidence in himself and boasting of his own attainments,—he is far more ready to doubt about his own salvation altogether and call himself " chief of sinners." He has no time to find fault with others, or be a busybody about his neighbours,—enough for him to keep up the conflict with his own deceitful heart, the old Adam within. No enemy so bitter to him as his own inbred corruption. Whenever I see a man passing his time in picking holes in other Churches, and talking about every one's soul except his own, I always feel in my own mind, " There is no work of the Spirit there." And it is just this humility and sense of weakness which makes God's children men of prayer. They feel their own wants and their danger, and they are constrained to go continually with supplication to Him who has given them the Spirit of adoption, crying, Abba Father, help us and deliver us from evil.

VII. The seventh mark of the new birth is a great delight in all means of grace. This is what Peter speaks of in his first Epistle : " As new-born babes, desire the sincere milk of the word, that ye may grow." This was the mind of David when he said, " A day in Thy courts is better than a thousand : I had rather be a doorkeeper in the house of my God, than to dwell in the tents of wickedness."

And oh, what a difference there is between nature and grace in this matter ! The natural man has often a form of godliness : he does not neglect the ordinances of religion, but somehow or other the weather, or his health, or the distance, contrives to be a great hindrance to him, and far too often it happens that the hours he spends in church or over his Bible are the dullest in his life.

But when a man is born again, he begins to find a reality about means which once he did not feel : the Sabbath no longer seems a dull, wearisome day, in which he knows not how to spend his time decently ; he now calls it a delight and a privilege, holy of the Lord and honourable. The difficulties which once kept him from God's house now seem to have vanished away : dinner and weather and the like never detain him at home, and he is no longer glad of an excuse not to go. Sermons appear a thousand times more interesting than they used to do ; and he would no more be inattentive or willingly go to sleep under them, than a prisoner would upon his trial. And, above all, the Bible looks to him like a new book. Time was when it was very dry reading to his mind—perhaps it lay in a corner dusty and seldom read—but now it is searched and examined as the very bread of life ; many are the texts and passages which seem just written for his own case ; and many are the days that he feels disposed to say with David, " The law of Thy mouth is better to me than thousands of gold and silver."

VIII. The eighth and last mark of the new birth is "love towards others." " Every one," says St. John, " that loveth is born of God, and knoweth God. He that loveth not knoweth not God ; for God is love."

He that is born of the Spirit loves his neighbour as himself; he knows nothing of the selfishness and uncharitableness and ill-nature of this world ; he loves his neighbour's property as his own; he would not injure it, nor stand by and see it injured ; he loves his neighbour's person as his own, and he would count no trouble ill bestowed if he could help or assist him ; he loves his neighbour's character as his own, and you will not hear him speak a word against it, or allow it to be blackened by falsehoods if he can defend it ; and then

he loves his neighbour's soul as his own, and he will
not suffer him to turn his back on God without endeavouring to stop him by saying, "Oh, do not so!"
Oh what a happy place would earth be if there was
more love! Oh that men would only believe that the
gospel secures the greatest comfort in the life that now
is, as well as in the life to come!

And such, beloved, are the marks by which the new
birth in a man's soul may generally be discovered.
I have been obliged to speak of them very shortly,
although each one of them deserves a sermon. I commend to your especial attention the two first: conviction
and forsaking of sin, and faith in Christ; they are marks
on which each must be his own judge. "Have I ever
truly repented? Have I really closed with Christ and
taken Him for my only Saviour and Lord?" Let these
questions be uppermost in your mind if you would
know whether you are born again or not. The six
last marks—viz. holiness, spiritual-mindedness, victory
over the world, meekness, delight in means, and love—
have this peculiarity about them, that a man's family
and neighbours do often see more clearly whether he
has got them than he does himself; but they all flow
out of the two first, and therefore I once more urge
the two first on your especial notice.

And now, brethren beloved, in concluding this course
of sermons, I desire to speak one word to the consciences of all who have heard them: old or young,
rich or poor, careless or thoughtful, you are all equally
concerned.

For three Sunday mornings you have heard this
new birth set before you according to my ability, and
have you ever thought upon your own state and looked
within? What of your own hearts? Are you living
or dead, natural or spiritual, born again or not? Are

your bodies temples of the Holy Ghost? Are your habits and characters the habits and characters of renewed creatures? Oh, search and see what there is within you: the language of the text is plain,—no new birth, no kingdom of God.

I know there is nothing popular or agreeable about this doctrine; it strikes at the root of all compromising half-and-half religion, and still it is true. Many would like much to escape the punishment of sin, who will not strive to be free from its power; they wish to be justified but not to be sanctified; they desire much to have God's favour, but they care little for God's image and likeness; their talk is of pardon, but not of purity; they think much about God's willingness to forgive, but little about His warning that we be renewed. But this is leaving out of sight half the work which Christ died to perform: He died that we might become holy as well as happy, He purchased grace to sanctify as well as grace to redeem; and now forgiveness of sin and change of heart must never be separated. "What God hath joined together, let no man presume to put asunder." The foundation of God stands firm: "If any man have not the Spirit of Christ, he is none of His."

Beloved, it is easy work to live unto ourselves and take no trouble about religion; the world approves it, and says we shall probably do well at last; but if ever we are to be saved there is another life, and that too on this side the grave, we must live unto God. It is easy to be natural men,—we give no offence, and the devil comforts us by saying, as he did to Eve, "Ye shall not surely die": but the devil was a liar from the beginning. So long as we are natural men, we are dead already, and we must rise to newness of life. And what know ye of the movements of the Spirit? I ask not

so much whether ye can say which way He came into
your hearts, but I do ask whether ye can find any real
footsteps or traces or tokens of His presence—for "if
any man have not the Spirit of Christ, he is none
of His."

Be not deceived and led away by false opinions.
Head-knowledge is not the new birth: a man may
know all mysteries like Balaam, and think his eyes
are opened ; or preach and work miracles and be an
Apostle like Judas Iscariot, yet never be born again.
Church-membership is not the new birth ; many do
sit in churches and chapels who shall have no seat
in Christ's kingdom ; they are not Israel who have the
circumcision of the flesh outwardly, they are the true
Israel who have the circumcision of the heart, which is
inward.

There were many Jews in the New Testament days
who said, "We have Abraham for our father, and we
have the temple among us and that is enough," but
Jesus showed them that they only are Abraham's
children who have the faith of Abraham and do
Abraham's works. And then water-baptism alone is
not the new birth : it is the sign and seal, and when
used with faith and prayer we have a right to look
also for the baptism of the Holy Ghost ; but to say
that every man who has been baptised has been born
again is contrary to Scripture and plain fact. Was not
Simon Magus baptised ? Yes, but Peter told him after
his baptism that he was in the gall of bitterness and
bond of iniquity, his heart not right in the sight of God.
" I would not have you ignorant," says Paul to the
Corinthians, that all our Fathers were baptised, ... but
with many of them God was not well pleased. " Baptism," writes Peter, "doth indeed save us"; but what
baptism? " not the putting away of the filth of the body,

not the washing of water, but the answer of a pure conscience," a conscience made pure by the baptism of the Holy Ghost.

Beloved, let no man lead you astray in this matter ; let no man make you believe that a baptised drunkard or fornicator or blasphemer or worldling has been born of the Spirit ; he has not the marks of the new birth, and he cannot have been born again ; he is living in sin and carelessness, and St. John has given us his character—" he that committeth sin is of the devil." Remember, the outward seal is nothing without the inward writing on the heart. No evidence can be depended on excepting a new life and a new character and a new creature ; and to say that men who want their evidences are born again is an unreasonable and unscriptural stretch of charity.

And now, in conclusion, if any one of you has reason to think that he still lacks this one thing needful, I entreat that man not to stifle his convictions or nip them in the bud. Do not go away like Cain and silence the voice of conscience by rushing into the vanities of the world, nor dream, like Felix, that you will have a more convenient season than the present ; but remember I tell you this day there are two things which make a death-bed specially uncomfortable : first, purposes and promises not performed ; and second, convictions slighted and not improved. And if any of you has satisfactory grounds for thinking that he has really tasted something of that saving and necessary change we have considered, I charge that man not to stand still, not to loiter, not to linger, not to look behind him ; I warn him that none are in so dangerous a way as those who have become cool and cold and indifferent after real and warm concern about salvation ; I urge him to press forward more and more towards the knowledge of Christ, and to remember it is a special mark of God's children that as they grow in age they grow in grace, and feel their sins more deeply and love their Lord and Saviour more sincerely.

V

SAVING FAITH

"God so loved the world, that He gave His only begotten Son, that whosoever believeth in Him should not perish, but have everlasting life."—JOHN iii. 16.

IN this verse, beloved, we have one of those "heavenly things," which our Lord had just spoken of to Nicodemus. Blessed indeed are the lips which spake it, and blessed are the hearts which can receive it! In this verse we find a treasury of the most precious truth, a mine of inexhaustible matter, a well of ever-flowing waters; and when we consider the simple words in which our Lord has here brought together the whole body of divinity, we must willingly confess, with those who heard Him preach, "Never man spake like this man." Listen, I pray you, once more—"God so loved the world, that He gave His only begotten Son, that whosoever believeth in Him should not perish, but have everlasting life." There is hardly an expression that a child could not easily explain, and yet there are doctrines here which the wisest upon earth must humbly receive, if they would enter into the kingdom of heaven and sit down at the marriage supper of the Lamb. We learn in it, what philosophers of old could never clear up—the history of God's dealing with mankind, and the terms which He offers for their acceptance. Here is life, and here is death; here you have the deserts

57

of man, and here you have the free grace of God ; here
you see what all may expect who follow their own
course, and here also the way, the truth, and the life
is directly pointed out.

And at this particular season of the year, when we
are about so soon to commemorate the mysterious birth
of Him who in mercy to our sins consented to take
our nature on Him and be born of a virgin, even Christ
Jesus, we cannot, I think, do better than examine the
things which are herein contained.   May the Eternal
Spirit, through whom He offered Himself, the great
Teacher whom He promised to send, be amongst us :
may He rouse the careless, fix the inattentive, and make
the subject profitable to all.

Now I conceive the chief things to be noticed in this
verse are :

    I. The state of the world, that is, of all mankind.

    II. The love of God.

    III. The gift of His Son.

    IV. The means whereby we enjoy this gift.

    V. And the promise attached to those who believe.

    I. First, then, let us inquire what the word of God
has taught us respecting the world and the *world's
character*.   Now, the testimony of Scripture upon this
head is so clear and explicit, that he who runs may read,
" The whole world," says St. John, "lieth in wickedness."
Our first father, Adam, was indeed created in the image
of God, pure and sinless ; but in one day he fell from
his high estate by eating the forbidden fruit, he broke
God's express command and became at once a sinful
creature ; and now all we his children have by inheritance from him a wicked and a corrupt nature, a
nature which clings to us from the moment of our birth.
and which we show daily in our lives and conversation.
In a word, we learn that from the hour of the fall our

character has been established, that we are a sinful, a
very sinful world.

Beloved, does this appear a hard saying? do you
think such a statement too strong? Away with the
flattering thought!—We see it proved in Scripture,
for every book of the Old Testament history tells the
melancholy story of man's disobedience and man's
unbelief in things pertaining to God. We read there
of fearful judgments, such as the flood and the
destruction of Sodom, yet men disregarded them,—
of gracious mercies, such as the calling and protection
of Israel, but men soon forgot them,—of inspired
teachers and revelations from heaven, such as the law
of Moses, and men did not obey them,—of special
warnings, such as the voice of the prophets, and yet
men did not believe them. Yes, beloved, we are a
sinful world! Think not to say within yourselves, " It
may be so, but this happened in days of old ; the world
is better now." It will not avail you. We have read
it in Scripture, but we see it also around us, and you
will find at this time, even under your own eyes, con-
vincing proof that the charge is literally true. Let any,
for instance, examine the columns of a county newspaper, and he will see there within a month enough
to make his ears tingle. I speak as unto wise men,—
judge ye what I say : will he not see accounts of nearly
every sin which is abominable in the sight of God?
Will he not read of anger, wrath, malice, blasphemy,
theft, adultery, fornication, uncleanness, lasciviousness,
emulations, variance, strife, seditions, envyings, murders,
drunkenness, revellings, and such like: " of the which,"
says the apostle (Gal. v. 21), " I tell you before, as I
have also told you in time past, that they which do such
things shall not inherit the kingdom of God." And
if such things take place in a land which is blessed with

so much light and knowledge as our own, how much more should we find in countries where there is neither one nor the other! If men do these things in a green tree, oh, what shall they do in a dry?

Can you still doubt? I will go further. We see proof in ourselves. Let the best among you search his own heart ; let him honestly cast up the number of evil thoughts and unholy ideas which pass through his imagination even in one single day—thoughts, I mean, which are known only to himself and the all-seeing God—and let him tell us whether it be not a most humiliating and soul-condemning calculation. Yes, dear friends, whether you will receive it or no, we are indeed a sinful world. It may be an humbling truth, but Scripture says it, and experience confirms it ; and therefore we tell you that the world spoken of in our text is a world which lieth in wickedness, a corrupt world, a world which our great Maker and Preserver might have left to deserved destruction, and in so doing would have acted with perfect justice, because He has given us laws and they have been broken, promises and they have been despised, warnings and they have not been believed.

II. Such is the world of which we form a part, and such is its character. And now let us hear what the feeling is with which God has been pleased to regard His guilty creatures. We were all under condemnation, without hope, without excuse ; and what could stay the execution of the sentence? *It was the love of God.* "God," says our text, "so loved the world." He might have poured on us the vials of His wrath, as He did on the angels who kept not their first estate ; but no! He spared us, "God loved the world." Justice demanded our punishment, holiness required we should be swept off the earth ; but "God loved the world." Praised be His name, we had not to do with man's judgment, which may not show mercy, when a crime is proved ; we were in the hands of One whose ways are not as our ways and whose thoughts are not as our thoughts, and hence, " God so loved the world." May we not well say with the Apostle, " O the depth of the riches both of the wisdom and knowledge of God ! " (Rom. xi. 33). Consider, I pray you, this incomprehensible goodness ! Do not many in this world think it no harm to remember injuries, and sometimes to resent them ? Do we not find it hard to love those who have given us some slight offence ? or if we do profess to love them, do we make any endeavour to promote their happiness? Such, alas ! is too seldom our practice ; there is but little real affection in these hard hearts ; but we are not dealt with according to our own ways, for the God of holiness has loved the sinful world, which has continually dishonoured and denied Him. Oh ! beloved, let us dwell much on such expressions as these, for they are more precious than rubies ; let us bear them continually in mind, for they will not fail us in the day of trial, when temptation is strong and faith weak ; let us write them on our hearts and in our memories, and we shall find them a strong consolation in the hour of death and on the bed of sickness. God is indeed love, and God loved the world.

III. Let us next inquire in what way it pleased God to manifest this love. We had all sinned. Who then could put away this sin and present us clean and spotless before His throne ? We had all failed utterly of keeping His holy laws. Wherewithal then could we be clothed for the wedding-feast of our Master ? Beloved, here is wisdom ! This is the very point which the learned of this world could never understand. How, they have asked, can perfect justice and perfect mercy be reconciled ? How can God justify His

sinful creature, and yet be that Holy One whose law
must needs be fulfilled? But all is explained in this
simple verse, if ye can receive it; and thus it was
—" *He gave His only-begotten Son*." Observe the mag-
nitude of this gift—" His only-begotten Son." Can
anything give you a more tender idea of God's love?
Observe again the expression " He *gave* ": not because
we had merited anything, for it was a free gift; not for
our deservings, for it was all of grace. " By grace are
ye saved," says Paul to the Ephesians. " The gift of God
is eternal life," says the same apostle to the Romans.

And for what purpose was His Son given? Beloved,
He was given to atone for our guilt, by the sacrifice
and death of Himself, as a lamb without spot and
blemish; and by so doing He made a full, perfect,
and sufficient oblation and satisfaction for the sins of
the whole world. He was given to bear our iniquities
and carry our transgressions upon the accursed tree,
the cross; for being innocent Himself He was for our
sakes accounted guilty, that we for His sake might be
accounted pure. Nor is this all: He was given to fulfil
the demands of that law which we have broken; and
He did fulfil them. He " was tempted in all points,"
says St. Paul, " like as we are, and yet without sin ": the
prince of this world had nothing in Him, and thus He
brought in an everlasting righteousness, which like a
pure white raiment is unto all and upon all them that
believe. (2 Cor. v. 21.)

IV. It would be easy to dwell upon this delightful
branch of our subject, beloved, but we must pass on.
How then are! the benefits of this gift made our own?
What are the means through which it is applied to our
souls? What is the hand by which we lay hold on
this remedy?

Here again our text supplies an answer. It is

FAITH. Whosoever believeth (not with the head, remember : but with the heart), and believing comes to Christ with a confession of his own unrighteousness, and accepts Him as his only hope of salvation— is saved by Faith.

Consider now the beautiful simplicity of this way of life : we do not see written on the gate, Whosoever has prepared himself by long repentance—whosoever has begun to lead a new life—whosoever has done so many good works—whosoever has attended church so many times—whosoever has given so much in charity—these shall enter in here, and none else. No, dear friends ; such announcements would frighten many a weary sinner, and these are fruits you will thankfully bring forth a hundredfold after you have entered : the only thing required of those who seek admission is faith, and he that approaches in simple childlike faith shall never be rejected. Hear how St. Paul speaks on this point (Rom. x. 5 to 10). And, lest any one should suppose that God is a respecter of persons, that there is one way for the rich and another for the poor, one for the learned, another for the unlearned, he adds these comfortable words : " For there is no difference between the Jew and the Greek : for the same Lord over all is rich unto all that call upon Him. For whosoever shall call upon the name of the Lord shall be saved." But remember also—and I solemnly warn every one of this—there is no other way than the way of faith. God has not left each man to choose his own road to heaven, or his own path for coming unto Christ, but He has appointed one and no more, and no man shall enter into life except by this.

" If ye will not believe," says Isaiah, "surely ye shall not be established." " If ye believe not," says our Lord,

" that I am He, ye shall die in your sins." And hence
we may learn this most important lesson, that although
God so loved the world that He gave for it His only-
begotten Son, still the benefits of that gift can never be
obtained by those who will not believe.

V. It remains for us in the last place to consider
the *promises and consequences* which our text holds
forth to the faithful. We read that " whosoever believeth shall not perish, but have everlasting life."

And is not this a promise the most acceptable to
our nature that a gracious God could have devised ?
We know there is nothing the unconverted fear so
much as death : people of the highest animal courage,
who would shrink from no danger and encounter any
difficulty, have been seen to tremble and turn pale
at the approach of some pain or complaint which seems
likely to bring their frail bodies to the grave. And
why should this be so ?—pain is not very bitter, and
life with its cares and anxieties is not so very sweet
as to account for it ! No, beloved, the reason is this.
Conscience tells every unconverted person, whether he
likes to confess it or not, that after death shall come
the judgment ; conscience tells him that all shall be
judged according to their works,—that he cannot abide
this fiery trial, because he has sinned and not sought
reconciliation, and he feels that he may one day have
his part in the lake which burns with fire and brimstone.
Hence it is that he thinks death a most unpleasant
subject, and with all his pride of life stands in cowardly
fear of his last day ; and hence you may understand
how blessed these words should be to a sinner's ear,
that "Whosoever believeth on Him shall not perish
but have everlasting life."

Observe now the contents of this promise ; look
narrowly into it, for it will stand a close examination.

The believer shall not perish; this earthly tabernacle may indeed be dissolved, and laid in the grave and see corruption, but the true sting of that death is sin, and this his Saviour has taken on Him and put away. He shall not perish in the day of judgment; the second death can have no power over him; hell has no claims upon him, and then the words of our blessed Master shall be found a truth. "This is the will of Him that sent Me, that every one which seeth the Son, and believeth on Him, may have everlasting life: and I will raise him up at the last day" (John vi. 40). " I am the resurrection and the life: he that believeth on Me, though he were dead, yet shall he live: and whosoever liveth and believeth in Me shall never die " (xi. 25, 26).

And more than this: the believer shall have everlasting life. He shall be raised body and soul at our Lord's second coming. He shall have part in that first resurrection, which belongs only to the saints, and finally shall dwell for ever in that blessed place where "there shall be no more death, neither sorrow, nor crying, neither shall there be any more pain: for the former things are passed away" (Rev. xxi. 4).

And now, beloved, judge for yourselves whether it be not true, that our text contains a treasury of precious and most consoling doctrines, and he that can hear it without feeling its value may indeed tremble for the safety of his immortal soul. Believer, let it be thy care to carry home these comfortable words on which we have dwelt, and meditate upon them as thy daily food throughout the week which is now before thee. Let them be ever in thy mind, and prepare thee for that holy sacrament which Jesus has mercifully ordained; let them add strength to thy faith and growth to thy sanctification; let them increase thy humility and thy

thankfulness, thy zeal for God's glory, and thy desire
to show forth His praise, thy love towards Christ and
thy love towards thy brethren ; for surely, dear friends,
if God so loved us, it is a small matter if we love our
fellow-sinners.

And you too, dear brethren, who have dared hitherto,
like Gallio, to care for none of these things, you also
are appealed to in this text.   Learn then now, if you
have not learned it yet, that this single verse, if there
were no other, would be sufficient to condemn you in
the last day, because it leaves you without excuse for
remaining in your sins.   You have deserved nothing but
wrath ; and yet, behold, here is God willing to save,
loving, giving, promising all things.   Oh ! remember
how great must be your guilt if you reject so great
salvation.   You are the very world that God has so
loved ; for your sakes He gave His only-begotten Son,
and even now, at this minute, He is inviting you, by
me, His minister, to accept the mercy which He freely
offers, to be reconciled with Him who will one day be
the Judge of all. (Isaiah lv. 1, 2¦; i. 18 ; Acts xvi. 31.)

Come then, I entreat you, to your Father, in the
name of Christ, for through Him we have boldness and
access with confidence.   Resist the attempts of the
world, the flesh and the devil to detain you ; resist
even your best friend, if he would keep you back from
God and tell you there will be a more convenient season
than to-day.   "As though God did beseech you by
us : we pray you in Christ's stead, be ye reconciled to
God.   For He hath made Him to be sin for us, who
knew no sin ; that we might be made the righteousness
of God in Him" (2 Cor. v. 20, 21).

May God the Holy Ghost bless the words which
we have spoken to the everlasting benefit of all your
souls.

VI

"COME UNTO ME"

"Come unto Me, all ye that labour and are heavy laden, and I will give you rest."—Matt. xi. 28.

THERE are few texts more striking than this in all the Bible—few that contain so wide and sweeping an invitation—few that hold out so full and comfortable a promise.

Let us consider—

I. Who it is that speaks.

II. Who they are that are spoken to.

III. What is the invitation.

IV. What is the promise.

I. WHO SPEAKS?—That is a most important question, and it is right to have it answered.

You live in a world of promise. "Come with us," says one party, and you will be rich. "Come with us," says another, and you will be happy.

The devil can promise. "Eat the forbidden fruit," he said to Eve, "and you shall be as gods, knowing good and evil. You shall never die." But he lied to her.

The world can promise. "Sell all and embark for California," says one man, "and you will soon roll in wealth." "Invest all your money in railways," says another, "and you will soon make your fortune." I never take up a newspaper without seeing many alluring invitations. I see page after page of advertisements, all full of high-sounding promises. I read of short ways to health, wealth, and happiness, of all descriptions. But it is all words and nothing more, and so many a man finds.

But He that promises in our text is One who can be depended on. It is the Lord Jesus Christ, God's own Son.

He is ABLE to do what He promises. He has all power in heaven and on earth. He has the keys of death and hell. The government is given to Him in time, and all judgment committed to Him in eternity.

He is FAITHFUL to do what He promises. He will not lie, nor deceive, nor break His promise. What He speaks that He will do, and what He undertakes that He will perform. Heaven and earth may pass away, but His word shall not pass away.

He is WILLING to do what He promises. He has long since proved this by the love He has shown to man, and the sacrifice He has made for man's soul. For man He came into the world; for man He suffered and died; for man He endured the cross and the shame. Surely He has a right to be believed.

Beloved brethren, see that you refuse not Him that speaketh to you this day. If a letter came to you from the ruler of this country you would not despise it. If you were sick, and advice came from a wise physician, you would not reject it. If you were in danger, and counsel came from your best and truest friend, you would not make light of it. Then hear the words that Jesus sends to you this day. Listen to the King of kings. Then body and soul shall be His.

II. WHO ARE THEY THAT ARE SPOKEN TO?—
Jesus addresses the "labouring and heavy laden":

" Come unto Me all ye that labour and are heavy
laden." Now, whom does this mean?

You must not fancy it describes the *poor in this
world*. That would be a great mistake. It is possible
to be poor in time and even poorer in eternity.

Nor yet must you fancy it describes the *sick and
the afflicted*. That also is a great mistake. It is very
possible to have trouble in this life and trouble in
that to come—and this some of you may find.

The " labouring and heavy laden " describes all who
are pressed down and burdened by a feeling of sin.
It describes all whose consciences are set at work, and
who are brought to concern about their soul—all who
are anxious about salvation, and desire to have it—
all who tremble at the thought of judgment, and know
not how to get through it, and of hell, and are
afraid of falling into it ; and long for heaven, and
dread not getting to it ; and are distressed at the
thought of their own badness, and want deliverance.
All such persons appear to be the labouring and heavy
laden to whom Jesus speaks.

This was the state of mind in which the Jews were to
whom Peter preached on the day of Pentecost. Their
consciences were awakened ; they felt convinced and
condemned ; and when he had finished, we are told
they said, " Men and brethren, what shall we do? "
This was the state of mind in which Saul was when
Jesus met him going to Damascus, and smote him
to the ground. A light seemed to break in on his
mind. He got a sight of his one enormous sin and
danger ; and we read that, trembling and astonished,
he said, " Lord, what wilt Thou have me to do? "
This was the state of mind in which we see the
jailer at Philippi. He was roused from sleep by an
earthquake. His fear brought his sin to his remem-

brance, and he came and fell down before Paul and
Silas, and said, "Sirs, what must I do to be saved?"
This is the state of mind I desire to see in each of
you, for the beginning of all saving religion. You will
never come to Christ till you feel your need.

You *ought*, every one, to feel labouring and heavy
laden. Truly it is a marvellous proof of man's corruption, that men can be so careless as they are.
Many, I do believe, *feel something* of it, but never
allow it. There are many aching hearts under silk
and satin. There are many merry faces which only
hide an uneasy conscience. All is not gold that
glitters in happiness that seems like it. Few, I believe,
are to be found who do not feel something of it
some time in their lives. Halyburton said, not a soul
in his parish, but once had conviction.

But to all labouring and heavy laden souls, whoever
they may be, to you Jesus speaks—to you is this word
of salvation sent. Take heed that it is not in vain.

Jesus speaks to ALL such: none are left out. Though
you have been a persecutor like Saul, though a murderer like Manasseh, though a cheating extortioner
like Zacchæus, though unclean and profligate like the
Magdalen, it matters nothing. Are you labouring and
heavy-laden?—then Jesus speaks to you. You may
tell me, "I am such a sinner, Jesus never speaks to
me." I answer, "It may be so; but are you labouring
and heavy-laden?—then Jesus speaks to you. You may
say, "I am not fit." I see nothing said of fitness; I
only see Jesus calling the labouring and heavy laden:
if this is your case, He calls you. You may say, "I
am not this—I am not converted." You do not know,
perhaps; but are you labouring and heavy laden?—
then Jesus is speaking to you.

Ah! brethren, I fear many of you know nothing

of the state of the soul here spoken of. Your sins
never cut you to the heart, or give you a moment's
sorrow. You never really felt the confession of the
Church this day—" no health in us." You know nothing of communion with Christ. The remembrance
of grievous burdens is not intolerable. You are satisfied
with your present state: like Laodicea, " rich and increased with goods," comfortable and content. And
what shall I say? I will say plainly, there is no hope for
your soul while in such a state. I say if your soul is
in such a state, better never have been born. Your
hard heart must be broken. You must be brought
to see your own guilt and danger, your eyes must be
opened to understand your sinfulness. All who have
entered heaven were once labouring and heavy laden ;
and except you are, you will never get there.

III. WHAT IS THE INVITATION TO THE LABOUR-
ING AND HEAVY LADEN? JESUS SAYS, " COME UNTO
ME."

I love that word " Come." To me it seems full of
grace, mercy and encouragement. " Come now," says
the Lord in Isaiah, " and let us reason together :
though your sins be as scarlet, they shall be white as
snow."

Come is the word put in the mouth of the king's
messenger in the parable of the guest-supper : " All is
now ready ; come unto the marriage."

Come is the last word in the Bible to sinners. " The
Spirit and the Bride say, Come."

Jesus does not say, " Go and get ready." This is the
word of the Pharisee and self-righteous. " Go and work
out a righteousness. Do this and that and be saved."
Jesus says, Come.

Jesus does not say " Send." This is the poor Roman
Catholic's word. " Put your soul in the hand of the

priest. Commit your affairs to saints and angels, and
not to Christ." Jesus says *Come*.

Jesus does not say "Wait." This is the word of the
enthusiast and the fanatic. "You can do nothing. You
must not ask ; you cannot pray ; you must sit still."
Cold comfort for troubled souls. Jesus says *come*.

Come is a word of *merciful invitation*. It seems to
say, "I want you to escape the wrath to come. I am
not willing that any should perish. I have no pleasure
in death. I would fain have all men saved, and I offer
all the water of life freely. So come to Me."

Come is a word of *gracious expectation*. It seems
to say, "I am here waiting for you. I sit on my
mercy-seat expecting you to come. I wait to be
gracious. I wait for more sinners to come in before I
close the door. I want more names written down in the
book of life before it is closed for ever. So come to Me."

Come is a word of *kind encouragement*. It seems to
say, I have got treasures to bestow if you will only
receive them. I have that to give which makes it
worth while to come : a free pardon, a robe of righteousness, a new heart, a star of peace. So come to Me.

Brethren, I ask you to hear these words and lay them
to heart. I plead for my Master ; I stand here an
ambassador ; I ask you to come and be reconciled
to God.

I ask you to *come with all your sins*, however many
they may be. If you come to Him they will be taken
away. I ask you *to come as you are*. You feel unfit ;
you say you are not good enough. The worse you think
yourself, the better prepared you are. Christ is not a
Saviour of the FIT, but of sinners. I ask you *to come
now*. No other time is your own. The opportunity
past, the door will be shut, and yourself dead. Come
now. Come to Christ.

Ah! brethren, I fear that many of you will not take one saving step—will not come to Christ. You go on content with your own devices, like Balaam ; like Felix, you never finally come to Christ.

I warn you plainly that you may come to church, and come to the table, and come to the minister, and yet never be saved. The one thing needed is actual coming to the Saviour, actual coming to the Fountain, actual washing in the blood of atonement. Except you do this, you will die in your sins.

Gird up your loins like a man, and resolve that you will come. Do you feel vile and unworthy to come? Tell it to Jesus. Do you feel as if you know not what to say and do when you come? Tell it to Jesus. Tell Him you are all sins ; tell Him you are all weakness ; tell Him you feel as if you had no faith and no power, no grace and no strength, no goodness and no love ; but come to Him, and commit your soul to His charge. Let nothing keep you back from Christ.

Tell Him you have heard that He receiveth sinners ; that you are such an one, and you want to be saved. Tell Him you have nothing to plead but His own word ; but He said Come, and therefore you come to Him.

IV. LET US CONSIDER THE PROMISE HELD OUT: " I WILL GIVE YOU REST."

Rest is a pleasant thing, and a thing that all seek after. The merchant, the banker, the tradesman, the soldier, the lawyer, the farmer, all look forward to the day when they shall be able to rest. But how few can find rest in this world! How many pass their lives in seeking it, and never seem able to reach it! It seems very near sometimes, and they fancy it will soon be their own. Some new event happens, and they are as far off rest as ever.

The whole world is full of restlessness and disappointment, weariness and emptiness.   The very faces of
worldly men let out the secret ; their countenances
give evidence that the Bible is true ; they find no rest.
" Vanity and vexation of spirit " is the true report of
all here below.   " Who will show us any good ? " the
bitter confession of many now, just as in David's time.

Take warning, young men and women.   Think not
that happiness is to be found in any earthly thing.
Do not have to learn this by bitter experience.   Realise
it while young, and do not waste your time in hewing
out " cisterns, broken cisterns, that can hold no water."

But Jesus offers rest to all who will come to Him.
" Come unto Me," he says, " and I will give you rest."
He will give it.   He will not SELL it, as the Pharisee
supposes—so much rest and peace in return for so many
good works.   He gives it freely to every coming sinner,
without money and without price.   He will not LEND,
as the Arminian supposes, so much peace and rest,
all to be taken away by-and-by if we do not please
Him ; He gives it for ever and for aye.   His gifts are
" without repentance."

" But what kind of rest will Jesus give me ? " some
men will say.   " He will not give me freedom from labour
and trouble.   What kind of rest will He give ? "   Listen
a few minutes, and I will tell you.

He will give you *rest from fear of sin.*   The sins of
the man who comes to Christ are completely taken
away ; they are forgiven, pardoned, removed, blotted
out.   They can no longer appear in condemnation
against him.   They are sunk in the depths of the sea.
Ah ! brethren, that is rest.

He will give you *rest from fear of law.*   The law
has no further claim on the man who has come to Christ.
Its debts are all paid ; its requirements are all satisfied.

Christ is the end of the law for righteousness. Christ has redeemed us from the curse of law. "Who shall lay anything to the charge of God's elect in the day of Judgment?" No believer can run his eye over the fifth chapter of Matthew, and not feel comforted. And that is rest.

He will give you *rest from fear of hell.* Hell cannot touch the man who has come to Christ. The punishment has been borne, the pain and suffering have been undergone by another, and he is free. And that, too, is rest.

He will give you *rest from fear of the devil.* The devil is mighty, but he cannot touch those who have come to Christ. Their Redeemer is strong. He will set a hedge around them that Satan cannot overthrow. He may sift and buffet and vex, but he cannot destroy such. And that, too, is rest.

He will give you *rest from fear of death.* The sting of death is taken away when a man comes to Christ. Jesus has overcome death, and it is a conquered enemy. The grave loses half its terrors when we think it is "the place where the Lord lay." The believer's soul is safe whatever happens to his body. His flesh rests in hope. This also is rest.

He will give you *rest in the storm of affliction.* He will comfort you with comfort the world knows nothing of. He will cheer your heart, and sustain your fainting spirit. He will enable you to bear loss patiently, and to hold your peace in the day of wrath. Oh! this is rest indeed.

I know well, brethren, that believers do not enjoy so much rest as they might. I know well that they "bring a bad report of the land," and live below their privileges. It is their unbelief; it is their indwelling sin. There was a well near Hagar, but she never saw it. There was safety for Peter on the water, but he did not look to Jesus, and was afraid. And just so it is with many believers : they give way to needless fear— are straitened in themselves.

But still there is a real rest and peace in Christ for all who come to Him. The man that fled to the city of refuge was safe when once within the walls, though perhaps at first he hardly believed it ; and so it is with the believer.

And, after all, the most downcast and complaining child of God has got a something within him he would not exchange for all the world. I never met with one, however low and desponding, who would consent to part with the rest and peace he had, however small. Like Naboth he prizes his little vineyard like a kingdom. And this shows me that coming to Christ can give rest.

Be advised, every one of you who is now seeking rest in the world. Be advised, and come and seek rest in Christ. You have no home, no refuge, no hiding-place, no portion. Sickness and death will soon be upon you, and you are unprepared. Be advised, and seek rest in Christ. There is enough in Him and to spare. Who has tried and did not find? A dying Welsh boy said, in broken English, " Jesus Christ plenty for everybody." Know your privileges, all you who have come to Christ. You have something solid under foot and something firm under hand. You have a rest even now, and you shall have more abundantly.

Let me speak to *those who have not yet come to Christ.*

Why do you not come? What possible reason can you give? What excuse can you show for your present conduct?

Will you tell me you have no need? What! no sin to be pardoned—no iniquity to be covered over! There is no state so bad as that of utter insensibility. Beware, lest you only awake to hear the word " Depart."

Will you tell me you are happy without Christ? I do not believe you. I know you are not. You dare not look into your heart,—you dare not search your conscience. It is the happiness of a tradesman who is bankrupt and does not look at his books. There is no happiness out of Christ.

Take heed. Every morning you are in awful danger. You stand on the brink of hell. Let a fever, an accident, an attack of disease carry you off, and you are lost for ever. Oh! take the warning. Escape for your life. Flee, flee to Christ!

Let me speak to those *who have not come to Christ, but mean to some day.* I marvel at your presumption. Who are you, that talk of meaning? You may be dead in a week. Who are you that talk of meaning? You may never have the will or opportunity, if not to-day. How long will you go on halting between two opinions? You must come to Christ some time—some day; why not now? The longer you stay away, the less chance there is of your coming at all; and the less happiness will you have in the world.

" Take heed, therefore, lest, a promise being left us of entering into His rest, any of you should seem to come short of it."

Many meant to have come in the robes, but put it off till too late. If like the Levite you put off your journey till late in the day, you must not wonder if the sun has gone down when you are far from home. Come now.

Let me speak to *those who have come to Christ indeed.*

You are often cast down and disquieted within you. And why? Just because you do not abide in Christ

and seek all rest and peace in Him. You wander from
the fold : no wonder you return weary, footsore, and
tired. Come again to the Lord Jesus and renew the
covenant. Believe me, if you live to be as old as
Methuselah, you will never get beyond this : a sinner
saved by the grace of Christ. And think of the
sinner's end.

Rest in Christ, and so rest indeed.

VII

THE LORD OUR RIGHTEOUSNESS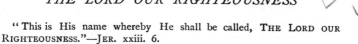

"This is His name whereby He shall be called, THE LORD OUR
RIGHTEOUSNESS."—JER. xxiii. 6.

THE time is short. It is but a little while, and
the Lord Jesus shall come in His glory. The
judgment shall be set and the books shall be opened.
"Before Him shall be gathered all nations," "that every
one may receive the things done in his body, according
to that he hath done, whether it be good or bad." The
inmost secrets of all hearts shall be revealed; "and the
kings of the earth, and the great men, and the rich
men, and the chief captains, and the mighty men, and
every bondman, and every freeman," will stand together
on a level at the bar, and will see each other face to
face, and one by one will have to give account of
themselves to God before the whole world. Thus it
is written, and therefore it is true and sure to come
to pass.

And what does each of you intend to say in that
hour? What is the defence you are prepared to set
up? What is the answer you propose to give? What
is the cause you mean to show why sentence should
not be pronounced against you?

Verily, beloved, I do fear that some amongst you
do not know. You have not thought about it yet—
you have resolved to think about it some day soon;

79

or you are not quite clear about it at present ; or you
have made out some ingenious, plausible scheme which
will not stand the touchstone of the Bible. Oh, what
a fearful case is yours ! Life is indeed uncertain ; the
fairest or the strongest here may perchance be taken
next—you cannot make an agreement with death—and
yet you cannot tell us what you are resting upon for
comfort. You do not know how soon the last trumpet
may sound, and yet you are uncertain as to the ground
of your hope. Surely these things ought not so to be.

Did any of you ever happen to visit a court of justice
just before the prisoners are tried ? Have you not
remarked how anxiously each one is consulting with
his friends and his lawyers as to the defence he shall
make—how earnest they are, how careful to leave no
stone unturned that may help to prove their innocence ?
And yet the greater part of them are liable to no more
than a few months' imprisonment, or a few years'
transportation ; perhaps they may get off altogether
by a quibble of the law, or through want of evidence.
See now how differently you act in the matter of
your souls. In the great day there will be no want
of witnesses ; your thoughts and words and actions
will appear written in the book one after another.
Your Judge is a searcher of hearts. And yet, in spite
of all these facts, too many of you sleep on as if
the Bible were not true ; too many of you know not
how or why you are to escape God's wrath and condemnation.

Hearken then, if you love life, while I endeavour
to give you some instruction from the words of my
text. The great question to be made known is, " How
shall man be just with God ? wherewithal can I come
before the Lord ? " and I wish this morning, if the
Lord will, to make you understand : I. That you must

have *some* righteousness, or you will not be saved.
II. That you have no righteousness of your own of
any sort, and therefore by yourself you cannot be
saved. III. That the Lord Himself must be your
Righteousness, and so you shall be saved. May God
the Holy Ghost, who can convert the most aged, the
most careless, the most sinful (I speak that which I
do know myself), accompany the words I am about
to speak, and make them seasonable to all your souls !

I. First, then, I am to show you you must have
some righteousness. The Bible says plainly, " The
wrath of God is revealed against all ungodliness and
unrighteousness of men." " The unrighteous shall not
inherit the kingdom of God." " Let me die the death
of the righteous," says Balaam, "and let my last end
be like his." " The Lord loveth the righteous, but the
way of the wicked He turneth upside down." " The
righteous hath hope in His death." Thy people,"
says Isaiah to his God, " shall be all righteous." " The
cursed shall go away into everlasting punishment,
but the righteous into life eternal." " Have on the
breastplate of righteousness," says Paul to the Ephesians. And how shall any one presume to say that
he can enter into heaven without it !

But I wish here to expose the folly of all those who
talk in a loose and general way about God's mercy.
Men will often say, when urged to think about their
salvation, "Indeed I know I am not what I should be ;
I have broken God's law very often, but He is very
merciful, and I hope I shall be forgiven." Truly, I
do believe that the religion of many goes no further
than this. This is the only point they can lay hold
of ; this is the only rock on which they build : press
them for a reason of their hope, and there is no answer ;
ask them to explain the ground of their confidence,

and they cannot do it. "God is merciful" is the Alpha
and the Omega, the beginning and the end, the first
and the last, of all their Christianity. Now, I am bold
to say, beloved, this is an immense delusion; a refuge
of lies that will not stand being compared with Scripture, and, more than this, it will not last one instant
in the fire of trial and affliction.

Have you not ever heard that God is a God of perfect
holiness—holy in His character, holy in His laws, holy
in His dwelling-place? "Speak unto the children
of Israel," says the Book of Leviticus, and say unto
them, "Ye shall be holy; for I the Lord your God
am holy." "He is a holy God," says Joshua; "He
is a jealous God; He will not forgive your transgressions nor your sins." "Thou art of purer eyes than
to behold evils, and canst not look on iniquity," says
Habakkuk. "Without holiness no man shall see the
Lord." And the book of Revelation, speaking of
heaven, says, "There shall in no wise enter into it
anything that defileth." "It shall be called the way
of holiness," says Isaiah; "the unclean shall not pass
over it." And will you tell us, in the face of all these
texts, that man, corrupt, impure, defiled—as the best of
us most surely is—shall pass the fiery judgment of our
God and enter into the heavenly Jerusalem by simply
trusting in the mercy of his Maker, without one single
rag to cover his iniquities and hide his natural uncleanness. It cannot be: God's mercy and God's
holiness must needs be reconciled, and you have not
done this yet.

And have you never heard that God is a God of
perfect justice, whose laws may not be broken without
punishment, whose commandments must be fulfilled
on pain of death? "All His ways are judgment," says
the book of Deuteronomy; "a God of truth and

without iniquity, just and right is He." " Justice and judgment are the habitation of Thy throne," says David. " The just Lord is in the midst," says Zephaniah ; " He will not do iniquity : every morning doth He bring His judgment to light; He faileth not." " Think not that I am come to destroy the law or the prophets," said Jesus : " I am not come to destroy, but to fulfil. For verily I say unto you, Till heaven and earth pass, one jot or one tittle shall in no wise pass from the law till all be fulfilled." I cannot find that these verses have ever been declared useless ; I cannot discover any place which says the law is now let down, and need not be fulfilled ; and how, then, can I teach you that it is enough to look to God's mercy ? I read of only two ways in the Bible : One is, to do the whole law yourself ; the other is, to do it by another. Show me, if you can, one single text which teaches that a man may be saved without the claims of the law having been satisfied. An earthly prince, indeed, may forgive and pass over men's transgressions ; but God never changes. " Hath He spoken, and shall He not make it good ? " I tell you, then, God's mercy and God's justice must be reconciled ; and this you have not done yet.

You must have something to appear in at the marriage supper of the Lamb. You would not say a murderer should be acquitted, because he said he was sorry and hoped to be forgiven ; you must make some amends to justice and to holiness ; you cannot shut your eyes against the plain declarations of the Bible. You must have some good reason to give, why you should not be judged for all your sins and backslidings ; you must show some cause why the punishment threatened for breaking God's law is not to fall upon you ; there must be satisfaction for your sins, or you will perish everlastingly.

You tell us fairly you are not what you should be, but you say that God is merciful. I answer you this will not stand before the Bible : the wages of sin is death, he that offendeth in one point is guilty of all. God loves you, but He will have His demands paid in full : your debt must be discharged by yourself or by some one else ; choose which you please, but one thing at least is certain—payment must be made. God is indeed all love : He willeth not the death of any sinner; but, however small your iniquities may be, they cannot possibly be put away until the claims of His law have been satisfied to the uttermost farthing. By some means, then, you must have righteousness, or else it is clear you cannot be saved.

II. I promised in the second place to show you that we have *no* righteousness of our own, and therefore by ourselves we cannot be saved. I trust I need not dwell upon this point long, and therefore I shall only say a few words to enforce it on your notice.

Look at the law of God, and measure its requirements. Does it not ask of every man a perfect, unsinning obedience from first to last, in thought and word and deed, without one single failure in the slightest jot or tittle? And where is the son or daughter of Adam who can say, " All this I have performed "? Who is not conscious of a daily falling short in everything he does ? I do not speak so much of thieves and liars and adulterers and drunkards and the like, for these are walking towards their own place, leaning on Satan's arm. I speak rather of those who do not live in gross vices ; I would even take the case of the best Christian among ourselves, and ask him if he can name a single day on which he has not sinned in many things. Oh, how much he would tell you of wandering in his prayers, of defilement in his thoughts, of coldness toward God, of want of love, of pride, of evil tempers, of vanity, of worldly-mindedness!—and all, remember, in the heart of one of those few who are travelling in the narrow way which leadeth unto life. And how shall we then believe, though all the world persuade us to the contrary, that man can ever purchase his acceptance in the sight of God? So true are the words of that clear-sighted witness the apostle Paul, " By the deeds of the law shall no flesh living be justified."

But here I take occasion to answer the reasoning of those Pharisees, who would have men believe they can assist in the work of salvation by their own performances. They cannot submit to the idea that we are naturally so helpless, and so they go about to establish their own righteousness, and this in a variety of ways.

Some tell us that repentance and amendment will enable us to stand in the great day, but the Bible does not warrant it. No doubt, without them none of you will enter into the kingdom of heaven ; but they cannot put away your sins nor endure the severity of God's judgment ; they cannot open that strait gate which must be passed before you get into the narrow way, although they may lead you up to it ; they cannot blot out one single page of that black book in which your iniquities are written. John Baptist preached repentance, but he never told his hearers it would save them.

Some say they put their trust in well-spent lives: they never did anybody any harm ; they have always done their best, and so they hope they shall be accounted righteous. Beloved, this is miserable trifling. Let them tell us of a single day in which they have not broken that spiritual law laid down in the Sermon on the Mount. What! never thought an unkind thought ? never looked an unchaste look ? never said an uncharitable thing ? never coveted ? Oh, that tenth commandment: how utterly it seems neglected!—and yet it goes along with murder and adultery. Or let them tell us of a single hour in which they have not left undone something it was in their power to do; and this must be accounted for. They cannot do it; they are silent; and yet these things are written plainly in the Bible. Is it not clear, then, that they do not read the Scriptures, or neglect their precepts if they do, and so, at any rate, they are not doing their best?

Some tell us that they hope sincerity will carry them safe through their trial. They may not perhaps have quite clear views, but still they have always meant well, and so they hope to be accepted. I cannot find there is any place for them in heaven. I read in the book of Kings that the priests of Baal called on their God for half a day, and cut themselves after their manner with knives, until the blood gushed out upon them. That was sincerity at any rate, and yet, a few hours after, Elijah commanded them to be put to death as soul-destroying idolaters. I read that Paul himself, before conversion, was zealous toward God: he thought within himself he ought to do many things contrary to Jesus of Nazareth, and shut up many of the saints in prison, and was exceedingly mad against them. Here was sincerity and earnestness; and yet we find him saying, when his eyes were opened: "I was a blasphemer and a persecutor, and injurious. . . . I am the least of the apostles, the chief of sinners . . . I am not meet to be called an apostle, because I persecuted the Church of God." And so it seems a man may be in earnest, and yet going towards the place of torment.

Lastly, some tell us that they go through all the forms and ordinances of religion, and build their claim to righteousness on that. " Hath not God commanded us," they say, " to honour His word, His house, His

ministers, His sacraments?" All this we do, and surely
He will accept us. I cannot find it written. But I do
remember that the Jews had ceremonies and observances
in abundance; and I have found many passages which
seem to show that men may pay attention to these
things, and yet be abominable in the sight of God.
Hear the judgment of Samuel: "Hath the Lord as
great delight in burnt offerings and sacrifices as in
obeying the voice of the Lord? Behold, to obey is
better than sacrifice, and to hearken than the fat of
rams. For rebellion is as the sin of witchcraft, and
stubbornness is as iniquity and idolatry." Listen to
the voice of Isaiah: "To what purpose is the multitude
of your sacrifices unto me? saith the Lord: I am full
of the burnt offerings of rams, and the fat of fed beasts;
and I delight not in the blood of bullocks or of lambs
or he-goats. When ye come to appear before me,
who hath required this at your hand, to tread my
courts? Bring no more vain oblations; incense is an
abomination unto me; the new moons and sabbaths,
the calling of assemblies, I cannot away with; it is
iniquity, even the solemn meeting. Your new moons
and your appointed feasts, my soul hateth; they are
a trouble unto me; I am weary to bear them. And
when ye spread forth your hands I will hide mine eyes:
yea, when ye make many prayers I will not hear:
your hands are full of blood. Wash you, make you
clean; put away the evil of your doings from before
mine eyes; cease to do evil; learn to do well; seek
judgment." "I spake not to your fathers," says the
Lord by Jeremiah, "concerning burnt offerings or
sacrifices: but this thing commanded I them, saying,
Obey my voice, and I will be your God, and ye shall
be my people: and walk ye in all the ways that I have
commanded you, that it may be well with you."

I trust it will not seem to you unprofitable to have taken up so much time in exposing these delusions. In one way it is very useful. They all show that conscience tells every man he must have something wherewith to appear before God. Now, I wish to show you plainly that we have nothing of our own; the doctrine may seem hard and disagreeable, and yet there are few who do not allow it at one important period in their lives, if they never did before. I mean the hour of death. Mark then how anxious almost every one becomes, whom God permits to keep possession of his senses. The judgment day appears then in its true light. Man feels naked and empty. He knows he is about to be asked that awful question, "What hast thou to say, why thou shouldst not perish for this long list of sins?" and if he has not furnished himself with the only answer that can be given, the view before his eyes cannot possibly look anything else than dreary, black, and hopeless. Ask those who have been brought to death's door by sickness, whether this be not true, and they will tell you. In short, both Scripture and your own experience prove most fully that nothing we can do will stand God's examination; repentance, works and services, all necessary and useful in themselves, are so tainted, so infected and imperfect, that they cannot justify us. We have no righteousness of our own, and therefore by ourselves we cannot be saved. "We are all as an unclean thing," says Isaiah, "and all our righteousnesses are as filthy rags; and we all do fade as a leaf; and our iniquities, like the wind, have taken us away."

III. "But what are we to do?" perhaps you will ask. "You seem to have shut us up without hope. You told us first that we must have some righteousness, and now you have told us further that we have not any of our own. What are we to do? Which way are we to turn? What would you have us say? To whom are are we to look?" Praised be God, beloved, I am not obliged to leave you here. I will not lead you into the wilderness and terrify you, and then point out no path towards the heavenly Canaan. I promised in the third place to tell you how God can be a just God and yet show mercy and justify the most ungodly: and this is all contained in the words of my text—" The Lord " must be "our RIGHTEOUSNESS."

I show you here a mystery of wisdom and of love. The Lord Jesus Christ has done what we ought to have done, and suffered what we ought to have suffered; He has taken our place and become our substitute both in life and death, and all for the sake of miserable, corrupt, ungrateful beings like ourselves. Oh, is not His name then rightly called, " The Lord our Righteousness "?

Beloved, I ought to dwell upon this point. It is so highly important to have a clear view of it, and Satan does so much to prevent your seeing it distinctly, that I must try to unfold it before your eyes, that all of you may be able to understand what a minister means when he urges you to trust in the Lord Jesus as your righteousness.

Consider now: there were two things to be done before guilty man could be saved. The law was to be fulfilled, for we had all come short of it; justice was to be satisfied, for we had all deserved punishment. And how was this effected? Hearken! The Lord Jesus Christ, pitying our lost estate, covenanted and engaged to become our surety and substitute; and when the fulness of time was come, He left the bosom of His Father and took upon Him the form of a servant here on earth, being born of the Virgin Mary.

In that form, by a sinless obedience to the whole law, He wrought out and brought in a perfect and ever-lasting righteousness, and this He is both willing and ready to bestow on all who will put their trust in Him. And more than this: to complete the mighty work He consented to offer up Himself in our place as a victim to the wrath of God, to suffer instead of us, to bear that punishment which we had deserved,—and this He did by dying on the cross. It was there He satisfied the claims of justice. It was there He paid the heavy debt written against our names. It was there that God the Father laid upon Him the iniquity of us all, and made His soul a sacrifice for sin. It was there that He redeemed us from the curse of the law, being made a curse for us. Here, then, you see the plan of salvation which is offered to all the world. The believing sinner's guilt is taken away and laid upon Christ, for He has carried our transgressions, and all the merit of Christ's life and death, and all the value of His sufferings, are then made over to the sinner.

But see how great and glorious is this exchange between Jesus and our souls: the Father sees us now as members of His dear Son, in whom He is well pleased; He deals with us as if we had never sinned, as if we had ourselves fulfilled all righteousness; He looks on us as one with Christ, and acknowledges us as dear children and heirs of eternal glory. Do I say more than Scripture warrants? I think not. Listen to St. Paul: "God hath made Him to be sin for us who knew no sin; that we might be made the righteousness of God in Him." Are not these words strong? But so it is. "Christ was accounted as a sinner, and therefore punished for us: we are accounted as righteous, and therefore glorified in Him. He was accounted as

a sinner, and therefore He was condemned ; we are accounted as righteous in Him, and therefore justified." *
God's law has been satisfied, and now we may be saved. Sin has been punished, and now sinners may go free. God has shown Himself a just God, and yet He can be the Saviour of guilty men.

Beloved, are not these things wonderful? Are not these glad tidings to the labouring and heavy laden ? The Lord Himself is our RIGHTEOUSNESS. Who is there among you that is groaning under the burden of sin, trembling under a sense of innumerable transgressions ? Fear not, but come to Jesus ; He has paid your debt in full ; believe, and you shall be free. Who is there among you that is tried with manifold temptations— slipping, stumbling, walking in darkness and seeing no light, and often ready to say with David, " I shall one day perish "? Fear not, but look to Jesus ; He has secured your entrance into heaven ; He has fought and won the battle for you. The Lord is our righteousness. This shall be our defence and plea, when earth and its works are burned up, and the trumpet shall sound, and the dead shall be raised incorruptible, and the Chief Shepherd shall appear to judge the sons of men. Who shall lay anything *then* to the charge of those who have laid hold on Christ ? Shall any one presume to say they have not done everything required ? The Lord, we will answer, is our righteousness ; He is our substitute ; we have done nothing, but He hath done everything ; He is our all in all. And who is he that can condemn us ? shall death or hell or Satan lay a finger on us, and dare to say that justice has not been satisfied ? The Lord, we will answer, is our righteousness ; we have indeed sinned, but Christ hath suffered ; we have deserved wrath, but Jesus hath died and shed

* Beveridge.

His blood to make atonement in our stead. "Blessed,"
says holy David, "is the man to whom the Lord will
not impute sin." "I will greatly rejoice in the Lord,"
says Isaiah ; "my soul shall be joyful in my God ; for
He hath clothed me with the garments of salvation, He
hath covered me with the robe of righteousness, as a
bridegroom decketh himself with ornaments, and as a
bride adorneth herself with her jewels."

Now, I have preached to very little purpose, beloved,
if you do not this very morning ask yourselves, "Is the
Lord my righteousness, or is He not?" Remember this
mighty gift is offered unto all, but it is only placed
upon them that believe. "Faith is the only hand which
putteth on Christ to justification. Christ is the only
garment which can cover your defiled nature, and
present you blameless in the sight of God. Without
this faith it is clear you have neither part nor portion
in this righteousness." * I know not that I can put into
your heads a more important inquiry ; and yet, I sadly
fear too many of you will not think I am in earnest,
or else you will suppose the question may be useful
to your neighbours, but not so very necessary for
yourself.

Indeed, I am persuaded there are many persons in
every congregation who flatter themselves they are
in a kind of middle path. They do not, to be sure,
pretend they are in the number of the very good people,
but they would be very sorry to be thought ungodly.
They have a great respect for religion, and some time
or other they intend to take it up more seriously—
perhaps when they are married and have got a home
of their own (so the young say), or when they have
not so many cares or so much trouble about their
families and their relations, or when they get on in

* Hooker.

years (so the middle-aged say), or by-and-by, or when they become ill (so the old and grey-headed say). But in the meantime, they live on and move forward in a comfortable state of mind, take all the promises of God and all the smooth parts of a sermon to themselves, and leave the addresses to the unconverted and the careless for others.

But, once for all, I say to such persons, if there are any such here, your middle path seems right in your own eyes; but I have searched the Scriptures, and I cannot find it. I cannot meet with more than two descriptions of character: I read of a broad way, and I read of a narrow way; I read of converted men, and unconverted men; I read of heaven, and I read of hell; I read of those that are in Christ, and I read of those that are not in Christ; but nowhere can I find that road in which you put your trust,—and I do not hesitate to say you will find it in the end to be nothing better than a piece of that broad way that leadeth to destruction. Think not I wish to hurt your feelings; but I do wish to awaken you, to convince you of the folly of this sleepy, half-and-half religion, and to show you the necessity of being decided and in earnest on the side of Christ, if you would not be lost for ever.

I say this much by way of warning, and I now repeat to every man, woman and child here present, the plain question: "Is the Lord your righteousness, or is He not?" I know that there are here, two parties. One would reply, if honest, "I fear He is not"; and the other would answer, "I trust He is." I purpose, therefore, to conclude this sermon by a few words to each of these two classes.

First, then, I shall offer some counsel to those among you who are prepared to say: "The Lord Jesus is,

we trust, our righteousness." I say then, and I think
it safe to do so, You have made a good profession ; but
I would have you daily search and see that you are
not deceiving yourselves. See that your tongue does
not lay claim to more than your heart has received
and knows of; see that your life and lips are thoroughly
agreed. Show all the world that He in whom you
trust is your example no less than your righteousness,
and while you wait for His second appearing endeavour
daily to become more like Him. Study to be holy,
even as He who has called you and washed you in His
own blood is holy. Let not the righteousness of the
Lord be evil-spoken of through you ; let not Jesus be
wounded in the house of His friends. Think of His
love ; let that constrain you to obedience—having much
forgiven, love much. Beware that you give the Lord's
enemies no occasion to blaspheme. They are watching
you much ; you cannot be hid. Be always saying to
yourself, " What shall I do, and how shall I behave,
to show my gratitude to Him who hath carried my
sins and given me His righteousness ? " But know ye
for a certainty, if the world says " What do these
persons more than others ? " if those who live with you
cannot take knowledge of you that you are much with
Jesus ; if you have no fruit to show of any sort ; if you
are not habitually and daily sober, just, holy, temperate,
humble, meek, loving, watchful, fervent in spirit, serving
the Lord, hungering and thirsting after righteousness ;
if you have none of these things, you are little better
than sounding brass and a tinkling cymbal, you are
ruining your own soul, and in the day of Judgment you
will plead in vain the name of Jesus. The Lord will
say, " I know you not ; you never really came to me ;
I cannot see my seal upon your forehead, of which my
servant Paul spake—' Let every one that nameth the

name of Christ depart from iniquity.'" "There shall be weeping and gnashing of teeth."

It only remains now to speak to all among you who cannot say "The Lord is our righteousness." Indeed, beloved, I am distressed for your condition. I cannot understand, I never can, what arguments you use to quench the striving of God's Spirit, to stop the prickings of your own conscience. In truth, I do suspect you never argue, you never reason ; you shut your eyes and try to forget your own perishing souls. But know ye not that verse of the Bible which declares "the wicked shall be turned into hell, and all the people that forget God,"—not ridicule, or insult, but simply all who forget. And know ye not the verse "How shall we escape if we neglect so great salvation?" It does not say abuse, or disbelieve, or deny, but simply "neglect," and this, I fear, is a charge you cannot turn aside. Oh, think of death ; it may be near at hand. Your careless indifference will alter then, but without Christ you will find a sting in that hour which no power of your own will ever remove. Think of eternity in hell: no merry companions, no comfortable gossiping, no noisy revelling at night, nothing but unchanging misery, unceasing torment, and unutterable woe. Think of thy judgment : your name will be called in turn, and you will stand in the sight of assembled millions— ministers, father, mother, wife, children, relations, all will see you—you will have to give account of your actions, and you know you will be condemned. But who will then pass sentence ? Not an angel, not even God the Father ; but the Lord Himself (Oh ! cutting and heartrending thought)—the Lord Jesus, whose blood and righteousness you now refuse, will pronounce your condemnation.

These things perhaps sound terrible ; perhaps they

may be treated with ridicule ; but the day is at hand
which will bring every one to their senses, and make
everybody sober, and you will then find that they are
true.   Knowing, therefore, the terrors of the Lord, let
me persuade you to close with the gracious invitation
of your Saviour, and never rest until you can say from
your hearts, " The Lord is my righteousness."

I know not anything that should prevent your
salvation if you are willing and obedient.   I cannot see
in what respect your happiness on earth would be
diminished.   You are discontented with yourself, and I
offer in the name of Christ, joy, pardon, and peace ;
you are poor, and I offer unsearchable riches ; you are
naked, and I offer you a spotless robe in which you
shall sit down at the marriage supper of the Lamb,
and none shall cast you out.

But mark, I will not promise you anything beyond
to-day. " Now is the accepted time." Thus far I can go,
but one step further I cannot proceed upon sure ground.
If you reject the counsel of God now, I cannot promise
even the youngest of you another opportunity.   Before
to-morrow your last home may be fixed unalterably ;
to-morrow death may interfere, or Jesus may return
to judgment, and it would be too late.

Go home, then, if you value your soul, and turn the
words of the text into a prayer, and entreat the Lord
to receive you and become your righteousness.

Even so, Lord Jesus, come quickly into every heart.
Amen and Amen.

VIII

SELF-RIGHTEOUSNESS.

"He spake this parable unto certain which trusted in themselves that they were righteous, and despised others."—LUKE xviii. 9.

ARE there none to whom this parable is applicable in the present day? Truly, if it were so, the ministers of Jesus would have comparatively a light employment and an idle post. We do not often meet with men who deny the divinity of Christ, or the personality of the Holy Ghost, or disbelieve the Bible, or doubt the existence of a God, and so bring upon themselves swift destruction ; but, alas! we have daily proof that the disease spoken of in our text is as deep-seated and hard to cure as ever, and of all the mischievous delusions that keep men out of heaven, of all the soul-destroying snares that Satan employs to oppose Christ's Gospel, there is none we find so dangerous, none so successful, as self-righteousness.

Perhaps you think this strange, and I daresay there are few who would not say, if asked the ground of their hopes, and how they expect to be saved, "We trust in the merits of Christ" ; but I fear that too many of you are making the Lord Jesus but half your Saviour, and could never stand the sifting of an inquiry which would draw out into daylight the secrets of your hearts. How much would then come out by degrees about doing as well as you could, and being no worse than

others, and having been sober and industrious and well-
behaved, and having attended church regularly, and
having had a Bible and a Prayer book of your own
ever since you can remember, and the like; besides
many other self-approving thoughts, which often never
appear until a death-bed, and all prove the root of all
evil, which is pride, to be still vigorous and flourishing
within.

Oh this pride of heart, beloved!—it is fearful to see
the harm that it does, and the carelessness with which
it is regarded : it is melancholy indeed to think of a
man, weak frail man, the descendant of fallen Adam,
the inheritor of a corrupt nature, forgetting his own
countless shortcomings and backslidings, trusting in
himself, and despising those who are his brethren
according to the flesh ; and wisely has our Lord spoken
the parable immediately following my text, which I
propose to bring under your notice this afternoon.

" Two men went up into the temple to pray ; the one
a Pharisee, and the other a publican. The Pharisee
stood and prayed thus with himself: God, I thank Thee
that I am not as other men are, extortioners, unjust,
adulterers, or even as this publican. I fast twice in
the week, I give tithes of all that I possess. And the
publican, standing afar off, would not lift up so much
as his eyes unto heaven, but smote upon his breast,
saying, God be merciful to me a sinner. I tell you,
this man went down to his house justified rather than
the other: for every one that exalteth himself shall
be abased ; and he that humbleth himself shall be
exalted (Luke xviii. 10-14).

Observe now how much more striking the lesson
sounds when conveyed to us in the form of an example.
How little many persons would have been affected if
our Lord had given a general discourse about the evil

of pride and the excellence of humility, about the danger of formality and the importance of a truly penitent frame of mind, if he had merely said, " Be not self-righteous in your dealings with God, but be lowly and self-abased "!—and how much more are our hard hearts likely to be moved when we see, as it were, living specimens of two sorts of worshippers, placed vividly before our eyes!

May God the Holy Ghost direct the instruction here contained to the awakening of the self-righteous, to the comfort of those who labour and are heavy-laden, and to the edification of all!

Now, before entering closely into the parable, I would have you mark, that the first verse tells us there was one point on which the Pharisee and the publican were agreed—one point which they had in common, and one only—and this was, " They both went up into the temple to pray." They both set their faces the same way, they walked in the same path, they entered the same house, and so far we can discover no difference whatever between them, in their outward behaviour at least ; but we shall soon find that their hearts were far asunder, and like the first worshippers recorded in the Bible, even Cain and Abel, there was a mighty gulf between them—for God, we shall see, accepted the sacrifice of the one, but rejected that of the other.

Oh, beloved, this passage suggests very awful reflections, and for our sakes no doubt it was written. Both these men, it appears, "went up to the temple to pray," and yet how fearfully the narrative ends! Jesus had just been speaking of the necessity of constant prayer, in the parable of the unjust judge, and immediately, without anything happening to break the thread of his discourse, he adds the parable we are now con-

sidering. Surely, then, this must be meant to remind
us, as a thing we are liable to forget, that, however
important prayer may be, we are not to suppose all
who pray have a prayerful spirit, and that outward
service is often given where there is no real dedication
of the heart to God.

Truly it is cheerful and encouraging to see a
multitude going up to the house of God, but still
it is painful to remember that too many go in the
spirit of the Pharisee and far too few in that of the
Publican. They all use the same prayers, they bow
the knee, they move the lips together, and yet they
are as widely different as gold and base metal. All
are not Israel, who are called Israel ; all are not
Christians who name the name of Christ ; all are not
acceptable worhippers who are found in the temples
of the Most High ; and what is the line of distinction ? We learn this in the parable. Some come
as Pharisees, and some as publicans ; some appear
with a broken and a contrite heart, such as the Lord
will not despise, and others with an unhumbled and
self-exalting spirit, wise in their own eyes and pure
in their own sight, and the sacrifice of all such is
abominable in the sight of God. Oh that you would
try to bear in mind more constantly, that "the Lord
seeth not as man seeth, for man looketh on the outward
appearance, but the Lord looketh on the heart " ; that
to Him "all hearts are open, all desires known, and
from Him no secrets are hid " !—and if you felt this
more, you would be more careful about the spirit in
which you draw near to His throne, you would avoid
anything like vain or trifling ccnversation both before
and after service, and so observe the advice of Solomon,
" to keep thy foot when thou goest to the house of God."

Let us, however, return to the parable from which

I have been led to turn aside. I have shown you
that there was one point in common between the
publican and the Pharisee ; and I shall now proceed
to call your attention to the main object of the parable,
by tracing out distinctly the four great points of
difference which we perceive existed between these
fellow-worshippers. I observe, then,—
    I. There was a difference in their character.
    II. There was a difference in their behaviour.
    III. There was a difference in their prayers.
    IV. And, lastly, there was a difference in the
reception their prayers met with.
    I. With respect to their *characters*, the parable,—
or rather narrative, for it is probably a true story,
adapted by our Lord to the purpose of the moment—
begins by stating that " One was a Pharisee, the other
a publican." Now, it is almost impossible to imagine
a more striking contrast, in the opinion of a Jewish
congregation. The Pharisees were the strictest sect
among the Jews : " I was of the strictest sect of the
Pharisees," says St. Paul. They prayed often—which
was very right ; but they also made long prayers for a
pretence, and they would pray at the corners of the
streets where two roads met, that they might be seen
by people going and coming both ways and so get a
name for uncommon sanctity. There is no reason for
supposing they were generally anything but moral men,
but their grand fault was that they relied on their
outward performance of the things written in the law
as a ground of acceptance before God. They seem to
have been indifferent as to the real state of their hearts,
and to have cared only for keeping up a fair appearance
before men, for they loved the praise of men more than
the praise of God. We may get some idea of their
real character from our Lord's saying, that they gave

tithe of mint, anise, and cummin, while they neglected the weightier matters of the law, judgment, mercy and truth, and from His comparison of them to whitened sepulchres, which indeed appear beautiful before men, but inwardly are filled with dead men's bones and all corruption. They " made broad the borders of their phylacteries," they had pieces of parchment sewed to the edge of their long robes, on which some texts of Scripture were written, that people might see them and infer therefrom that they were great lovers of the law of God. They were very strict about outward purifications, and set great value on the washing of pots, brazen vessels and tables, and many other such-like things that they did. They were particularly zealous for the traditions of the fathers, and for the observation of the rites and ceremonies of the Church, and yet they often made the law of God void by their traditions. They were exceeding exact in the outward observation of the Sabbath—so much so that they called our Lord a sinner, and said he was not of God, because upon the Sabbath day He had healed a man who was born blind. And for all these reasons they were held in high esteem by the people ; for men always prefer the things of sight to the things of faith, and think more of outward service than of heart ; they had the uppermost places in the synagogues and greetings in the market-places, and were called of men Rabbi ; and, in short, they got such a reputation for piety, that it became a proverb among the Jews, that if there were but two men saved, one of them must be a Pharisee.

Such were the Pharisees. But what was the character given to the publicans ? It was very different in every respect. They were generally Jews who were employed to collect the Roman taxes ; and as the Jews always disliked to pay tribute to the Gentiles, their office as

collectors was looked upon as disgraceful and dis-
reputable. Besides this it is pretty clear that they used
to exact much more than their due, and to amass much
wealth by false accusations, to the great disgust of
their fellow-countrymen. On these accounts they were
so universally infamous, that our Lord Himself tells
His disciples that if any man would not hear the
church, he must be to them as a heathen man and
a publican. The enemies of Jesus thought it a heavy
charge against Him that He was a friend of publicans
and sinners ; and in one place we find the publicans
and harlots mentioned together, as people of like reputation. On the whole, then, we may fairly conclude
that in teaching the nature of acceptable worship, our
Lord could not have chosen two examples more unlike
each other than a Pharisee and a publican. One is of
great repute with his fellow-creatures, while the other
is peculiarly offensive ; but which will God respect ?
We shall soon see.

II. Let us in the second place consider the different
behaviour of these two worshippers. Behold the
Pharisee. " He stood and prayed thus with himself."
Observe this : he went to some conspicuous part of the
temple, where he could stand alone near the altar,
separate from the rest of men, that all might see what
a devout man he was, and not lose sight of him in
the crowd. He stood " with himself," not among the
congregation, lest he should be defiled by touching
them ; he was too good for them. We do not read of
anything like humility here ; we do not learn that he
even bowed his head, as a mark of respect to his
Creator ; but there he stood erect, like one who felt
that he had done all that God required of him, that he
had no sin to repent of, that he had a right to expect
a blessing as a profitable servant.

Turn now to the publican. " Standing afar off, he would not lift up so much as his eyes unto heaven, but smote upon his breast." He stood afar off—probably in the outward court, as one who did not feel himself worthy to come beyond the threshold of Him whose name is Holy. " He would not lift up so much as his eyes to heaven." He felt the remembrance of his sins so grievous, and the burden of them so intolerable, that, like a child who has offended its father, he dare not look his Almighty Maker in the face. " He smote upon his breast." He could not control the feelings that arose in his mind : he recollected the mercies he had received and his own neglect of them, the life he had led and the God he had despised, and, like those who saw Jesus hanging on the cross, " he smote his breast," in sorrow, self-abasement and godly fear. Beloved, the posture of the body and the expression of the face are certainly not always sure signs of the state of a man's heart, but you may rest assured that a truly humble and devout worshipper will generally be distinguished by his conduct in the house of God.

He that is duly sensible of his own guilt, and is ever coming to Jesus as his Advocate ; he that is acquainted with the sinfulness of sin and the devices of Satan, and the value of the means of grace and the necessity of using them if he would save his soul,—such a one will never show any want of reverence, any levity or care-lessness of manner, when he has entered any place where prayer is wont to be made and the gospel preached, and Christ Himself is standing in the midst. But if a person comes to church with an air of indiffer-ence, as if he did the minister a favour by coming and cared not if he never came again, and does not join in the prayers, and looks as if he would be ashamed if any one thought he did, and does not listen to the

word of God, and does not pay attention to the sermon ;
if he employs himself with looking at other people's
dress, or deliberately goes to sleep, or talks to his
neighbours, or makes plans for the next week—he may
have his own reasons for coming here, but it is pretty
clear to me that he does not come in the way that
Jesus loves, as a miserable sinner who sees nothing but
evil in himself, nor in the spirit that Jesus loves, that
is in the spirit of the publican.

III. In the third place let us attend to the difference
in the *prayers* of these two characters. Hear the
Pharisee : " God, I thank thee that I am not as other
men are, extortioners, unjust, adulterers, or even as
this publican. I fast twice in the week, I give tithes
of all I possess." Mark these words : there is no expression of any want here ; he seems perfectly self-satisfied ;
he recites complacently what he is not, and he proudly
brings forward what he is. Remember, beloved, there
is ground for much thankfulness if God enables us to
resist gross sins, but then there is no excuse for boasting ;
none of us have anything which we did not receive,
and we cannot do better than follow the example of
St. Paul, who said, " By the grace of God I am what
I am." But the Pharisee had none of this spirit. He
was wrong on every point. He was wrong in supposing,
as he evidently did, that his own power and strength had
kept him from these vices ; he was wrong in believing
that he could lay any claim to the title of a perfect
observer of the law on these points. It is one thing
to keep God's commandments in the letter, and another
to keep them in the spirit ; the one may think they
do, like this Pharisee, but the other no man ever
did but our Lord Jesus Christ. " In many things we
offend all," says St. James. " Who can tell how oft
he offendeth ? O cleanse thou me from secret faults,"

is the language of the psalmist. Lastly, he was wrong
in supposing that this literal fulfilment of the law would
give him a title to justification in the sight of God.
Salvation is all of grace, not of works, lest any man
should boast. " By the deeds of the law shall no flesh
living be justified."

But the Pharisee, besides this, was especially wrong
in going out of his way to make unnecessary and uncharitable remarks upon the publican. He talks like
one who had no account to settle about his own soul ;
he assumes as a matter of course that the publican
was more vile in God's sight than himself, and he
proves himself a child of the devil by usurping Satan's
office—he becomes an accuser of his brethren. " I am
not as other men are, or even as this publican." Beloved,
I must call your particular attention to this language,
for I declare unto you with grief that I have heard
people say things, which in effect are very much the
same about themselves, who yet profess and call themselves Christians. Many say, if they are urged about
their own sinfulness in God's sight, " Well, at any rate
I am no worse than my neighbours : I am thankful I
do not drink, like such a one next door ; I am no
fornicator, like such a one over the way ; I do not miss
church altogether, like such a one who lives down the
road." Listen to me, I beseech you : is not this the
very mind of the Pharisee ? You are not to be judged
by the standard of those around you ; it will be no
excuse before God to talk about your neighbours—sin
is sin whether you live in it in company or alone ; and
be sure it will not diminish your misery in hell, to find
that all your neighbours are there as well as yourself.
Oh, beloved, beware of this delusion ; not a few allow
such thoughts to dwell within them, who never express
them with their lips, and even in the presence of God

they flatter themselves they are acceptable to Him, because they are free from open and gross vices, and perform certain known duties. All such are Pharisees; they use the Pharisee's prayer, and they will meet with the Pharisee's reception at the hand of God.

Hearken now to the publican. " He smote upon his breast, saying, God be merciful to me a sinner." He does not say " Be merciful to all sinners," thus leaving it doubtful whether he means himself or not, but " Be merciful to *me*," a sinner in whom there is no health, in whom there is no good thing—a sinner in thought, word and deed ; and he gives the ground of his hope too, not like some among you, who hope to be forgiven without exactly knowing how or why. The words trans-lated " be merciful," go further. They mean, " make a propitiation for me, offer an atonement for me, be reconciled unto me, through the sacrifice Thou hast appointed." Do you think he would have been offended, as some are now, if he had been called a child of the devil, utterly corrupt, full of iniquity and worthy of nothing but wrath ? Far from it : he knew he was a sinner, he felt his lost condition, he made no excuses, he offered no justification, he did not talk about his temptations, he did not make great professions of amendment, as if that could make up for the past ; he presented himself at the throne of grace, as he was, weary and heavy laden, casting himself on the long-suffering of God with all his iniquities, and pleading the blood of the atonement : " God be merciful to me a sinner." Blessed indeed are all among you who have done likewise !

IV. Lastly, it remains to consider briefly *the reception* the worshippers respectively met with. " I tell you," says Jesus, " this man went down to his house justified rather than the other." The publican came poor in spirit, and he was filled ; the Pharisee, rich in merits and self-esteem, went empty away. The penitent was not only pardoned, but justified ; he had left his house heavy and afflicted by a sense of sin, he returned with joy and peace ; he had asked mercy and received it, he had sought grace and found it, he had come hungering and thirsting after righteousness and he had been satisfied : " he went down to his house justified." But the proud Pharisee, not feeling his own wants, not acquainted with his own sinfulness, had sought no mercy, and had found none, and he departed unblessed and unheard ; and from the saying the " publican went down to his house justified rather than the other," we may fairly suppose this man of self-righteousness and self-dependence had none of that sense of favour and acceptance which the repenting sinner enjoyed.

See now the general application which our Lord makes : " Every one that exalteth himself shall be abased, but he that abaseth himself shall be exalted." Mark these words—" every one that exalteth himself." High or low, rich or poor, young or old, it matters not ; for God is no respecter of persons, " every one that exalteth himself " and not free grace, that trusts either in whole or in part in his own righteousness and performance and not entirely in Jesus Christ—though he go to church twice a day, though he keep the letter of the Ten Commandments, though he pay everything he owes, though he be sober and moral and decently behaved—every one that exalteth himself shall be abased and condemned when Jesus Christ shall come to judgment.

But on the other hand remember, " he that humbleth himself " as a sinner before God and comes unto Christ, though he may have been the most wicked of transgressors, though he may have broken all the commandments, though he may have been a Sabbath-breaker,

a drunkard, a thief, an adulterer, an extortioner—
whatever his sin may have been, if he act as the
publican did, "he shall be exalted," he shall be
pardoned, and washed and sanctified and justified
for the sake of Jesus Christ, and shall have his place
with David and Manasseh and Mary Magdalen and
the thief upon the cross in the everlasting kingdom of
our God and of the Lamb.

And now, beloved, in conclusion let me urge upon
all the lesson conveyed in this parable. It is a picture
of a very large portion of professing Christians ; some,
to be ·sure, are called by that name, but they never
think at all about Christ or their own souls—it would
make no difference if all the Bibles in the world were
burned to-day—and of course they are going straight
to destruction ; but all others, rich or poor (there is no
distinction), are either Pharisees or publicans. There
is no half-way house : they either trust to themselves
wholly, or in part, which is much the same, or else they
are always self-condemned and have no confidence in
anything they can do for justification.

You cannot search your heart too diligently, for
this is the subtlest enemy of all. Beware of thinking,
as the devil would have you, that the parable is a
very good one for everybody else, but does not exactly
touch your case. Be sure in this way you will lose
your own souls. The faithful Church of England has
provided you with an admirable Prayer-book, which
you use, and using it call yourselves "miserable sinners"
every Sunday of your lives. Do you really feel this?
Know for a certainty, if you never groan under the
burthen of sin and never make the publican's prayer
your own, you cannot be saved. And if you feel this
minute any doubt about your salvation, it were far
better to give your soul the benefit of it, and re-lay

the foundation of your faith. But let none forget the point of the parable : the Pharisee was not rejected because he was a moral man, but because he was proud and self-righteous ; the publican was not accepted because he was a sinner, but because he was eminently penitent. True repentance is necessary for all, whatever be their lives and outward conduct : it is not your morality and your virtues, O ye Pharisees, which hinder your salvation, but that proud feeling of something worthy in yourselves, which prevents you from clinging simply and entirely to the cross and blood of Jesus Christ.

Carry home, then, I entreat you, all of you, that as there is no way to salvation but Jesus Christ, so there is no character for entering that way but that of the publican, and no prayer so acceptable in the sight of your Redeemer and your Judge as " God be merciful to me a sinner."

IX

THE CHARACTER OF THE TRUE CHRISTIAN

"My sheep hear my voice, and I know them, and they follow me! and I give unto them eternal life ; and they shall never perish, neither shall any man pluck them out of my hand."—JOHN x. 27, 28.

THAT is a glorious saying, a perfect and complete text ; containing all I need to know for my soul's comfort, full of privileges and mercies for true believers and penitent sinners, and at the same time shutting the door effectually against self-righteous Pharisees and whitened sepulchres and painted hypo-crites. It shows us two things : the character of real Christians, and the spiritual treasures they possess ; or, in other words, what they are to their Saviour, and what their Saviour is to them. I propose this morning to consider these two things in order, and I pray God you may all be led to examine yourselves by the light which the text affords.

I. First, then, with respect to true Christians—their names, their marks, their character : what does the text say about them ? " My sheep," we read, " hear my voice and follow me." The Lord Jesus Christ likens them to sheep ; and He declares "they are mine, and they hear me and follow me." There is matter we shall do well to consider in each of these expressions.

True Christians, then, are compared to sheep, and we shall find a great depth of meaning in the comparison if

we look into it. Sheep are the most harmless, quiet,
inoffensive creatures that God has made. So should it
be with Christians: they should be very humble and
lowly-minded, as disciples of Him who said, "Learn of
me, for I am meek and lowly in heart." They should
be known as persons of a very gentle and loving spirit,
who desire to do good to all around them, who would
not injure any one by word or deed ; who do not seek
the great things of this world, but are content to go
straightforward on the path of duty and take whatever
it shall please God to send them. They ought to show
forth in their lives and outward conversation that the
Holy Ghost has given them a new nature, has taken
away their old corrupt disposition and planted in them
godly thoughts and purposes and desires. When, therefore, we see people biting and devouring one another,
saying and doing uncharitable things to their neighbours, fierce, and passionate and evil-tempered and
angry on the slightest occasion ; full of envy and strife
and bitter speaking,—surely we are justified in saying,
"Ye do not belong to Christ's flock ; ye have yet to
be born again and made new creatures ; there must be
a mighty change. Profess what you please, at present
we can only see in you the mind of the old man, even
Adam the first, but nothing of the Second Adam, even
Christ Jesus the Lord ; we can discern the spirit of
the wolf, however fair your clothing, and we want instead
to discover in you the spirit of the lamb."

But again, sheep are of all animals the most useful ;
none are so serviceable to man, none so necessary in
every way for his comforts and conveniences ; and
such should be the character of a true Christian. We
must study to do good in our day and generation, and
lay ourselves out for the spiritual and temporal advantage of our brethren. All can do much: it is not

the rich alone, and the great, who are able to be useful;
there are a hundred ways of conferring benefits beside
the form of giving gold and silver; and each in his
respective station can do good if he will. Has not
a poor man a tongue? Then surely, if he is a sheep
of Christ's flock, he will use it for his neighbours' profit,
when occasion is afforded; he will warn and entreat
and counsel and persuade; he will reason and argue,
as a witness and servant of God, against sin and carelessness in every shape; he will show himself an affectionate
lover of men's souls, who would fain impart to others
the knowledge he has found valuable to himself. He
will never suffer wickedness to pass unnoticed if, by
saying a quiet word on the Lord's side, he may perchance restrain it. He will never allow anger and strife
to continue, if he can be the means of making peace.
And then has not a poor man a feeling heart? Then
surely, if he is a true sheep of Christ's flock, he will
remember them that are in adversity, as being himself in
the body; he will not shun the house of mourning, but
strive to be a comforter, bearing in mind the proverb
" A word spoken in season, how good is it "; he will
weep with them that weep, as well as rejoice with them
that rejoice; he will let men see that he is a real child
of his Father in heaven, who doeth good to the just
and the unjust too, and is kind even to the unthankful
and the evil. And cannot a poor man pray? Yes! and
effectual fervent prayer availeth much, and if he prays
for the souls of others, who knows but he may draw
down benefits on all around him? Oh! but a real
praying Christian, a man who is constantly asking for
the Spirit to come down on the place in which he dwells
and convert the sleepers, that man is a mighty bene-
factor; he is working a powerful engine, and if he is
the cause of one single person being converted, he has

done something that makes all heaven rejoice. Brethren, let it be written on our minds that all *can* do much, and they that belong to Christ's flock *will* strive to do much. No man is so really useful in a parish as a true Christian, and no one can have much real Christianity about him who does not endeavour to do good either by his advice or by his example or by his prayers. Are we indeed the sheep of Christ? Let us never forget this point of our character.

A genuine Gospel-faith has nothing selfish about it—it never makes a man think only of his own salvation ; it stirs him up, on the contrary, to anxiety about the souls of others. I always suspect that those who care nothing whether their brethren are saved or not, must in reality be ignorant or thoughtless about their own state.

Again. Sheep love to be together; they do not like being alone ; there are no animals which seem to take such pleasure in being in a flock, and cling to each other's company so faithfully. And so is it with true Christians : it is their delight to meet each other and be together, if possible. It is their continual sorrow and complaint that far too often they have to journey on alone, without any that are like-minded to commune with about the things which their souls love most ; and this is a very sore trial. Friends and relations may be kind and affectionate, they may have everything to make this world enjoyable, but what they sigh and crave after is to have with them persons who can enter into their secret feelings, who understand the unseen workings of their inward man, who can comprehend the hidden warfare which goes on in their hearts,—persons with whom they can take sweet counsel about their souls' health and souls' trials, with whom they can converse freely and unreservedly about their Lord and

Master and their hopes of forgiveness through His name. Who, indeed, can describe the pleasure with which the members of Christ's flock do meet each other face to face? They may have been strangers before; they may have lived apart, and never been in company; but it is wonderful to observe how soon they seem to understand each other, there seems a thorough oneness of opinion, and taste and judgment, so that a man would think they had known each other for years; they seem, indeed, to feel they are servants of one and the same Master, members of the same family, and have been converted by one and the same Spirit; they have one Lord, one faith, one baptism; they have the same trials, the same fears, the same doubts, the same temptations, the same faintings of heart, the same dread of sin, the same sense of unworthiness, the same love of their Saviour. Oh, but there is a mystical union between true believers, which they only know who have experienced it; the world cannot understand it—it is all foolishness to them. "Whatever can you find," they say, "to make you take such interest in each other's society?" But that union does really exist, and a most blessed thing it is; for it is like a little foretaste of heaven.

Beloved, this loving to be together is a special mark of Christ's flock,—nor is it strange if we consider they are walking in the same narrow way, and fighting against the same deadly enemies,—and never are they so happy as when they are in company. The unconverted know nothing of such happiness; they meet each other, and are civil and polite, and even kind in their way; but how seldom do they open their whole hearts, how much of jealousy and cold suspicion there is about their very friendships, how much they conceal from their nearest acquaintances! The sheep of Christ know nothing of all this ; it is their hearts' desire to be together, and when together they have all their thoughts in common, there is no reserve, no keeping back. No doubt there are false professors in the world, who have a form of godliness without the power—tinkling cymbals whose religion consists only in talk, all sound and no substance ; but notwithstanding the number of these hypocrites, I still say that true believers are remarkable for their love of communion and intercourse with each other ; they are ready to pine away with heaviness when separate ; it is the very life-breath of their nostrils to be together.

The last thing I would remark about sheep is this : they are of all animals most helpless, most ready to stray, most likely to lose themselves and wander out of their pasture ; and so it is with Christ's people. They are far too ready to turn aside and go in ways that are not good ; in vain they are warned and advised to be watchful and take heed to their path ; they often get into a drowsy, sleepy frame, and fancy there is no danger, and so they wander down some bypath, and are only wakened by some merciful chastisement or heavy fall. They will have it they are strong enough to get on without this constant vigilance, and so they take their eye off the Chief Shepherd, and wander on from this field to that, after their own desires, until they find themselves at last in darkness and doubt. And Christ's sheep, too, like other sheep, do seldom return to the fold without some damage and loss, for it is far more easy to get out of the right way when you are in, than to get into it when you are out.

There are some people who fancy Christians are perfect and faultless creatures, but this is indeed an opinion far wide of the truth. No doubt they aim at perfection, but the very best come far short of it ; they would tell you

that in many things they offend daily, that they are
continually erring and straying and backsliding, that
the most fitting prayer they could offer up would be
this : " Lord, we are no better than wandering sheep.
God be merciful to us unworthy sinners ! "

And then, too, like sheep, true Christians are easily
frightened. It takes very little to alarm them and make
them fearful about their own condition ; they are jealous
and suspicious of danger from every quarter, and, like
creatures who know their own weakness and the number
of their enemies, they will often imagine there is something to be feared where no fear really is. But still
this godly fear is an eminent sign of Christ's flock—it
proves that they feel their own helplessness ; and when
a man knows nothing of it, and is full of presumptuous
confidence, there is but too much reason to suspect he
knows little of Christianity as he ought to know it.

Such appear to be the reasons why true believers
are compared to sheep. They may not always be
discerned in this corrupt and naughty world ; you may
often see no great difference between them and the
unbelievers, but still they have a nature of their own,
and sooner or later if you observe you will see it. You
may put a flock of sheep and a flock of swine together
in a broad green meadow, and an ignorant man might
say at first their natures were the same ; but drive
them together in a narrow road, with a puddle at one
side, and the mind of the animal will soon come out.
The swine may have looked clean in the meadow, but
as soon as they have the opportunity they will wallow
in the mud. The sheep were clean in the meadow, and
when they come to the dirt they will keep clean there
too if they possibly can. Just so is the case of the
Christian and the world: when things run smoothly,
and there is no particular inducement to sin, there

seems no mighty difference between them ; but when there comes a temptation, and self-denial is required, immediately the disposition of the heart comes uppermost—the Christian holds on his way, however narrow it may be, the worldly-minded turns down that broad lane which leads to destruction, and the real character of each is revealed.

II. The second thing to be considered in our text is that word " My." Our Lord does not simply call His people sheep, but He says also " My sheep." It is as though He would have us understand He looks upon them as His property; they are, as it were, stamped and sealed and marked as the possession of the Lord Jesus Christ Himself, and it is a blessed, comfortable thought that even as men are careful and tender about their earthly belongings, and will not willingly allow them to be lost and damaged, so is our Lord and Saviour careful of the souls that belong to Him.

But why are Christ's people called Mine, in this particular manner ? There are many sufficient reasons. We are " His " by *election*. We were chosen and given to Him by the Father before the foundations of the world were laid ; our names were written in the covenant of salvation before we were born, we were predestined or fore-ordained to be His people from all eternity. That is a glorious, a soul-comforting doctrine, however some abuse it : a man may doubtless get to heaven and never feel sure that he was a true sheep of Christ's flock until he gets there ; he may walk in much darkness and uncertainty all his days ; but to all who really feel in themselves the working of Christ's Spirit, the doctrine that we are *His* by everlasting election, is full of sweet, pleasant and unspeakable consolation.

But again : Christ's people are " His " by *purchase.* Death and hell had claims upon every one of them, they had all broken the law and forfeited eternal life, but Christ has redeemed them. Christ paid the heavy price of their salvation, even His own most precious blood, and well may He call them " Mine," for He has bought them off from captivity and Satan at the cost of His own life. He can say " They are Mine by fair purchase in time as well as Mine by free election in eternity."

And lastly, Christ's people are " His " by *adoption.* He has put His Spirit in them, and overturned the power of sin in their hearts ; He has given them a child-like frame of mind, so that they cry Abba Father ; they are become part of His family, the very sons and daughters of the Almighty ; He looks upon them as a portion of Himself, as members of His body and flesh and bones, and loves them and cherishes them accordingly. See then, beloved, what great things that little word " My " contains : " My sheep " is the name that Jesus gives to Christians—" Mine " by election, by purchase, by adoption. Oh, believe : you may sometimes be cast down and faint-hearted, but if you have any real interest in that blessed title, if you are really in the number of Christ's sheep, you have indeed good reason to rejoice.

III. But I must hasten on to the third point which our text lays down in the character of true believers : "My sheep," says Jesus, "hear My voice." This hearing of Christ's voice, what is it? It cannot be the mere hearing of the ears, for many do that who die in their sins ; it must be the hearing with the heart, the listening with attention ; the believing what is heard,—the acting manfully on what is believed. And where may Christ's voice be heard? It sometimes whispers in a sinner's *conscience,* saying, Oh, do not these abominable things :

turn, turn, why will you die? it sometimes speaks solemnly, in a visitation of *providence*, as a sickness or an accident or an affliction or a death, saying slowly but clearly, " Stop and think ; consider your ways: are you ready to die and be judged? " But it generally is to be heard in the reading of *Scripture* or the preaching of the Gospel ; then the voice of the Lord Jesus may be heard plain and distinct. One day it is sharp and piercing: " Except ye repent ye shall all likewise perish " ; "Ye must be born again " ; " Awake, thou that sleepest, and arise from the dead." Another day it is gentle, winning, entreating : " Come unto me, O weary and heavy-laden one, and I will give thee rest " ; " If any man thirst, let him come unto me and drink ;" " Whosoever will, let him take the water of life freely." In all these ways and manners the voice of Jesus may be heard. And here comes in the distinction between the converted and the unconverted : they that are converted hear Christ's voice, but they that are unconverted hear it not. The true sheep of Christ were once foolish and disobedient, serving divers lusts and pleasures, dead in trespasses and sins ; but they heard their Redeemer's voice at last, and when they heard they lived ; they knew not at first who called them, but they heard a voice they could not disobey, and now they can tell you they are sure it was the Lord's. They heard His voice, they listened to His invitation, they believed His promises, they confessed themselves sinners, and in Him they found peace. And now without His voice they will do nothing ; His word, His saying, His command, His will is their rule of life,—to be taught of Him by His Spirit and His Bible is their hearts' desire and prayer, to hear about Him from His ministers is the meat and drink of their souls   Their ears are like a dry soil, ever thirsting to drink in the water of life. Sometimes they may be tempted to turn aside to hear what the world can offer, but they soon go back again to sit at Jesus' feet and hear His voice, with sorrow and shame and wonder for their own backslidings. The world cannot see that Christ's voice is such a joyful sound ; they dislike it—it offends them ; to be told they are sinners, and must repent and believe or perish, is a stumbling-block. But Christ's sheep are never offended ; day after day they listen diligently to their Shepherd's teaching ; no music is so sweet to their ears as Jesus' voice, and whether preached or written there is nothing they love so much. It seems as if it were spoken for their own particular case, and they cannot, they dare not, they would not for all the world disregard it.

IV. I must go on to the fourth and last mark of a true believer. " My sheep," says the text in St. John, " hear my voice and follow me." To *follow* Christ, that is the grand mark of Christians. No man shall ever say of them, they profess and do not practise, they say and do nothing for their Master's sake ; they must not only hear their Master's voice, but follow Him. To follow Christ is to place implicit trust in Him as our Redeemer, Saviour, Prophet, Priest, King, Leader, Commander and Shepherd, and to walk in His ways, straightforwards. It is to take up our cross and subscribe our name among His people, to look to the Lamb as our Guide and follow Him wheresoever He goes. We are not to follow our own devices and trust in ourselves for salvation ; we are not to follow that vain shadow of a hope, our own doings and perform-ances, but we are to fix our eyes and hearts on Christ ; on Him we are to rest our faith for free and full forgiveness, to Him we are to pray for grace to help in time of need, after Him we are to walk, as the best, the brightest, the purest example. The way may be narrow and steep, we must press forward, not turning to the right hand or the left ; the way may be dark, we must keep on,—there will be light enough in heaven. O that Christians, the very best of them, were not so slack in following ! Some stop to trifle with the perishable things of earth ; some stop to pick up the gaudy, scentless flowers by the wayside ; some stop to sleep, forgetting this is not our rest, it is enchanted ground ; some stop to pick holes and find fault with their fellow-travellers ; few even of Christ's sheep do hold on their way as steadily as they might. But still, compared with the world, they are following Christ Jesus (Oh that they would only remember, those who follow Him most fully shall follow Him most comfortably !) ; they are following Christ Jesus, and they know where they are going ; and even in the dark river, in the valley of the shadow of death, they feel a confidence that their Shepherd will be with them, and His rod and His staff will comfort them. They would all tell you they are poor wandering sheep, less than the least of all God's mercies, ashamed of the little fruit they bear ; but still, weak as they are, they are determined to follow on to the end, and to say, " None but Christ, in life and in death, in time and in eternity."

Such is the character which the text gives of true Christians. They are compared to sheep ; they are called Christ's property ; they hear His voice, and they follow Him. To go further at this time would be plainly impossible, and I therefore purpose, if the Lord will, to speak to you about the other branch of the text—the privileges of Christians—this evening. By God's blessing you shall then hear what their Saviour is to His people. It only remains to wind up what has been already said by personal application.

I told you this was a text for *self-inquiry* ; and in
that light I press upon each of you now. I call upon
thee, O man or O woman, to put thy hand upon thy
heart and ask that little question, " Am I a sheep of
Christ's flock, or am I not ? Do I hear His voice or do
I not ? Do I follow Him or do I not ? " Does not thy
Redeemer and thy Judge say plainly, " This is the
character of my people ? " Does He not give thee the
most certain marks by which to try thy state ? and if
thou canst not see in thyself these marks, where and
what are thy claims to eternal life ? without them thou
art, for the present, no better than a lost soul. Dost
thou not know there are only to be two sorts of characters
before the judgment-seat—sheep on the right hand in
honour, and goats on the left hand in disgrace? And
dost thou not know it is just the same even now?
There are only two classes of characters upon earth—
men who hear Christ and follow Christ and are in a
way to be saved, and men who neither hear nor follow
Him and are in a way to be lost? And which flock
dost thou belong to? There is no middle state. Examine
thyself and be wise in time.

Think not to put off this question by saying, " I shall
do as well as the rest of the world,"—that well may
be doing very badly. The way of the world, indeed !
Bring the world to the bar, and try it by the text,
" Does the world hear Christ ? " Who will stand forth
and say it does ? Christ's promises and invitations and
warnings and threatenings and instructions and exhorta-
tions are all alike disregarded and despised ; the world
is deaf to them ; they might never have been spoken.
" Oh," says the world, " we shall do very well without
minding all that ; it was not meant for us." And who
was it meant for, then ?

But again, does the world follow Christ? Who will

stand up and say Yes to that? No, indeed! Christ's
ways and Christ's example, holiness and love and meekness and temperance and self-denial, are the exceptions—
the rare, scarce things in the world; and the things most
frequent are anger, wrath, malice, blasphemy, adultery,
fornication, uncleanness, lasciviousness, hatred, variance,
emulations, wrath, strife, seditions, heresies, envyings,
drunkenness, revellings, wantonness, pride, vanity, idleness, spiritual sloth, Bible-despising, prayer-neglecting,
church-forgetting, worldliness, and the like. "Oh, never
mind," says the world; "we shall do very well without
being so strict." Very well in the devil's opinion, who
would love to ruin every living soul, but not very well
in God's. No; indeed the world will neither follow
Christ nor hear Christ, anything else sooner—and yet
remember it is the character of those who are to have
eternal life that they hear Christ's voice and follow
Him. Sinner, remember, to-day I have told you.

And think not, O man, to put me off by saying, "At
this rate very few will be saved." Thou sayest very
truly, and the Lord Jesus Christ Himself foretold it;
but let me tell thee a secret: Why is it so few are likely
to be saved? God would have all men brought unto
the knowledge of the truth: why do so many, so very
many, come short and take the broad way? Simply
because they will not believe what God has told them
in His word; simply because they will have it God
will not stand to what He has written in His Bible;
they will fancy heaven is to be entered without being
Christ's sheep—will have their own way and not God's.

Remember, then, this day, I tell thee, that God is
willing to receive thee *if thou wilt only turn to Him*:
if thou wilt only resolve to think for thyself and never
mind the world, if thou wilt only hear the voice of
the Lord Jesus Christ and follow Him, if thou wilt

only be in earnest and come unto Him for forgiveness and His Holy Spirit, He shall grant thee thy heart's desire, and thou shalt never perish but have eternal life. But whether thou wilt hear or whether thou wilt forbear, Christ and Christ only is the way, the truth, and the life, and whatever the world may tell thee, no man shall ever come unto the Father but by Him.

X

THE PRIVILEGES OF THE TRUE CHRISTIAN

" My sheep hear my voice, and I know them, and they follow me : and I give unto them eternal life ; and they shall never perish, neither shall any man pluck them out of my hand."—JOHN x. 27, 28.

ABOUT the first part of this text, beloved, I spoke to you this morning. I told you then that this passage contains two things—first the character of true Christians, and secondly their privileges—first what they are to their Saviour, and secondly what their Saviour is to them.

Let me, then, remind you what the text says of their character. We found on examination that God's children, His real believing people, are compared to sheep, because they are gentle, quiet, harmless and inoffensive ; because they are useful and do good to all around them ; because they love to be together, and dislike separation ; and lastly because they are very helpless and wandering and liable to stray.

We next found that Jesus calls them " My sheep," as if they were His peculiar property ; "Mine," He would have us know, by election, " Mine " by purchase, and " Mine " by adoption. We found in the third place that Christ's sheep hear His voice, they listen humbly to His teaching, they take His word for their rule and guide. Lastly we found that they follow Him, they walk in the narrow path He has marked out, they do not refuse because it is sometimes steep and narrow, but wherever the line of duty lies they go forward without doubting.

It only remains for us now to consider the other part of my text, which respects the *blessings* and *privileges* which Jesus the Good Shepherd bestows upon His people. The Lord grant that none of you may take to yourselves promises which do not belong to you, —that none may take liberty from God's exceeding mercy to continue sleeping in sin. Glorious and comfortable things are written in this passage, but remember they are given to Christ's flock only; I fence it out against all that are unbelieving and impenitent and profane. I warn you plainly, except you will hear the voice of Christ and follow Him, you have no right or portion in this blessed fountain of consolations.

Hear now what Jesus says of His believing people : " I know them. . . . I give unto them eternal life ; they shall never perish, neither shall any man pluck them out of my hand."

Before we look into the meaning of these words more closely, I wish to answer two questions which may arise in the minds of some before me. Of whom is the Lord Jesus speaking ? Are we to suppose He only has in view patriarchs and prophets and apostles—men like Abraham and David and Job and Daniel, men who through faith subdued kingdoms, wrought righteousness, stopped the mouths of lions, quenched the violence of fire, worked signs and miracles, and shed their blood for the kingdom of God's sake ? Are these the sort of persons who alone can take comfort from those blessed words—" I know them . . . . they shall never perish ? " Is every one else to go on doubting to his life's end ? God forbid that I should tell you so ! it were doing Satan's work to preach such doctrine. This text may

become the property of the worst of sinners, if he only
will : scribes and Pharisees, Sadducees and Herodians,
publicans and harlots, drunkards and fornicators,
murderers, thieves and adulterers, liars and blasphemers.
worldly-minded and covetous ones,—all and each of
them may lay firm hold on this text, and inherit its
precious treasures, if they will only hear Christ's voice
and follow Him. It is for all who repent and believe
the Gospel ; it is for all who mourn over their past
sins with a true godly sorrow, and flee to the Lord
Jesus Christ with faith and prayer as their only hope,
their all-sufficient Saviour, their all in all ; there is not
one single man or woman of whom it shall not be
written in the Lamb's book of life, " This is one known
of God, this is an heir of eternal life, this is a man or
a woman that is never to perish, never to be plucked
out of the Lord's hand," if you will only give up
your sins and take Christ Jesus for your Shepherd and
Redeemer. Your repentance may seem very faint, your
faith may appear weak as water, but if there be so
much as a grain of mustard seed, if there be enough
to lead you a penitent to the foot of the cross, you shall
find yourself one day numbered with the saints in
glory everlasting.

The other question I wish to answer is this : why
did the Lord Jesus Christ give us this full and complete
promise ? Because He knew that true Christians would
always be a very doubting, fearful, faint-hearted generation, always ready to believe they shall not be saved,
always afraid they shall never see the New Jerusalem,
because of the inbred corruption which they find continually in their hearts. He saw they would require the
strong wine of assurance like this, and so He has provided this and like texts, as a reviving cordial to cheer
and enliven their hearts, whenever they feel desponding

and feeble-minded and ready to halt, in their pilgrimage
through this weary world.

We will now look narrowly into the parts of this
promise. First, says the Lord Jesus Christ of His
sheep who hear His voice and follow Him—" I know
them." I know their number, their names, their particular characters, their besetting sins, their troubles, their
trials, their temptations, their doubts, their prayers,
their private meditations ; I know everything about
every one of them. Think what a comfortable saying
that is ! The *world* knows nothing about Christ's sheep ;
to be sure, the world remarks there are a few people,
here one and there one, who live differently to others,
who seem to be more serious in their deportment, who
appear to be taken up with some important consideration or other ; but the world only wonders they can be
so particular about little sins, and when their ways run
counter to the world, the world is vastly offended. But
as for their fear of sin, and their carefulness about souls,
the world neither knows nor understands what they are
about ; the secret springs of their conduct are all hidden.

Again, a Christian's *friends* do often know him not.
They may possibly respect him and allow him to hold
on his way unopposed—though this, alas ! is not always
the case—but as for his pleasures and his pains, his
constant warfare with the flesh, the world and the devil,
his dread of falling into temptation, his delight in all
means of grace, they can neither explain nor comprehend it ; there is a something hidden in his character
of which they know nothing.

Be ye comforted, all you who are tried and buffeted
with difficulties in your way towards heaven, difficulties from without and difficulties from within,
difficulties abroad and difficulties at home, grief for
your own sins and grief for the sins of others :

the Good Shepherd Jesus knows you well, though you may not think it. You never shed a secret tear over your own corruption, you never breathed a single prayer for forgiveness and helping grace, you never made a single struggle against wickedness, which He did not remark and note down in the book of His remembrance. You need not fear His not understanding your wants, you need not be afraid your prayers are too poor and unlearned to be attended to ; He knows your particular necessities far better than you do yourselves, and your humble supplications are no sooner offered up than heard. You may sometimes sigh and mourn for want of Christian brethren, you may sometimes lament that you have not more around you with whom you might take sweet converse about salvation ; but remember there is a Good Shepherd, who is ever about your path and about your bed, His eyes are on all your movements, and no husband, brother, father, mother, sister, friend, could take more tender interest in your soul's welfare than He does. If you transgress He will grieve, but He will chasten and bring you back ; if you bear good fruit, He will rejoice and give more grace ; if you sorrow He will bind up your broken heart and pour in balm ; He is ever watching and observing and listening ; none so humble and lowly but He is acquainted with all their ways.

And does not Jesus know the men of this world, the faithless and ungodly ? Unquestionably He does. He knows their proceedings ; there is not a single sin they have committed but will appear written down in full in the great book ; but He only knows them as His enemies—as careless, thoughtless ones, who will not take the trouble to hear His voice and follow Him—and in the last day, when all shall stand before Him, He will say, " I know you not : you would not seek to know me on earth, and I know nothing of you in heaven ; depart, ye cursed, into everlasting fire, prepared for the devil and his angels." No doubt there will be many a Balaam there, many a barren fig-tree, many a foolish virgin, many a fruitless vine, many a loud-talking hypocrite, who will say, " Lord, Lord, open to us : have we not taught in Thy name, and in Thy name quoted many texts, and in Thy name made a great profession ? " but still the answer will be, " I never knew you . . . depart from Me, ye that work iniquity."

Oh, what a blessed and comfortable thing to be known of Christ, known and marked as His friends, His relations, His dear children, His beloved family, His purchased possession ! Here we are often cast down, often discouraged, often persecuted, often spoken against, often misunderstood,—but let us take courage, our Lord and Master knows all. A day shall come when we shall no longer see through a glass darkly, but face to face—a day when we shall know even as we are now known ; for the union between us and our Redeemer, which we so often feel disposed to doubt, shall then be clearly seen, and we shall no more go out to battle.

II. What is the next part of my text? The Lord Jesus says of His sheep, " I give unto them eternal life." What is the portion which Jesus gives His people ? " ETERNAL LIFE "—a perfect, never-ending happiness for that which is the most important part of a man, his immortal soul. They shall not be hurt of the second death, which alone is to be really feared. What greater things could our Lord bestow upon His people ? Health and riches and honour and pleasures, houses and lands, and wives and children, what are they ? how long do they last ?—it is but threescore years and ten, and we must leave them all, and six paces of the

vilest earth is room enough for us. Naked came we
into the world, and naked must we return unto the
dust, and carry nothing with us. Where is the difference between the rich and the poor in death? They
both go unto one and the same place; the worm
feeds sweetly on them both; it is but a short time,
and you would not be able to distinguish between
their bones. But if the poor man sleeps in Jesus,
while the rich man dies in his sins, oh, what a mighty
gulf then is between them! The rich will take up his
abode in that fire which is never quenched; the poor
will awake to find he has an everlasting treasure in
heaven, even eternal life. Eternal life! compared to
which this world's concerns, weighty and important as
they seem, are like a drop of water. Wonderful indeed
that men should disquiet themselves about the things
of earth, and sweat and toil after a little more gold
and silver, and spend their strength upon these frail,
sickly bodies of ours, to get enjoyment for them, and
yet remain careless and dead and frozen about the
life of that precious talent the soul!

But about eternal life? "I," says the Lord Jesus
Christ, "do give it to my people." Who says this?
He says it who bought and paid the full price; He
who has in His hands the keys of death and hell; He
who opens and no man shuts, He who shuts and no
man opens; He says it who is the Amen, the faithful
and true Witness, who is not a man that He should
lie, who never breaks His promise; He says it who
has a right to say it, for He came down to do His
Father's will and die in our stead to obtain redemption
for us, and when He declares "I give eternal life," death
and hell must be silent, none can gainsay Him.

"I give," He declares, "eternal life." He does not
speak after the fashion of the world; this world is cold,

and calculating and heartless; there is little giving,—it is all bargaining and selling and paying what is the value of things. Blessed be God, the Lord Jesus does not deal with sinners as they deal with each other. He gives eternal life *freely*, and of grace, and for nothing, without money and without price; He does not give it because we are worthy or deserving, nor yet because we shall show ourselves worthy and deserving; but He gives it as a free gift, because He loves us and has set His affection upon us.

Consider with yourselves how glorious that doctrine is; how thoroughly it takes away all excuse from the impenitent: pardon and forgiveness are here unconditionally bestowed; we are not told that we must pay off so much every day, and then shall be saved—that would drive us to doubt and despair—but if a man will only hear Christ's voice and follow Him, "Behold" says Jesus, "I give unto him eternal life, there remaineth no condemnation for him."

III. The third promise in my text is as follows: Jesus says of His sheep, "They shall never perish," —they shall never be finally cast away, if they have once been sealed and numbered in my flock. They may have many a slip and many a fall, they may experience many a shortcoming and many a backsliding, but they shall never be lost eternally, they shall be kept by the power of God through faith unto salvation. Where are those fearful Christians, who will have it they may be Christ's sheep and yet come short at last? behold the assurance of Him who cannot lie,— "they shall never perish."

Yes; true Christians shall never perish! Is not that great work begun within their hearts by the Holy Ghost? has not the power of God Himself been employed in converting them from darkness to light?

and shall we dare say that God will take in hand the
smallest thing, and yet leave it unfinished and not
bring it to perfection? Have they not been born again
of incorruptible seed, and shall this seed be choked
and bear no fruit? Have they not been made by
grace new creatures, and is it possible that grace can
have raised them to newness of life in vain? Where
in the whole world can you find a work which the Lord
has attempted, and yet been obliged to give up and
leave all incomplete? Then far be it from us to suppose
that a true believer can ever be cast away! If man had
any share in his conversion one might reasonably doubt;
but it is not so, it is the work of God, and what He
does shall always be brought to perfection. The
building which the Holy Ghost has founded shall
never be suffered to decay, it shall never be left half
finished, and the top stone shall certainly be one day
laid on with shouting.

True Christians shall never perish. Are they not
Christ's special property, the servants of His house, the
members of His family, the children of His adoption?
Then surely He will never let them be overthrown, He
will watch them as tenderly as we watch over our
own flesh and blood, He will guard them as we guard
our valuable and precious possessions, He will cherish
them as we cherish that which is most dear to our
hearts; He never would have laid down His life for
their sakes if He had intended to give them up.

"Never perish"! Kings of the earth and mighty
men shall depart and be no more seen; thrones and
dominions and principalities, rich men and honourable
men shall be swept into the tomb, but the humblest
Christian cottager shall never see death everlasting,
and when the heavens shall pass away as a scroll, and
earth with all its fair clothing shall be burned up, that

man shall be found to have a house not made with hands, eternal in the heavens. That man may be poor in this world and lightly esteemed, but I see in him one who shall be a glorious saint, when those who perchance had more of this life's good things shall be in torment ; I am confident that nothing shall ever separate him from the love of Christ. He may have his doubts, but I know he is provided for, he shall never be lost.

IV. There remains one thing more. Jesus adds, " Neither shall any man pluck them out of my hand." There is assurance upon assurance, that none may have an excuse for doubting. There is always something plucking at Christ's sheep : the lust of the flesh, the lust of the eyes, the pride of life, the devil, and the world are ever striving hard to destroy them ; but they shall not succeed. Think you the devil will give up his kingdom without a mighty struggle ? Oh no, he goes about as a roaring lion seeking whom he may devour ; he wars a constant warfare with all who keep the commandments of God and have the testimony of Jesus Christ, but the word of God is pledged that he shall never prevail. Not all the powers of darkness shall avail to quench one single spark of real gospel faith.

And now, beloved, in conclusion, let me speak a word of exhortation to all among you who hear Christ's voice and follow Him. O that the Spirit may come down among you, and add to your number a hundredfold ! Are ye indeed Christ's sheep ? Can you feel within yourselves the working of His blessed Spirit, mortifying the works of the flesh and drawing up your minds to heavenly things ? have you the witness in yourselves that you have gone through a real spiritual change, that you hate the sins which once you loved, and love the

things which once you despised? have you good reason
to believe that you have indeed put off the old man
with his deeds, and put on the new man with the lamb-
like nature of your blessed Master? Then, oh, rejoice
with joy unspeakable and full of glory; pray that you
may not stand still, but go on from grace to grace and
strength to strength; pray that you may bear much
spiritual fruit, for thus is your Father glorified, and then
will you make your own calling and election sure
to yourselves.

Are ye indeed Christ's sheep? *Then beware of ever
trusting to yourselves;* nothing offends the Good
Shepherd more than to see the members of His flock,
forgetting that in Him alone is all their safety, and
glorying in their own attainments and performances.
Think not of your weak endeavours; think not to say,
" I do very little, and therefore have very little hope,—
by-and-by I trust I shall do much, and then I shall
have much hope "; your best performances and attempts
towards heaven are in themselves but broken reeds,
and can bear no weight; they are precious as evidences
of spiritual life, but they cannot justify. Think only of
your Saviour Jesus Christ, trust Him entirely, love Him
affectionately, look to Him continually : as long as you
lean on Him you are strong and none can touch you,
without Him and in your own might you are weak and
unstable as water.

Are ye indeed Christ's sheep? *Then beware of
wandering from the pasture He has provided.* The
devil and the old Adam would often persuade you there
is no need for this diligence in using means of grace :
" Surely," they will say, " you are not such a babe but
you can leave these fields for a short season ; surely
you need not keep so closely in your Shepherd's sight."
Christian, take heed and beware of the charmer, charm

he never so wisely : diligent private prayer, diligent Scripture searching, diligent gospel hearing,—these are the pastures in which Jesus feeds His flock, and if you turn aside, if you become slack in using them, be sure your soul will soon starve for want of its accustomed nourishment, and you will return to the fold weak and lame and lean and diseased.

Once more, and I have done. Are ye indeed Christ's sheep ? *then be sure you will have many a trial ;* where indeed would be the value of a Saviour, if there were not enemies to be saved from? Yes ! you will have many a trial ; Satan has great wrath with all who have escaped his snares, and he will bring every engine to bear against your peace ; he will start many a doubt within your mind, he will stir up many a vile and blasphemous imagination within the chambers of your heart, many a horrid thought you once would have believed impossible ; but still remember those words, "never perish." Yes ! you will have many a trial : when did the world ever patronise and encourage a true Christian ? Oh no, the world will mock and despise, and laugh and frighten, and misrepresent you, and spread false reports, and throw traps in your way, and if it dares it will persecute you ; and then there is the flesh, sleepy and drowsy and fond of excuses, always trying to make you believe you have more difficulties than anybody else, deceitful, treacherous, needing constant watchfulness ; but still the world and the flesh can never turn you back, except you are a graceless traitor ; remember those blessed words "never perish." Christian, you may be perplexed, but you never need despair ; you may be persecuted but you are not forsaken, cast down but not destroyed ; you may have tribulation, but you shall not have condemnation ; you shall be saved from your enemies and from the hand of all that hate you. Fear none of these things which ye shall suffer ; be faithful unto death, and your Good Shepherd shall give you a crown of life.   Verily He is gone before to prepare a place for those whom He knows, and where He is in glory there they shall be also.

" For I am persuaded," says Paul, " that neither death nor life, nor angels, nor principalities, nor powers, nor things present, nor things to come, nor height, nor depth, nor any other creature, shall be able to separate us from the love of God, which is in Christ Jesus our Lord."

XI

THE GRACE OF GOD IN VAIN

"We then, as workers together with him, beseech you also that ye receive not the grace of God in vain."—2 COR. vi. 1.

ALTHOUGH the Church of Corinth, to which these words were written, was certainly not a body without spot and blemish; although we learn by Paul's first Epistle that in many things its members were to be blamed; still, with all its faults, it is plain this Church was very different from the churches of our own day; there was less profession without practice, more fruit in proportion to the branches, a stronger leaven of faith and holiness and love, a more abundant crop of wheat in proportion to the tares. And yet you see by the text how solemnly the apostle warns them of danger, how earnestly he entreats them not to hear the gospel only to their condemnation; he would not have them rest upon their outward privileges and opportunities, he would not have them soothe their consciences with the idea that all was safe because they were baptised in the name of Jesus, but as a faithful labourer in God's vineyard he calls on them to examine themselves, and beware lest they receive the grace of God in vain. And are we better than they? Can we produce a greater list of evidences that God· is in us of a truth? I speak as unto wise men, judge ye what I say. Verily, beloved, we are guilty in this matter.

Let us rather confess that we have nothing whereof to glory, and as a shortcoming generation let us humbly consider what this text contains for our particular instruction. It is an easy matter to say, "one minister is too sharp, we do not like him, and another is too high, we cannot understand him, and another makes the way so narrow that no one can be saved, and another is so dull that we do not care to hear him"; but consider, O ye men and women who are so difficult to please, consider, O ye who are so backward to search the Scriptures for yourselves, ye have a great work to do, the time is short, the fashion of this world passeth away, and tremble lest ye go on doubting and trifling and fault-finding till the end, and so be found among that wretched company who have received the grace of God in vain.

Now, there are three points to be considered in our text.

I. What you are to understand by the grace of God.

II. What it is to receive it in vain.

III. The reasons why we beseech you so earnestly not to receive it in vain.

I. First, then, what is this grace of God, which the apostle here speaks of? It is an expression which has different meanings in Scripture; sometimes it signifies the free favour of God, as when we read, "By grace are ye saved, not of works"; sometimes it means the operation of the Holy Spirit in a man's conversion, as when St. Paul tells the Galatians, it was "God who called me by His grace"; but in our text I conceive it has a wider, broader signification. I take it to mean that gracious offer of free salvation for the worst of sinners which is commonly called the gospel, and so called because it is in every way good tidings, that free gift of righteousness, peace and pardon, which is provided for all who will believe in the Lord Jesus. Now, what

is it that makes this offer so important and so precious ?
It is simply this, that we are all by nature sinful and
corrupt. We are born into the world with a disposition
inclined to evil and not to good ; we show it in our
infancy by angry tempers, by jealousy, by selfishness ;
we show it in our youth by deceit, by idleness, by
unwillingness to learn, by disobedience to parents, by
unthankfulness, by self-conceit ; and when we come
to man's estate we show it in a hundred fashions,—by
giving way to our lusts and passions whenever we
dare, by loving pleasure more than God, by Sabbath-
breaking, and swearing, and drinking and fornication,
by uncharitable conduct to our neighbours, by pride
and vanity, by neglecting God's Bible, by staying away
from His church, by despising His sacraments, by dis-
honouring His ministers, by worldly-mindedness, by
living on from year to year without a spark of love
to Him who gave us life and breath and all things
that we enjoy. This is the manner in which we naturally
like to pass our time ; and thus it is that one way or
another we prove our hearts to be " deceitful above all
things and desperately wicked." No doubt it was not
so in the beginning : man was created upright, and his
Maker pronounced him, like His other works, to be
very good in the day when everything was finished ;
but Adam did not keep his first estate, he ate the
forbidden fruit and fell ; and in that hour there came
an awful change over his nature : he lost the holy image
and likeness of God, and from that time the imagination of man has had a continual bent towards evil.
And yet the God with whom we have to do is holy :
He is of purer eyes than to behold iniquity, the least
speck of sin is an abomination in His sight ; the heaven
that He dwells in is a holy place, and the general
judgment which he hath appointed as the end of all

things will be a judgment of holiness and a judgment of righteousness. And how can we expect to face this fiery trial? wherewith can we come into our Maker's presence? The laws we have insulted, and the mercies we have lightly esteemed, would all rise up against us; by nature we are all shut up unto condemnation, there remains nothing for us to look forward to, but the worm that never dies and the fire that shall not be quenched.

But here, in this deplorable case, the grace of God has come in: the Lord of all, out of pure love and mercy for we deserve nothing but wrath and condemnation—out of pure love and mercy, for He was not obliged to redeem us—the Lord of all has sent His beloved Son Jesus Christ to take our nature upon Him, and suffer death upon the cross, "that whosoever believeth in Him should not perish, but have everlasting life." It is the grace of God that, when we were all without hope, Christ came into the world, to do the things we never could have done, to fulfil that holy and just and good law which brings us all in guilty, and He did fulfil it to the last jot and tittle; to suffer the punishment which we deserved, and He did suffer it upon the cross, and drank the bitter cup to the very dregs; and by the things He did and the things He suffered He provided a perfect righteousness for every one that is willing to believe.

It is the grace of God that He came to do His Father's will, and to satisfy His Father's justice, by standing in our place and taking upon Himself the sins of the whole world; and though the burden was so heavy that He sweat great drops of blood, yet He proved "mighty to save," and won a victory over our great enemies upon the cross—here is the grace of God, of which the apostle spake; here is the message we are charged to deliver. We offer to you Christ

and a free pardon, Christ and everlasting life ; you may
have been fornicators and adulterers, and thieves and
covetous and drunkards, and revilers and extortioners,
and yet you are not shut out from this salvation ; only
believe—all things are possible to him that believeth.
You tell me you have been a sinner before God exceedingly—I answer the blood of Christ cleanseth from all
sin ; you tell me you have broken God's laws a million
times—I answer Christ is the end of the law for righteousness to everyone that believeth ; you tell me you have
no righteousness, you will never be fit for heaven—I
offer you the perfect righteousness of the Lord Jesus
Himself, all that He hath done shall be accounted yours.
I repeat, the complete righteousness of the Lord Jesus
shall be placed upon you as a pure white garment, which
shall cover all your iniquities, and who shall dare to raise
his voice against you ?   But you tell me you have such
a cold, dead, wicked heart,—I answer, if you come at
once unto the Lord Jesus He shall pour the Holy
Ghost upon you and give you a new one, and you
shall become a new creature.

This very day I set before the worst among you
pardon and peace and immortality, without money
and without price : I do not tell you to go and become
saints, to go and live a new life before you can receive
these blessings ; I call upon to return at once, with all
your sins upon you, and lay them at your Saviour's
feet, and they shall be forgiven.   I know nothing of
conditions ; I am not sent to one and not to another.
I am commissioned to invite you all to my Master's
banquet, and whatever your character may have been
in time past, however thoughtless and profane you
may have been, I am charged to offer you the gospel
of the grace of God, to tell you all shall be pardoned
and forgotten if you trust in Jesus' name.   Here is

bread for the hungry and water for the thirsty—healing
balm for the wounded and rest for the weary—light
for those that are in darkness and life for those that
are dead—riches for those that are poor, and joy for
those that mourn ; Christ's precious blood shall wash
away every single sin, Christ's everlasting righteousness
shall be all your own.   Return unto Jesus all ye that
are far off in this congregation, old or young, high
or low, rich or poor—whether ye be now sleeping in
utter carelessness, whether ye be godless blasphemers
of the truth, whether ye be talking, self-deceiving
hypocrites, whether ye be self-righteous, formal Pharisees,
whether ye be cold, heartless listeners to truth, whether
ye be wretched backsliders from the narrow way—
return unto Jesus, I beseech you, for He hath redeemed
you.

What fruit have ye in the life ye now live ?   Ye are
not really happy ; ye tremble at the thought of judgment : return unto Jesus and ye shall be welcome ;
all things shall be yours, the world or life or death, or
things present or things to come, all shall be yours,
for ye shall be Christ's and Christ is God's.   Come to
your Father's house ; the price of your redemption has
been paid, and He prays you to enter in ; He tells the
very guiltiest of you all that if you will only come
to Him through the appointed Mediator, He will
blot out as with a thick cloud your transgressions,
and as if carried into a land that is not inhabited
He will make mention of them no more.

Such, then, beloved, is the mighty doctrine which
Paul had in view when he spoke of " the grace of God "
in our text.   He did not merely mean that spiritual
help is promised to those who want to set up a
righteousness of their own ; he had before his mind
that grand offer of full reconciliation which is made by

our Heavenly Father to His rebellious children through
Christ's atonement ; he meant that new and living way
which Jesus hath opened for disobedient man to draw
near his holy Maker ; that mystery of undeserved love
and mercy which angels desire to look into ; and so
deeply does he dread the corruption of man's heart,
that he seems to tremble lest the Corinthians should
hear of this grace of God and go no further, should
listen to the report of the gospel and yet perish in
their sins.

II. Let us, then, next inquire how and when it may
be said that a man receives the grace of God in vain.
Now, I have nothing to do in this matter with the
open unbeliever, the man who deliberately forsakes
the house of God, and turns his back upon the simplest
elements, the first principles of Scriptural religion.   Of
such a one I can only say that he is not receiving the
grace of God at all ; he will not even listen to our
message ; he has not even an outward form of
Christianity, and to all intents and purposes he is
living without God in the world.   The persons whom
I wish to deal with are those who profess and call
themselves Christians, the men and women who
generally make up our congregations.   You must know
well that a vast proportion of them hear the gospel
and yet are never the better for it ; they receive the
grace of God into their ears and their mouths and their
heads, aye, sometimes even into their houses, and yet
they do not receive it into their own hearts, and
therefore they are said to receive it in vain, unprofitably,
to no purpose ; and the point I want to establish in
your minds at present is how and why and when these
things are so.   And be ye very sure there never was
a time when such inquiry was so necessary : you live
in days which prophets and kings of old did wish to

see and never saw, days when many run to and fro,
and light and knowledge is marvellously increased,
days when there are opportunities for getting spiritual
wisdom which your grandfathers never enjoyed, but
days, alas! when there is much profession without
practice, and there is need for much self-examination,
lest perchance we deceive ourselves.

Now, I say that all are receiving the grace of God in
vain who have never been convinced of the guilt and
corruption of their own hearts, who have never found
out that they are sinners and must be born again of
the Holy Ghost, who are altogether at ease about
their own souls, and cannot see the need for such
anxiety as Christ's people show, and wonder at
people who think much about religion ; who cannot
believe themselves to be so desperately wicked, and
cannot think that God will be so particular. These
are the men who in their own opinion are rich and
increased with goods and have need of nothing, and to
this hour know not that they are wretched and
miserable and poor and blind and naked ; all such
have hitherto received the grace of God in vain. I say
in vain, for how can a man know the value of a remedy
until he has felt his disease? how can you love the
light if you never discovered yourself to be in darkness ?
how can you see the excellence of the gospel if you
never found yourself condemned by the law? how
can you understand your need of a Saviour if you
never groaned under the burden of sin ? Oh no!
beloved, if your spirit has never witnessed within you
that you have really erred and strayed from God's ways
like a lost sheep, that you have really followed too
much the devices and desires of your own hearts, that
you have really offended against God's holy laws,
that there really is no health in you,—if you have

never mourned over your transgressions with a true
godly sorrow, and hated them with a true godly hatred,
—if you are hitherto a stranger to these feelings,
it is impossible you can regard Christ crucified as the
one thing needful ; you may have heard of the grace of
God, but you know nothing of it as you ought to know.

But again, there are many who are convinced of
sin, and yet will not come to Christ and the hope set
before them in the gospel. Some are so melted under
the word that rivers of tears run down their eyes,
they cannot speak bad enough of their past lives, they
will have nothing more to do with the accursed thing ;
and yet the first temptation carries all before it, and
their goodness proves no better than the morning dew
and the cloud which passeth away—and all because
they made resolutions in their own strength, they
did not build upon the sure corner-stone, even the
Lord Jesus Christ, without whom nothing is strong,
nothing is holy. Others, perhaps, appear to make surer
work : they put away the evil of their doings ; they
give up outward vices, they put on a whitewashed
garment, and are beautiful in the eyes of men, and
they are regular and decent in the formal duties of
religion—but there they stop. They flatter themselves
that all is safe ; that they have whereof to boast before
God ; and that persons so sober, so honest, so just,
so reformed, cannot miss of attaining everlasting life.
But if the word of God be true, their hopes are false ;
they are looking to themselves while Scripture says,
" By the deeds of the law shall no flesh living be justified " ; they are building on the sand.

" I am the way, the truth, and the life," saith
Jesus ; " no man cometh unto the Father but by me."
A simple faith in the blood of Christ is the very
alphabet in the school of Christianity ; and if your

conviction never bring you to it, it is plain you have something at the bottom which you have not given up—and that is pride.

There can be no true repentance without faith. You may cast away your old habits, as the serpent casts his skin ; but if you are not resting all upon the Lamb of God which taketh away the sins of the world, and looking to be saved by simple faith in Him, you may be wise in your own eyes, but you are just ignorant of the root and fountain, the Alpha and the Omega, the beginning and the end, the first and the last, in all true gospel religion. You may tell us you have repented ; but if you have not at the same time laid hold on Christ, you have hitherto received the grace of God in vain.

Lastly, there can be no doubt that they who do not follow after holiness, who do not strive to glorify their Lord with their bodies and spirits, have received the grace of God in vain. About all other men we may not be able to decide with certainty ; but about them the rule is laid down clearly.

" By their fruits ye shall know them." The fruit of the Spirit is love, joy, peace, long-suffering, gentleness, goodness, faith, meekness, temperance. "And they that are Christ's have crucified the flesh with the affections and lusts." They that are true believers in the Lord Jesus do love to tread in their Master's steps and learn of Him, and endeavour to be as like Him as possible in all their habits and tempers. I never can believe that men and women who name the name of Christ and yet neglect His will, and speak of the Holy Spirit while they resist Him, and talk of faith while they plainly do not believe, and of repentance while they continue impenitent, and of a heavenly life while they continue carnal—I never can believe that

such, for all their fine words, have any portion or lot
in the kingdom of God. These are like sign-posts:
they point the way towards Zion, but they never
get one yard nearer to it themselves. Such people
build with their lips, but pull down with their lives;
they warn others of hell, and yet are on the high road
to it. I read that Christ redeems His flock from all
iniquity, that He may purify unto Himself a peculiar
people, zealous of good works; and therefore, when
I see men or women walking in the counsel of the
ungodly and standing in the way of sinners and
sitting in the seat of the scornful, making provision
for the flesh to fulfil the lusts thereof, conforming to
the world in its vain and idle customs—I am at no
loss about their character. They may often look like
saints and talk like angels—they may be acquainted
with all mysteries and all knowledge; but if sin reign
in their mortal bodies that they can obey it in the
lusts thereof without a struggle to be free, I hesitate
not to tell them to their face—whoever they may
be—"You have, so far, received the grace of God in
vain."

But I may not go further on this point. Indeed,
I tremble to think how many of you may come under
the three classes that I have named. All who have
never been truly penitent for sin,—all who have never
rightly closed with Christ,—and all who do not strive
to walk worthy of their high calling,—all those have
received the grace of God in vain. And if He whose
fan is in His hand were now to come amongst you, an
thoroughly purge His floor and cast out all the unprofitable hearers, oh, what a poor little handful might
possibly be left!

III. I promised in the third place to say a few words
about the reasons why ministers are so anxious that

you should not receive the grace of God in vain. Oh!
it is a strange thing we should have to beseech at all;
you would not need it if we every Sunday had a purse
of gold to divide amongst a congregation, but when we
have to set before you the kingdom of God, righteousness, peace and everlasting life, alas! it is a great
matter if we can get you to give your attention to our
invitations, it is a great matter if you can be brought
to listen patiently to the messengers and ambassadors
of your Maker, your Redeemer, and your Judge.

Know, then, that we beseech you earnestly that ye
receive not the grace of God in vain, because the time
is short, and every day that you continue lingering and
undecided doth shorten your opportunity for repentance
and make your heart more dull and harder to be
moved. The time you have is short for praying, short
for Bible reading, short for breaking loose from this
deceitful world, short for preparing for the world to
come; those fevers and diseases, which God doth shake
over the heads of many, might easily cut off twenty or
thirty of the strongest of you, and where would your
souls be? We beseech you because you have a battle
to fight; the world, the flesh, the devil have all to be
opposed; you have to put on the whole armour of
God, to strive, to wrestle manfully against temptation;
and if you really love the crown of glory, you cannot
too soon come out from sinful ways and take your
stand among the valiant for the truth upon the earth.
But if there were no other reason, we beseech you
because of death and judgment. I urge upon you that
an hour is meeting each of you like an armed man,
when this body shall become the food of creeping things
and the soul shall be called to its last account; I see
in my mind's eye the business of that awful day—the
great white throne, the assembled millions, the open

books, the heavens departing as a scroll, the earth and the works that are therein melting with fervent heat ; I hear the archangel's trump summoning the dead from north and south and east and west, and I tremble to think how those will fare who have received the grace of God in vain. I tremble to think how they will be dealt with, who have a long account of Bibles unread and prayer neglected, churches despised and sacraments dishonoured, ministers disregarded and sermons scorned, all standing in full array against their names. I tremble to find it plainly declared by Christ Himself, Christ the compassionate and tender-hearted, that even Sodom and Gomorrah shall be mercifully treated, compared with those who have been called upon to repent and have not repented, who have been invited to believe in Jesus and have not believed. And for all these causes, and for many more of which we cannot speak particularly, we do beseech you and implore you to beware lest ye receive the grace of God in vain, to beware of hearing without improving, to beware of professing while you are not growing, to beware of giving your ears to God but not your heart.

See, now, most dearly beloved, does not this text divide you all in twain ? Does it not separate the good fish from the bad ? You know in your own consciences it does. And where are the few among you who humbly trust that they have not altogether heard the gospel in vain ? Hearken, O ye that are really followers of Christ. Can you see in yourselves a feeling of hatred towards sin that once you never knew, a dependence on the blood of Jesus only to which ye were once strangers, a thirsting after holiness with which ye were once unacquainted ? Then O rejoice with humble fear, and go forward in faith and hope ; and though iniquity abounds, let not your love wax cold ; but grow in grace

and every day bring forth more fruit, and unto the God
of gods ye shall every one of you appear in Zion.

But are there not many of you who have all your lives
received the grace of God to no purpose, and sided with
the world? You know there are. I speak not these
things to shame you, but as beloved to warn you, for
it is my heart's desire and prayer to God that every soul
among you may be saved; and I ask all such to listen
to a word of exhortation. Consider, I beseech you, O
ye thoughtless ones, consider the madness, the folly of
your conduct. Surely you must feel that in the ways
of worldly-mindedness and sin there is no real satisfaction, and you must know the end of these things is
death. Surely your Father's offer of forgiveness is a
gracious and a loving one. Oh, do not sell your souls for
such miserable rewards as this world can give, and let
it not be written of you this day that you were asked
to turn and refused. You cannot really suppose that
God's beloved Son was crucified and put to open
shame, while heaven became black and the earth
quaked and the veil was rent at the fearful sight, that
you might be careless and live as you please, and
yet be saved. Oh, but you must have a low view of
heaven if you think it can be won so cheaply! Let
me plead with you, let me plead the cause of your
everlasting souls. I do not want to make you
wretched, melancholy beings; the devil, who was a
murderer and a liar from the beginning, tries to make
you believe this, but it is not so; I want to provide
you with a solid peace, such as this perishable world
can neither give nor take away. Why will you cleave
so closely to the lust of the flesh and the lust of the
eye and the pride of life?—they cannot comfort you in
the days of trial which you must go through. Why
is the everlasting gospel, which alone is good for every

season, good for time and good for eternity, good for
sorrow and good for joy, good for youth and good for
age, good for life and good for death,—why is the gospel
to be treated as a thing that will do you harm and poison
the springs of your happiness? You cannot answer
me ; you know that I am speaking the words of sober-
ness and truth. This very day I call upon you to
begin a change—to forsake your sins, to care nothing
for the opinion of the world, to receive your Father's
invitation readily and willingly, meekly and honestly ;
I beseech you to turn and live, to repent and be
converted, to believe and be saved.

Let not another harvest ripen on this earth and
find you still among the number of those who are
called the tares, still spiritually dark, sleeping and dead,
still unprepared and unforgiven ; sow to yourselves
in righteousness, break up your fallow ground with
the plough of repentance, seek your loving Redeemer
with the publican's prayer, " Jesus, have mercy on me
a sinner,"—and thus, and thus only, when the mighty
harvest of the earth is reaped, the angels shall gather
you as precious wheat into the treasure-house of God,
and you shall not be burned up as worthless chaff with
unquenchable fire.

XII

THE CHRISTIAN RACE

" Seeing we also are compassed about with so great a cloud of witnesses,
let us lay aside every weight, and the sin which doth so easily beset us,
and let us run with patience the race that is set before us, looking unto
Jesus the author and finisher of our faith."—HEBREWS xii. 1, 2.

BELOVED, I have lately spoken to you much
about the character and experience of true
believers in the Lord Jesus Christ, the men who are
sowing for everlasting life.

Before, however, we continue this inquiry, I wish to
warn you against forgetting the sure foundation ; I wish
to caution you most strongly against losing sight of the
root of the whole matter—a simple faith in the Lord
Jesus Christ. You must not stumble at the outset by
supposing I want you to set up a righteousness of your
own. Some think their own endeavours after holiness
are to make up their title to salvation ; some think
that when they come to Christ, their sins past alone
are forgiven, and for the time to come they must
depend upon themselves. Alas ! there always have
been mistakes upon this point : men toil and labour
after peace with God as if their own exertions would
give them a right to lay hold on Christ, and when
they find themselves far short of the Bible standard
they mourn and grieve and will not be comforted ;
and all because they will not see that in the matter
of forgiveness, in the matter of justification in the sight

of God, it is not doing which is required, but believing ; it is not working, but trusting ; it is not perfect obedience, but humble faith. Now, once for all, let us understand, that all who have really fled for mercy to the Lord Jesus Christ are, as Paul assures the Colossians, complete in Him ! In themselves they may be poor shortcoming sinners, but seeing they have laid hold on Christ, God looks upon them as complete—completely pardoned, completely righteous, completely pure—no jot or tittle of condemnation can be laid to their charge.

They have nothing more to do with the law as a covenant of works, as a condition they must fulfil or die : the Lord does not say, " Be perfect and then you shall live," but "Christ has given you life, and for His sake strive to be perfect." But you will ask me, " Why do they hunger and thirst so much after holiness, since all their debt has been paid ? " I answer, They work for love's sake—for gratitude ; they do not work and strive after holiness in order that they may be forgiven, but because they are forgiven already, chosen and sealed and saved and redeemed and bought with a price, and they cannot help desiring to glorify Him with their bodies and spirits who loved them and gave Himself for them. They thirst after holiness because their Father loves holiness ; they thirst after purity because their Master loves purity ; they strive to be like Jesus because they hope to be one day for ever with Him.

But seeing they have many a difficulty in doing the things that they would, and are continually warring with the world, the flesh, and the devil, and sometimes are so ready to faint that they doubt whether they really are of Christ's family or not,—seeing these things are so, I have tried to give you a faint outline of their experience

on late occasions, and I purpose this afternoon to lay
before you shortly the advice which the apostle gives
them in my text.

Now, I say that the text contains five points :

I. We have all a race to run.

II. Many have gone before us.

III. We must lay aside every weight.

IV. We must run with patience.

V. We must be continually looking unto Jesus. The
Lord pour down His Spirit upon each of you, and
bow the hearts of all here present, as the heart of
one man, that you may seek the Lord while there is
yet time, and set your faces towards Jerusalem, and
not die the death of the faithless and unbelieving.

I. First, then, we have a *race to run*. By this you are
not to understand that our own right arm and our own
strength can ever open for us the gates of everlasting
life, and win us a place in heaven. Far from it : that
is all of grace—it is another question. It simply means
that all who take up the cross and follow Christ must
make up their minds to meet with many a difficulty,
they must calculate on labour and toil and trouble, they
have a mighty work to do, and there is need for all their
attention. Without there will be fightings, within there
will be fears ; there will be snares to be avoided, and
temptations to be resisted ; there will be your own
treacherous hearts, often cold and dead and dry and
dull ; there will be friends who will give you unscriptural
advice, and relations who will even war against your
soul ; in |short, there will be stumbling-blocks on every
side, there will be occasion for all your diligence and
watchfulness and godly jealousy and prayer,—you will
soon find that to be a real Christian is no light matter.

Oh what a condemnation there is here for all those
easy-going persons who seem to think they may pass

their time as they please, and yet be numbered with the saints in glory everlasting ! Are those who show less earnestness about their souls than about their earthly amusements, and those who have much to tell you about this world's business but nothing about heaven, and those who think nothing of neglecting the commonest helps towards Zion, and count it much to give religion a few Sunday thoughts,—are these men running the Christian race, and straining every nerve after the prize ? I leave the answer with yourselves : judge ye what I say.

And those who profess to have entered the course, and yet find time to rest by the wayside and trifle with temptation, and find fault with the anxiety of others,—and those who stop to take breath and boast of their attainments, and look behind them,—are such running the race set before them as if it was a matter of life and death ? Oh no ! They may get the name of Christians, but they are not so running that they shall obtain. But they who are taught and called of God may soon be distinguished from the sleeping children of this world. These have no leisure for vain amusements ; their eyes are fixed and their thoughts are engaged upon the narrow path they have to tread and the crown they hope to receive ; they have counted the cost, and come out from the world ; and their only wish is that they may finish their course with joy.

II. The second thing you may learn from the text is this : " Many have gone before us ; we are encompassed with a great cloud of *witnesses*." The witnesses here spoken of are those patriarchs and prophets who are mentioned in the eleventh chapter, and the apostle calls upon us to remember them and their troubles and take courage. Are we frail earthen vessels ? so were they. Are we weak and encompassed with in-

firmities? so were they. Are we exposed to temptation and burdened with this body of corruption? so
were they. Are we afflicted? so were they. Are we
alone in our generation, the scorn of all our neighbours?
so were they. Have we trials of cruel mockings? so
had they. What can we possibly be called upon to
suffer which they have not endured? What consolations did they receive which we may not enjoy? You
may talk of your cares and business and families, but
their portion was just like yours; they were men of
like passions; they did not neglect business, and yet
they gave their hearts to God. They show the race
can always be run by those who have the will. Yes,
they were all flesh and blood like ourselves, and yet
by grace they became new creatures; and so by faith
they "obtained a good report;" by faith they confessed
themselves strangers and pilgrims on the earth; through
faith they "subdued kingdoms, wrought righteousness,
obtained promises, stopped the mouths of lions, quenched
the violence of fire, escaped the edge of the sword, out
of weakness were made strong, waxed valiant in fight,
turned to flight the armies of the aliens: women received
their dead raised to life again; and others were tortured
not accepting deliverance, that they might obtain a better
resurrection; and others had trial of bonds and imprisonment: they were stoned, they were sawn asunder,
were tempted, were slain with the sword; they wandered
about in sheepskins and goatskins, being destitute,
afflicted, tormented." But grace exceedingly abounded,
and all fought a good fight and finished their course
and kept the faith, and to the God of gods appeared
every one of them in Zion. Take courage, fainting
Christians: you are encompassed with a great cloud of
witnesses; the race that you are running has been
run by millions before; you think that no one ever had

such trials as yourself, but every step that you are journeying has been safely trod by others ; the valley of the shadow of death has been securely passed by a cloud of trembling, doubting ones like yourself ; they had their fears and anxieties, like you, but they were not cast away ; the world, the flesh and the devil can never overwhelm the weakest woman who will set her face towards God ; these millions journeyed on in bitterness and tears like your own, and yet not one did perish—they all reached home.

III. The third point to be considered is the apostle's advice, to " lay aside every weight." By this he means that we must give up everything which is *really hurtful to our souls.* We must act like men who throw off all their long and flowing garments, as an encumbrance, when about to try their speed in running. We must cast away everything which hinders us upon our road towards heaven—the lust of the flesh, the lust of the eye, and the pride of life ; the love of riches, pleasures, and honours, the spirit of lukewarmness and carelessness and indifference about the things of God, all must be rooted out and forsaken if we are anxious for the prize. We must mortify the deeds of the body, we must crucify our affection for this world ; we must look well to our habits and inclinations and employments, and if we find anything coming in as a stumbling-block between ourselves and salvation, we must be ready to lay it aside as if it were a millstone about our necks, although it cost us as much pain as cutting off a hand or plucking out a right eye. Away with everything which keeps us back ; our feet are slow at the very best, we have a long course to run, we cannot afford to carry weight, if we are really contending for everlasting life.

But above all we must take heed that we lay aside the sin which doth most easily beset us, the sin which from our age, or habit, or taste, or disposition, or feelings, possesses the greatest power over us. I know of two which are always at our elbows, two sins which try the most advanced Christians even to the end, and these are pride and unbelief—pride in our own difference from others, pride in our reputation as Christians, pride in our spiritual attainments : unbelief about our own sinfulness, unbelief about God's wisdom, unbelief about God's mercy. Oh, they are heavy burdens, and sorely do they keep us back, and few really know they are carrying them, and few indeed are those who will not discover them at the very bottom of the chamber of their hearts, waiting an opportunity to come out.

But there are particular besetting sins, of which each separate Christian can alone furnish an account ; each single one of us has some weak point, each one has got a thin, shaking spot in his wall of defence against the devil, each one has a traitor in his camp ready to open the gates to Satan, and he that is wise will never rest until he has discovered where this weak point is. This is that special sin which you are here exhorted to watch against, to overcome, to cast forth, to spare no means in keeping it under and bringing it into subjection, that it may not entangle you in your race towards Zion. One man is beset with lust, another with a love of drinking, another with evil temper, another with malice, another with covetousness, another with worldly-mindedness, another with idleness ; but each of us has got about him some besetting infirmity, which is able to hinder him far more than others, and with which he must keep an unceasing warfare, or else he will never so run as to obtain the prize. *Oh these bitter besetting sins !* How many have fallen in their full course, and given occasion to God's enemies to blaspheme, from

thinking lightly of them, from not continually guarding
against them, from a vain notion that they were
altogether cut off!—they have been over-confident and
presumptuous; they have said "We are the temple of
the Lord, and we cannot greatly stumble," and they
have forgotten that hidden root, that branch of the
old Adam; and so day after day, little by little, shoot
after shoot, it grew, it strengthened, it filled their
heart, it blighted their few graces; and suddenly, without
time to think, they have slipped and fallen headlong
in the race, and now they are hurrying down stream
amidst that miserable party, the backsliders, and who
can tell what their end may be? But what was the
simple cause? They disregarded some besetting sin.
Go, child of God, and search the chamber of thine
imagination: see whether thou canst find there some
seed of evil, some darling thing which thou hast
tenderly spared hitherto, because it was a little one;
away with it—there must be no mercy, no compromise;
no reserve: it must be laid aside, plucked up, torn up by
the roots, or it will one day trip thee up, and prevent
thee running thy race towards Zion. The gates of heaven
are broad enough to receive the worst of sinners, but too
narrow to admit the smallest grain of unforsaken sin.

IV. The fourth point to be noticed in the text is
the frame of mind in which we are to run: "let us run
with *patience*." I take this patience to mean that meek,
contented spirit, which is the child of real living faith,
which flows from a confidence that all things are
working together for our good. Oh, it is a most
necessary and useful grace! There are so many crosses
to be borne when we have entered the course, so many
disappointments and trials and fatigues, that, except
we are enabled to possess our souls in patience, we
shall never persevere unto the end. But we must not

turn back to Egypt, because some bring up an evil
report of the promised land ; we must not faint because
the journey is long and the way lies through a wilderness, we must press forward without flagging, not
murmuring when we are chastened, but saying, with
Eli, " It is the Lord let Him do that which seemeth
Him good." Look at Moses, in Hebrews xi. : " When
he was come to years, he refused to be called the
son of Pharaoh's daughter ; choosing rather to suffer
affliction with the people of God, than to enjoy the
pleasures of sin for a season ; esteeming the reproach
of Christ greater riches than the treasures of Egypt :
for he had respect unto the recompence of the reward ;
he endured as seeing Him who is invisible." Look at
Job, when God permitted Satan to afflict him : " Naked,"
he says, " came I out of my mother's womb, and naked
shall I return thither : the Lord gave, and the Lord
hath taken away ; blessed be the name of the Lord."

" What ? shall we receive good at the hand of God,
and shall we not receive evil ? " Look at David, the
man after God's own heart, how many waves of trouble
passed over that honoured head ; how many years he
fled from the hand of Saul, how much tribulation did
he suffer from his own family ; and hear what he says
when he is fleeing from his own son Absalom, and a
certain Benjamite came forth and cursed him. " Behold,
my son, which came forth of my bowels, seeketh my
life : how much more may this Benjamite do it ? Let
him alone, and let him curse ; for the Lord hath bidden
him. It may be that the Lord will look on mine
affliction, and that the Lord will requite me good for
his cursing this day." Mark too, as you read his Psalms,
how often you come on that expression, " waiting
upon God " : it seems as if he thought it the highest
grace a Christian can attain to.

Look lastly at your blessed Lord Himself. St. Peter says, "He left us an example, that we should walk in His steps: who did no sin, neither was guile found in His mouth: who when He was reviled, reviled not again; when He suffered, He threatened not; but committed Himself to Him that judgeth righteously." Paul says: "For consider Him that endured such contradiction of sinners against Himself, lest ye be wearied and faint in your minds. Ye have not yet resisted unto blood, striving against sin. And ye have forgotten the exhortation which speaketh unto you as unto children, My son, despise not thou the chastening, of the Lord, nor faint when thou art rebuked of Him: for whom the Lord loveth He chasteneth, and scourgeth every son whom He receiveth." O yes, beloved, we must run with patience, or we shall never obtain. There may be many things we cannot understand, much that the flesh could perhaps wish otherwise; but let us endure unto the end, and all shall be made clear, and God's arrangements shall be proved best. Think not to have your reward on earth, do not draw back because your good things are all yet to come: to-day is the cross, but to-morrow is the crown; to-day is the labour, to-morrow is the wages; to-day is the sowing, but to-morrow is the harvest; to-day is the battle, but to-morrow is the rest; to-day is the weeping, but to-morrow is the joy; and what is to-day compared to to-morrow? to-day is at most but threescore years and ten, but to-morrow is eternity. Be patient and hope unto the end.

V. The last point is the most important in the text. It is the object on which our eyes are to be fixed: we are to run our race "*looking unto Jesus.*" We are to run, depending on Him for salvation, renouncing all trust in our own poor frail exertions,

and counting our own performances no better than
filthy rags, and resting wholly and entirely, simply
and completely, upon that perfect righteousness which
He worked out for us upon the cross. We need not
run uncertain of the end, we need not fight in ignorance of what shall follow ; we have only to behold
the Lamb of God who taketh away the sin of the
world, and believe that He hath borne our griefs and
carried our sorrows, and will soon present us spotless
and unblameable in His Father's sight. And then we
are to run, making Jesus our Example, taking no lower
pattern than the Son of God Himself, endeavouring
to copy His meekness, His humility, His love, His
zeal for souls, His self-denial, His purity, His faith,
His patience, His prayerfulness, and as we look we
shall daily become more like Him. And then we are
to run, looking for our blessed Lord's appearing, praying always with all prayer and supplication that He
will hasten His coming and kingdom and accomplish
the number of His elect. Unto them that look for
Him shall He appear the second time without sin
unto salvation, and their vile bodies in a moment, in
the twinkling of an eye, shall be made like unto His
glorious body, and they shall be for ever with their Lord.

Oh, this looking unto Jesus ! here is the secret cause
which kept that cloud of witnesses steadfast and unmoveable in this narrow way ! here is the simple rule
for all who wish to enter on the course which lands
a man in Paradise ! Look not to earth : it is a sinful,
perishable place, and they that build upon it shall find
their foundation of the earth earthy ; they will not stand
the fire. Set not your affections upon it, or else you
will perish together ; the earth shall be burned up, and
if you cling to it in death you shall not be divided !

Look not to yourselves ! you are by nature wretched

and miserable, and poor and blind and naked ; you
cannot make atonement for your past transgressions,
you cannot wipe out a single page in that long black
list, and when the King shall ask you for your wedding-
garment you will be speechless. Look simply unto
Jesus, and then the weight shall fall from off your
shoulders, and the course shall be clear and plain, and
you shall run the race which is set before you. Truly
a man may be mistaken for a season, and walk in
darkness for a time, but if he once determine to look
to Jesus he shall not greatly err.

Who now are the men and women in this congregation who have not entered on the grand struggle for life ?
This day, ye Christless, sleeping ones, this day I charge
you to be honest and merciful to your souls. Turn
ye, O turn ye from your evil ways, turn ye from
your self-pleasing and self-indulging ; seek ye the Lord
while He may be found, call upon Him while He is
near ; cry mightily unto the Lord Jesus Christ, before
the night cometh and you sleep for evermore. I know
the thoughts that are in the hearts of those among
you who ever think, (for many come and go without
thinking) : I know your thoughts ; you cannot make up
your mind to lay aside every weight, you cannot throw
overboard the sin that doth so easily beset you. Alas !
like Herod you would do many things, but not all : you
will not give up that Herodias, that darling bosom-sin—
the world, the business, the drink, the pleasure—you
cannot give it up, it must have the first place in your
heart. I testify, I warn you, I take you to record,
that God hath declared there shall in no wise enter
into heaven anything that defileth, and if you are
determined not to give up your sins, your sins will
cleave to you like lead and sink you in the pit of
destruction. You need not wait : you must show some

inclination ; God will not convert you against your will ; except you show the desire, how can you expect He will give you the grace ?

But where are the men and women who are running the race and struggling towards the heavenly Jerusalem ? Think not that you have anything which makes your journey more difficult than others' ; the saints at God's right hand were perfected through sufferings ; and you must run with patience ; millions have gone safe through, and so shall you.

Beware of cumbering yourselves with any weight of earthly chances ; examine your hearts most closely, and purge out each besetting sin with a godly prayerful jealousy. Remember that blessed rule, " looking unto Jesus." Peter did run well for a time, when he left the ship to walk upon the sea to Jesus ; but when he saw the waves and the storm he was afraid and began to sink. Thus many a one sets out courageously ; but after a while corruptions rise high within, corruptions are strong without, the eye is drawn off Jesus, the devil gets an advantage, and the soul begins to sink. Oh, keep your eye steadily fixed on Christ, and you shall go through fire and water and they shall not hurt you. Are you tempted ? look unto Jesus. Are you afflicted ? look unto Jesus. Do all speak evil of you? look unto Jesus. Do you feel cold, dull, backsliding ? look unto Jesus. Never say, " I will heal myself and then look unto Jesus, I will get into a good frame and then take comfort in my Beloved." It is the very delusion of Satan. But whether you are weak or strong, in the valley or on the mount, in sickness or in health, in sorrow or in joy, in going out or in coming in, in youth or in age, in richness or in poverty, in life or in death, let this be your motto and your guide—" LOOKING UNTO JESUS."

Why those fears? behold, 'tis Jesus
  Holds the helm and guides the ship:
Spread the sails, and catch the breezes
  Sent to waft us o'er the deep
      To the regions
Where the mourners cease to weep.

Could we stay when death was hov'ring,
  Could we rest on such a shore?
No, the awful truth discov'ring,
  We could linger there no more;
      We forsake it,
Leaving all we loved before.

Though the shore we hope to land on
  Only by report is known,
Yet we freely all abandon
  Led by that report alone:
      And with Jesus
Through the trackless deep move on.

Render'd safe by *His* protection,
  We shall pass the wat'ry waste;
Trusting to *His* wise direction,
  We shall gain the port at last,
      And with wonder
Think on toils and dangers past.

XIII

"WHAT THINK YE OF CHRIST?"

"What think ye of Christ? whose son is he? They say unto him,
The Son of David."—MATT. xxii. 42.

BELOVED, I have told you more than once, and
I tell you now again, that since I have had the
charge of this House and district it has been my heart's
desire and prayer to promote your salvation. Morning
and night I make my petition to my Father which is
in heaven, that it will please Him to pour out the Holy
Ghost upon you all, and bring you unto Christ. Hath
not He said "Ask, and ye shall receive"? and shall
I not bring your case before Him?

But you little know what an anxious situation a
minister of the Church is placed in at all times, and
never more so than when preparing for the pulpit.
Perhaps you may think I have nothing to do but open
my Bible, take the first text that meets my eye, and
write off a sermon in two or three hours. But it is
far otherwise. I have to watch for your souls, as one
that would give account; and if you will not think
about them yourselves, I must try to persuade you to
it. Now, I search the Scriptures and compare them
with what I see and observe and hear of those who live
about me; and I declare to you, with grief and sorrow,
in many many cases I cannot make the two agree.
I find there are some persons ruining body and soul

KINGSTON LIBRARIES

OLD MALDEN LIBRARY
CHURCH ROAD
WORCESTER PARK KT4 7RD
Tel: 01-337 6344   Fax: 01 330 3118

MONDAY
10.00 a.m. - 12.30 p.m.
1.30 p.m. - 5.00 p.m.

TUESDAY
10.00 a.m. - 12.30 p.m.
1.30 a.m. - 7.00 p.m.

WEDNESDAY
10.00 a.m. - 12.30 p.m.
1.30 p.m. - 5.00 p.m.

THURSDAY – CLOSED

FRIDAY
10.00 a.m. - 12.30 p.m.
1.30 p.m. - 7.00 p.m.

SATURDAY
10.00 a.m. - 12.30 p.m.
1.30 p.m. - 5.00 p.m.

*Books and spoken word tapes
to borrow*

Children's Books to borrow

Foreign Language Tapes

Prestel Information Service

*KINGTEL, Local
Information Service*

Fax Facilities

ROYAL
KINGSTON

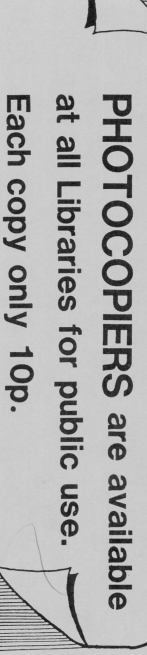

PHOTOCOPIERS are available
at all Libraries for public use.
Each copy only 10p.

by drunkenness and immorality ; some who only come
to church once, and that without any conceivable reason
that I can discover ; others who do so very irregularly,
and on some Sundays do not come at all. Oh, beloved,
I tell you again, as I have told many from house to
house, if it is worth while to come at all, it is worth
while to come regularly. One person told me the other
day he never went anywhere, either to church or chapel,
he had given it up ; and I fear there are others like
him. Believe me, when I see all this, it becomes a very
difficult matter to make up my mind what texts will
do you the most good.

What, I say to myself, will most awaken this people ?
What will most startle them ? What will arouse them
and make them think ? What will most likely lead
them to see the sinfulness of sin, the danger of trifling
with their Maker and their Judge, the real value of
their own souls, the exceeding mercy of God in Christ
Jesus ? Such were some of the reflections that passed
through my mind when I chose the text you have
heard : " What think ye of Christ ? "

Beloved, the present state of your souls depends on
the nature of the answer your conscience gives : " What
think ye of Christ ? " You cannot answer this satis-
factorily unless you are true members of His body—
really united to Him by a living faith, really renewed
by the Holy Ghost. There is no middle path here.
You cannot make it a matter of indifference whether
you think rightly of Christ or not ; the question is very
short, very simple, but the answer to it involves life
or death. The book of Judges tells us that the Gileadites
slew forty-two thousand men of Ephraim, because they
could not pronounce a word aright ; but the pronun-
ciation of that single word was the proof whether they
were enemies or not. And just so stands the case

between you and God in the matter of my text. I
ask you a little, plain question ; but if you cannot
give the answer God requires, I warn you, in love and
tenderness, you are travelling on the broad way that
leadeth to destruction.

There are some, I know, who would fain believe
that to think and preach so much about Christ is no
true religion, that it would be better if I spoke more
about plain practical duties, that it does not signify
so much what men think about Christ ; but I trust
they are so few, that I shall say nothing to them.
Plain practical duties are very well, but they cannot
put away sin, or give men new hearts, or save souls :
all that is Christ's office ; Christ is the mainspring
and subject of all Scripture ; Christ, we read, is the
Bishop of souls, the Author and Finisher of faith, the
Bread of life, the Captain of salvation, the Corner-stone,
the Door, the Mediator, the Prince of life, the Prince
of peace, the Rock, the Shepherd, the Sun of righteousness, the Light of the world ; and surely, then, I may
fairly tell you that to think rightly of Jesus Christ is
the sum and substance of religion.

1. Let us then inquire, beloved, what it is to think
rightly of Christ.   First, then, with respect to *His
Person*, we must think that He is perfect God, equal
with the Father, and together with Him and the Holy
Ghost, making up the ever-blessed Trinity.   If we do
not think this we contradict the words of Scripture.
If we do not think of Christ as God, we cannot
explain how He can be so mighty to save, or why
His fulfilment of the law and crucifixion can have
been so meritorious, so complete a sacrifice for sins
in the sight of His Father.   If Christ had been at
all inferior to God, the work that He worked upon
earth for our sakes would have been the act of a

servant, performing the commands of his master and doing no more than his duty. Nothing less than God could have made atonement for this guilty world.

2. We must think of Him as *perfect man*, of like nature with ourselves in everything, sin only excepted. If Christ had not been man He could not have suffered the punishment of our iniquities by dying on the cross; if He had not taken on Him a body and a nature liable to temptation like our own, He could never have fulfilled the law for us and in our stead; and we could not have looked upon Him with a brotherly confidence, as one who can be touched with the feeling of our infirmities.

3. We must think of Him as the great *Redeemer* and Saviour, who by the voluntary sacrifice and death of Himself made atonement for the sins of the whole world, provided a means of reconciliation between His Father and mankind, and brought in an everlasting righteousness which is unto all and upon all them that believe.

4. We must think of Him as a *King*: He is the great head of a spiritual dominion over the heart of all whom He chooses and calls out of the world; the chief of a spiritual kingdom which confers peculiar blessings and privileges on all who become subjects of it—a kingdom which is unseen, invisible at present, but shall be known and acknowledged by all at Christ's second coming.

5. We must think of Him as the *great High Priest*, who, like the Jewish high priest of old, has gone alone before us into the Holy of Holies, that is Heaven, to make satisfaction for the sin of His people with blood, even the blood of Himself, who ever stands at the right hand of God to make intercession for them; and can always feel for and pity them, because as man He was tempted like as they are.

6. We must think of Him as the *Prophet* that
should come, foretold by Moses shortly before His
death, who has shown to mankind the way of salvation,
who has clearly explained how God's mercy and God's
justice can be reconciled when sinners are accounted
righteous, who has taught us how God would have
men to live, and has placed duties and morality upon
their right foundation, and these are the inward motives
and the heart.

7. Lastly, we must think of Him as the great
Example, who has left men a pattern that they should
walk in His steps, who has given them, in His own
person and behaviour, a model of conduct in nearly
every department of life which they cannot strive too
much to imitate.

Now, I doubt not the greater part of you will feel
disposed to say, " Do we not certainly know all these
things ? We have learned them long ago ; we have heard
them continually in church ; if this is all you mean
by thinking rightly of Christ, none may feel more
comfortable than we do in answering the question of
your text."

Yes, beloved, but this is not all: there is the point
at which so many members of the Church of England
stop short ; here lies the snare into which so many of
you fall ; hitherto the devil himself will accompany you,
and perhaps go further, for he believes, he trembles,
he confesses Jesus to be the Holy One of God.
Hearken, therefore, I beseech you, and understand that
there are two ways of thinking about Christ ; both
indeed are necessary to salvation, but one, alas, is very
often found to exist without the other. It is one thing
to think of Him with the head, and another to think
of Him with the heart ; it is one to think about His
offices as a matter of opinion, it is another to rejoice

in them as infinitely important to your own soul ; it
is one to know these things correctly, it is another
to live as if you felt them ; it is one to acknowledge
that Christ is a mighty gift to ruined man, it is quite
another to apply this healing medicine to your own
case.

Indeed I would not have you ignorant that this error
is a most poisonous one, it is the very seat of Satan ;
and in charity to your souls I beseech you, if you love
life, to take heed to your ways, to search your hearts,
and come out from it. The Church of England has
many privileges and advantages—there is no communion
on earth has near so many to offer—but, like every
other Church, she is liable to be abused by her unworthy
members. She has placed in your hands a Prayer-book
of unequalled beauty, propriety and spirituality ; but
many of you turn it to a bad account, and because you
join in prayers which speak of Christ as *our* Redeemer,
our Mediator, *our* Advocate, you flatter yourselves that
you are in a fair way to be saved, that *you* are accepted
in the Beloved. But know ye, each one, for a certainty,
however suitable these prayers may be to those who
can say Amen in faith, they will be found to have
profited you very little if your conscience cannot also
say, " He is *my* Redeemer, *my* Mediator, *my* Advocate."
To attend the services of this house is indeed a privilege,
and one too that may not be lightly disregarded ; but
it is very possible to draw near with the lips and not
with the heart, there is such a thing as the form of
godliness without the power, and all the prayer-books
in England will never save your soul if you will not
give your whole heart to God. Be not deceived : I
want each one of you to make his salvation his own
personal concern, and for a time to forget there is any
but himself in the world to be saved,—to ask his con-

science "What do *I* think of Christ?" not What do *we*
think? "Is Jesus *my* Saviour?" not Is He *our* Saviour;
for men will not be judged in congregations, but separ-
ately, each standing by himself, and each in succession
will be condemned who cannot say "The life that *I*
have lived I have lived by the faith of the Son of God,
who loved *me* and gave Himself for *me*."

Beloved, this doctrine may seem to make the way
to heaven narrow; but did not Jesus say it was so,
and would not your profession be all useless, all un-
meaning, without it?

You say you think that Christ is perfect God? But
how can His ministers suppose you really feel and
believe this, when they see you show so little anxiety
to worship Him, to give Him thanks, to put your whole
trust in Him, to cast all your burden on Him, to fear
Him, and to love Him—while you appear to meditate
so seldom on the mighty work He alone could perform
for you, on the righteousness He alone could bring—
while you do not obey His expressed will—while He
says one thing and you do another? Surely, when
these things are so, He cannot be *your* God.

You say you think that Christ is a great Redeemer.
But how can we suppose you feel this, while you appear
so careless about the souls which He purchased with
His own blood—while you think so lightly of the sins,
which could only be atoned for by His death and
sufferings upon the cross—while you show so little
humiliation, so little sense of your own unworthiness
and desperate state without Him—while you do not
use every means of strengthening and refreshing your
weak spirits, that you may be meet for the inheritance
of His saints in light—while you live so much for this
perishable world, from the snares of which He died
to deliver you? Surely, whatever you may choose to

think, when these things are so He cannot be *your* Redeemer.

You say you think that Christ is a great Example. But how can we imagine you believe it, while you do not frame your own lives according to the pattern He has left—while you evidently do not struggle to imitate His faith, His love, His humility, His purity, His self-denial, His meekness, His gentleness, His unwearied zeal for the good of souls? Surely, whatever you may think and say, He cannot be your Example.

O beloved, this cold, lifeless acknowledgment, this dead belief of truths because you know nothing to the contrary, can never be thinking rightly of Christ! This cannot be that saving faith which works by love, overcomes the world, and purifies the heart. If this is all, you cannot be aware of your own sinfulness, you cannot be aware of the mighty remedy required ; you must be dead alike to your own necessities, and the mercy of God who has provided so great salvation. If the plague or the typhus fever were in this church, and there stood amongst you some sure and healing cordial, and none of you did more than look at it, and say you believed it was an infallible cure, but none stretched out a hand to lay hold upon it and use it, could any one suppose that you either believed the remedy to be certain, or the disease to be a dangerous one? But just such is your case, if you profess to believe in Christ and yet cannot call Him your own ; for you may depend upon it, that as far as *your* salvation is concerned Christ unapplied is no Christ at all.

I am at a loss whether it would be more fitting to call such thinking of your great Redeemer ungrateful or unreasonable. Judge now for yourselves. If an inhabitant of another world were to be told there was a certain place called earth, where God once placed a man and woman, gave them everything they could desire, and made them rulers over all, he would probably say: "What goodness! how great must have been their love! what pleasure they must have felt in doing His will!" Suppose then I went on to tell him this man and woman would not believe God's word, they thought themselves wiser than their Maker, and broke the only small command imposed upon them, he would say, perhaps, "What miraculous ingratitude, folly and unbelief! doubtless they were punished deservedly." Suppose then I proceeded to tell him that, on the contrary, God spared them, provided means of reconciliation, and in due time made manifest His mercy by sending His only-begotten Son to take guilty man's nature, fulfil the law and suffer punishment in his stead—declaring that whosoever throughout the world confessed his sins and put all his trust in this Almighty Saviour should be saved from wrath and accounted righteous as if he had never broken the law, —do you not think that, on hearing this, he would say, "Wonderful! of course there must be very few who do not seek this Saviour, make Him the chief subject of their thoughts and object of their love, the resting-place of their hope, their refuge in trial, the rock of their salvation ; there must be few who do not delight to hear of Him, read about Him, talk of Him, meditate upon Him, pray to Him, honour His word, His house and His services." Beloved, what could I say next? I have stated the case fairly so far, and would not this be my only honest reply? "Many, alas, are called, but few are chosen. Many name the name of Christ, but few depart from iniquity or believe in Him to the saving of their souls."

Suffer me once more to plead with you for your eternal good. Do not, I entreat you, leave this place in a state of lukewarm uncertainty as to whether ye think rightly of Christ or not. If the thought of Christ has never weaned you from the world, made a difference in your lives, and sanctified your hearts, it has hitherto profited you nothing. If the thought of Him dying for sin has not shown you how sinful sin is, how hateful in the sight of God, has never brought you on your knees grieving for your iniquity with heartfelt repentance, has never led you to that Bible which testifies of Him, believe me it has hitherto profited you nothing, it will only increase your condemnation. Remember, however lightly you may esteem your souls, God has set an untold value on them, for He gave His only Son for their redemption, but they cannot be saved, unless Christ dwells in your heart by faith. Awake, then, and cast away this icy garment of indifference, which is now your pride. Dare to go further than the world around you, and to think of Christ as a true Christian, as one who has sins to be atoned for, and rejoices to find a complete atonement.

I solemnly declare unto you, if you are content with a mere head-knowledge of these things and can be at ease without coming unto Jesus as your Saviour and your God, you are ruining your own souls, and you shall find that Sodom and Gomorrah will rise up in judgment against you and condemn you, for if they had known them they would have repented long ago in dust and ashes.

Come, then, unto Jesus ; think that He is ready to receive you, willing and mighty to save. You cannot say I wish you to do what is impossible ; you cannot say I tell you to fulfil the law and then come ; I do not ask you to make brick without straw, to make yourselves saints and then come. In my Master's name I offer you complete salvation if you will believe, free

salvation if you will believe ; everlasting life if you will
believe.   All things are yours if you will think rightly
of Christ.
   Christians, one word for you.   What think you of
Christ ?   Do you regret that you have made Him your
Redeemer and your Friend ?   Is His service wearisome ?
Is not your blessed Lord as good as His word, " I will
give you rest " ?   Are not His ways ways of pleasant-
ness and paths of peace ?   Can you not say of Him
what was said of Solomon by the Queen of Sheba :
" It was a true report that I heard in mine own land
of thy acts and of thy wisdom.   Howbeit I believed
not the words, until I came, and mine eyes had seen
it : and, behold, the half was not told me : thy wisdom
and prosperity exceedeth the fame which I heard.
Happy are thy men, happy are these thy servants,
which stand continually before thee, and that hear
thy wisdom " (i Kings x. 6)?
   Press forward, then, I beseech you, toward the mark
for the prize of your high calling.   Show forth the
praises of Him that hath called you out of darkness
into this marvellous light.   Let nothing tempt you
to cast aside your confidence, which hath great hope
of reward.   " Be not weary in well doing, for in due
time ye shall reap, if you faint not."

XIV

THE UNCHANGING CHRIST

"Jesus Christ the same yesterday, and to-day, and for ever."—HEB. xiii. 8.

"ALWAYS the same! unchanging!—that is a glorious character; a character which belongs to nothing that is of the earth earthy; a character which He alone deserves who is the Lord from heaven.

What of this very world in which we live and move and have our being? It has stamped upon it the marks of a tremendous change; it is no longer the same as it was in the beginning, it cannot be that fair creation of which God pronounced every part and portion to be very good. Doubtless we are not ignorant it is still a beautiful world, clothed with all that is lovely to the eye, furnished with all that is necessary to our comfort, stored with everything that can make life enjoyable: you may see everywhere the traces of a Father's hand. But still, we repeat, this world is not what it once was: it is no longer the same—no more the same than the gallant ship which yesterday did walk the waters like a thing of life, and to-day is dashed high on the beach and lies there a wreck, dismasted, shattered, and forsaken—no more the same than the ruin of some ancient house of God, which in days gone by was set apart and hallowed for religious services, and now stands desolate and silent and alone, with weeds and briars creeping over

its floor, and ivy hanging about its broken walls like
a widow's garment. Just so this world has gone
through a blighting, withering change ; and therefore
it is we see so much of lusts unbridled and tempers
ungoverned and passions unrestrained and intellects
degraded and affections misplaced and powers mis-
applied, and God neglected, dishonoured and lightly
esteemed. And the sicknesses which devour their
thousands, and the wars which cut off their tens of
thousands, and the graves of infants snatched away
in the spring-time of life, and the tears and distresses
and troubles and sorrows and afflictions which God
never placed in Eden, but of which we now hear
continually,—all these tell you the same tale, the
world is no longer the same. All these are the hand-
writing on the wall, to remind us that man, like an
unfaithful steward, hath marred and spoiled his Maker's
handiwork by his own sin, and so put the creation
out of order and course.

But we have not time, beloved, to compare earth as
it is with earth as it was before Adam fell : it is enough
to know that by his transgression all things suffered,
for after his transgression all things were altered. We
would rather go on to set before you proofs which
are more under your own eyes and come within your
own observation. We wish you to feel the full force
and blessedness of the character St. Paul has given
to your Lord and Saviour in our text ; and in order
to this we think it of first importance to establish in
your minds this grand point—that there is nothing on
earth of which you can say it is unchangeable, it is
always the same, yesterday, to-day, and for ever.

First, then, we ask you to mark that the empires
and kingdoms of this world continue not the same :
not all the victories which mighty conquerors have won,

not all the blood which they have spilt to cement and
make firm their thrones, not all the gold and treasure
they have heaped together, not all the territory they
have brought under their authority, not all the laws
they have carefully framed for their subjects, have
ever availed to build up one single kingdom that has
stood firm and undestroyed.

Some have endured for a longer space than others,—
some have appeared likely to remain until the end of
time,—but sooner or later all have wasted away, their
strength has gone from them, they have decayed and
passed by, and their place is no more found.

Where are the kingdoms of Judah and Israel, whose
power and magnificence we read of in the books of
Kings and Chronicles? Armies like the sand of the
sea for multitude, gold and silver abundant beyond
even our conceptions,—who would have thought such
greatness would come to nothing? But Judah and
Israel could not bear prosperity; they did not live
up to their privileges, they provoked God by their
wickedness; and so the chosen land became a desert,
and Jerusalem itself was given to be burned, and,
notwithstanding all their wealth and power, no sooner
did the Lord touch them than they fell.

And where, too, are those mighty nations whose names
so often meet our eyes in searching the Old Testament
Scriptures—Nineveh and Babylon and Egypt? Time
was when they had all the world at their feet, they
ruled over countless people and tongues, and none
could stand before them; and yet one after the other
they were overthrown and melted away. God used
them as instruments to punish and chastise His faithless
people, but after they had done His work He did not
forget to reckon with them for their own sins. And,
with all their pomp, and splendour, and majesty,

no sooner did He put forth His hand and touch them
than they too consumed away and fell. The very cities
where their kings did reign are no more, their palaces
are levelled with the dust, their lofty walls which were
their pride are utterly broken down: Nineveh, that
exceeding great city, has been so completely destroyed
that the exact spot where she once stood is no longer
known ; and Babylon, the wonder of the world, the
hammer of the whole earth, has become, as Jeremiah
foretold, a desolation, a dry land, a wilderness, a land
wherein no man dwelleth, neither doth any son of man
pass thereby.

O beloved, man in his best estate is altogether vanity ;
the works of his hands are, like himself, frail and short-
lived and perishable and ready to fade away ; with
all his boasted wisdom he can make nothing lasting,
he cannot secure his handiwork against change. The
oldest dominion in Europe, is so to speak, only of
yesterday ; and who knows but there may be a worm
at the heart of the strongest empire on earth, and a
few short years and she too may be gone ?

But again, we ask you to mark that even churches
continue not the same. Alas ! there is only too much
evidence that they too may fall to pieces and decay.
Where are the churches whose faith and patience and
love and zeal shine forth so brightly in the Acts and
Epistles of the New Testament? Where is the church
of Antioch and the church of Ephesus, the church
of Philippi and the church of Berea, the church of
Thessalonica and the church of Corinth—those holy
communions which once brought such glory and praise
to God, whose obedience was spoken of throughout
the world, whose children were ready to shed their
blood for the Gospel's sake? They are gone, they are
dead, they are fallen ; they kept not their first estate,

they became high-minded and puffed up with self-
conceit ; they did not persevere in well-doing, they
did not abound in the fruits of righteousness, and so
the Lord who had grafted them in, did also cut them
off like withered and useless branches,—and if anything
can be said to remain of them, it is but the wreck and
remnant of what they once were. Doubtless, beloved,
there are promises belonging to Christ's Church
generally,—the gates of hell shall not prevail against it ;
the Lord will never leave Himself without a witness,—
but there is no assurance that the church of any
particular place or nation shall abide unchanged, except
she continue faithful. Take any church on earth, the
most renowned for wisdom, the most famous for age,
the most apostolic in her government ; and we are bold
to tell you if that church is unfaithful to the Bridegroom
Christ Jesus, if she does not hold forth the light of the
pure gospel, if she leaves her first love, if she suffers
false prophets to teach and seduce, if she becomes
lukewarm, and says " I am rich and increased with goods,"
if she rests content with having a name to live while
she is dead, and plumes herself on keeping hold of the
truth while she does not witness to it,—we are bold to
tell you, however long God's mercy may spare her, her
candlestick shall sooner or later be removed, for we
know this fearful threat has been over and over again
made good.

Yes! even we have reason to watch and to pray
and to be humble and fear : the fine gold may become dim ; no home so strong but if the servants
sleep it may be broken up ; no church so well ordered
but through the sin and faithlessness of her members
she may be overturned. The Lord Himself once gave
the pattern of His temple, but when the Jews who
kept it turned their own way and repented not, when

they thought only of a form of godliness and despised
the power, that very temple was delivered over to be
destroyed, and of all His beautiful stones not one
was left upon another.

But we desire to bring this matter nearer home to
yourselves. Have you not ever observed that men's
circumstances are always changing—they are never
long the same? Few indeed are those who have not
learned this by bitter experience. Some begin life
with every prospect of earthly prosperity, and before
they have reached their prime their riches seem to
have melted away, and are scattered like the leaves
in autumn, and they find themselves stripped of their
possession; others, who know not what it is to want,
are smitten with some sore disease, they have no
power to enjoy the fortune God has given them, and
often, when ready to cry in the evening "Would God
it were morning," and in the morning "Would God it
were evening," often when faint and weary and cast
down with pain, often would they give all their riches
for a little health and think it cheaply purchased;
others with bodily strength and store of worldly
goods are bereaved of friends by death or separation:
the advisers of their youth, the comforters of their
sorrows, the companions of their joys are one after
the other taken from them; year after year their
beloved ones, with whom they have taken sweet
counsel, and who were as their own souls, are all cut
down or removed, until at length they stand, like the
last tree of the forest, all single and alone.

Remember, I say not but that this is good: well for
us that we are constrained to drink the bitter cup of
affliction; it is the rod by which many are brought
home to Christ,—none are in such fearful peril as those
who have never known a cross. But judge ye whether

it be not true that our own life is full of changes;
that man is a poor, frail, perishable creature, and never
continueth long in one stay; there is nothing about
his earthly condition certain and fixed and immovable
and sure. We never know, when we part from those
that are dear to us, that we shall meet again: we know
not what alterations time may work before we once
more meet face to face, before hand grasps hand and
we again take sweet counsel about our common faith
and our hopes of heaven. We may part rejoicing and
meet sorrowing, part with laughter and meet with
tears, part with many around us and meet with few:
strange if we part and meet the same!

Oh, changing, changing world!—miserable indeed are
they who look upon it as an abiding habitation, who
think themselves anything but strangers, who give to
anything but heaven the name of home.

Look at men's minds. They are not always the same.
The intellect of the prudent statesman, the talent of the
eloquent orator,—these are not proof against decay.
It is a beautiful thing, is the mind of man, by nature,
when trained and educated and polished as it may be.
But often we see that mind become a mere wreck,
the eye become dim and the natural force abated; the
memory fails, the senses are deadened. We see all
the weakness of childhood without its playfulness and
light heart. This is a grief, and one more proof that
we are not always the same.

Look at men's affections. They are not always the
same: They may be warm and strong for a season,
but even they cool. Often time and absence and the
world cause strangeness and coldness between spirit
and spirit, bitter and painful to bear but it must be
borne. Business and new ties and new residence and
new relations nip off old friendships. Our changing

affections are one more proof that nothing remains always the same.

Onwards, onwards we are all moving : there is no standing still. The infant will soon be a boy, and the boy a man, and the man will find gray hairs upon him long before he expects, and the grave will be ready for him probably before he is ready for it. And men plant and build and labour and toil and plan and contrive, and often never see their schemes completed. For we never know what is before us—what to-morrow may bring forth ; it may be, as the marriage service beautifully teaches, better or worse, richer or poorer, sickness or health ; we may find in our path towards Zion sweet flowers, but far more likely thistles and thorns ; we may have some season of sunshine, but far more often darkness and clouds ; but still, whatever happens, we are rolling onward towards the end, and this we may be sure of—we shall never be long without some change, we shall never find our state is long the same, to-morrow and yesterday may be widely different.

Once more. The holiest saints of God are not always the same. We have no fear that their names will ever be blotted from the Lamb's book of life ; but we believe their hearts are often filled with shame and confusion because of their own shortcomings and unsteady walk with God. Show me one single servant of the Lord in Scripture who did not at some time err and stumble in his course, who did not by his inconsistency or sin give occasion to the Lord's enemies to blaspheme. Oh, but the best of men have given melancholy proof that so long as we are in the body we are liable to change. We venture to assert there is not one in the white-robed company of the redeemed who would tell you he had always held on his way without wavering, always fought an equally good fight; not one but could remember that at his best there were days of spiritual sloth and drowsiness, days of unholy and unchristlike tempers, days of vanity and self-conceit, days of self-indulgence and conformity to this world, days of coldness and want of love—and each the cause of pain and sorrow and self-abasement.

Away with the idea of a sinless perfection on earth! We are bound to aim at it, we are sworn to strive after it ; that man is no true Christian who sits down lazily and thinks to be saved without striking a blow, who does not wish to be holy as God is holy and perfect as God is perfect ; but still we are confident the dearest children of God do never lay claim to any personal sinlessness and perfection ; their hearts' confession is, Lord, "we are exceedingly unprofitable servants, in many things we offend daily," and their hearts' prayer, "Jesus, Master, bear with our sins and pardon our iniquities."

No, beloved, there is nothing unchangeable and the same here below. Kingdoms, churches, human conditions, holy Christians, all are alike in this respect,—they are liable to alter, they are never long the same. There is but one account of everything we see around us : it is all fleeting, perishing, passing away. The sun, which has shone on so many births and lighted so many graves, shall one day be darkened ; the solid hills, which have looked down on generation after generation and been trampled on by one short-lived owner after another, shall melt away ; the glorious heaven above us shall pass away like a scroll ; all speak with one voice,—"We shall soon be changed, we shall not always be the same."

And where, beloved, are we to look for comfort and

rest to our souls? We want a sure and lasting foundation ; we want a hope in which there is no variableness
nor shadow of turning : and mark ye, every one, this
cannot be on earth —they who search for it here will
search in vain—a sure hope for the soul is not to be
found in the land of the living : "The depth saith, It
is not in me : and the sea saith, It is not with me.
It cannot be gotten for gold, neither shall silver be
weighed for the price thereof. . . ." But "God under-
standeth the way thereof, and He knoweth the place"
where peace may be found, and in the text He sets
it openly before our eyes : "Jesus Christ, the same
yesterday, and to-day, and for ever." Now, of this
sameness we desire to speak fully and freely, and to
show you the comfortable things which it contains.

We would remind you, then, that Jesus has ever been
the same in His office, person and nature. In these
latter days He has graciously made plain to our eyes
the way of salvation, by coming upon earth to teach,
to suffer and to die ; He has proved Himself the Son
of God with power by rising again from the dead. But
still we would not have you forget He was always the
same—yesterday as well as to-day.

Before the mountains were brought forth, or the earth
and world were formed, from everlasting Jesus Christ
was, like the Father, very God. From the beginning
He was foreordained to be the Saviour of sinners ; He
was always the Lamb slain from the foundation of the
world, without whose blood there could be no remission.
The same Jesus, to whom alone we may look for salvation, that same Jesus was the only hope of Abel and
Enoch and Noah and Abraham and all the patriarchs ;
what we are privileged to see distinctly they doubtless
saw indistinctly, but the Saviour both we and they rest
upon is one. It was Christ Jesus who was foretold in

all the prophets, and foreshadowed and represented in all the law : the daily sacrifice of the lamb, the cities of refuge, the brazen serpent, all these were so many emblems to Israel of that Redeemer who was yet to come, and without whom no man could be saved. There never was but one road to heaven : Jesus Christ was the way, the truth and the life yesterday as well as to-day.

But we must pass on to another point of even greater interest than this. We remind you that the character of Jesus Christ is always the same—in this too He is unchangeable. What He was in the New Testament days He continues now, and will be even to the end. Consider now, I pray you, what a mine of comfort and consolation lies in that single thought.

Always the same in love towards men's souls. It was love towards a fallen world which made Him lay aside for a season His glorious majesty and honour, and take upon Him the form of a servant upon earth ; it was love that constrained Him to endure the cross and despise the shame, and lay down His life for us the ungrateful and the ungodly ; it was love that moved Him to shed tears over bloody-minded, unbelieving Jerusalem, because she would not know the things belonging to her peace ; and it is just the same love which He feels towards sinners now—He never changes.

Again : Jesus is always the same in His power to save. It was He that cast forth seven devils from Mary Magdalen and raised her up to newness of life. It was He that poured comfort on that weeping penitent sinner in the Pharisee's house, and pronounced those blessed words, " Thy sins are forgiven thee, go in peace." It was He that entered the house of Zacchæus, chief of the publicans, and declared that salvation was

come unto him, that he was a true son of Abraham.
It was He that gave that blessed assurance to the
dying thief who prayed to be remembered, "This day
thou shalt be with me in Paradise." It was He that
met the persecuting Saul on his way to Damascus, and
cast him down to the ground with all his pride, and
put in him a new heart, and sent him forth to preach
the faith he had once destroyed. And, O brethren
beloved, who need despair? Christ Jesus is still just
the same—able to save to the uttermost all those that
come to God by him.

But again: Jesus Christ is always the same in His
willingness to receive the penitent. We never read of
any who sought Him in sincerity and sought Him in
vain, who came poor in spirit and were sent away empty.
Oh, no! far otherwise; there is everything to encourage,
to invite, to lead us on. Who was it that used those
comforting words, "Come unto Me all ye that labour and
are heavy laden, and I will give you rest;" "Him that
cometh unto me I will in no wise cast out;" "The Son
of man came to seek and to save that which was lost;"
"Every one who seeth the Son and believeth on Him
may have everlasting life?" Who was it but Jesus
Christ—ever the same? He will not go back from one
jot or tittle of His words, and what He hath spoken
He will still make good. "Heaven and earth," He
says, "shall pass away, but my word shall not pass
away."

Once more "Jesus Christ is always the same in
His power to preserve. He will not begin the work
of grace and leave it uncompleted; for it is His own
word, "My sheep hear my voice, and I know them,
and they follow me, and I give unto them eternal life,
and no man shall ever pluck them out of my hand."
It was He that raised the apostles after they had shame-

fully forsaken Him and fled; it was He that turned the heart of even Peter back again, though he had denied Him before His face. And what He did then, beloved, He will do now also, for every believer; it shall never be said that any trusted in Jesus and were confounded, for the Author and Finisher of our faith never changes.

Always the same! It is this which gives such value to the Gospels in which our Lord's history is told. We are not reading there the life and sayings of one fickle and changeable like ourselves, but the life and sayings of a Redeemer who is now what He was then. We tell you confidently that all that love and gentleness and compassion and long-suffering and tenderheartedness which you may there see in your Lord and Saviour's character are placed before you that you may understand the character of Him from whom alone we receive forgiveness and to whom alone your prayer must be made, and we say this because we know He is the same yesterday, to-day, and for ever.

Always the same! It is this which makes the gospel so excellent and precious. We do not bid you depend on anything less than the tried corner-stone, the fountain whose water shall never fail—the city of refuge whose walls shall never be broken down—the sure Rock of Ages. Churches may decay and perish; riches may make themselves wings and fly away; but he that builds his happiness on Christ crucified and union with Him by faith, that man is standing on a foundation which shall never be moved, and will know something of true peace.

There are men and women in the world who rest all upon their personal amendment, or upon an unwearied round of services and regular attendance upon holy ordinances; and they fancy their spiritual disease is healed and all is peace. But we believe it is the peace of those who never found out their enemy, the cure of those who have never really felt their hearts' ailments.

Oh no! we believe when a man is once aroused to see the extent of his soul's danger, when he has felt the burden of his sins indeed grievous and intolerable, when he has found out his debt and his own inability to pay,—we are confident that man will never get peace till he has sought the Lord Jesus Christ, till he has taken for a Friend and Advocate Him that is the same yesterday, and to-day, and for ever. That man will not be put off with the ornaments and trappings of the Church which is the bride, he will never rest content till he has laid hold of the Lord Jesus, the Bridegroom, and has become one with Christ and Christ with him.

One word in conclusion. Are there not some among you who in one sense have always been the same—thoughtless, careless about your eternal interests, always lovers of pleasure more than lovers of God, always more anxious about the life that now is than the life which is to come, always disposed to give your best things to the world and the leavings of your time and talent to God? We warn you plainly there must be a change, a deep foundation-searching change, a change of heart. We call on you to remember the words of Him who never goes back from what He says "Except ye repent, ye shall all likewise perish." "Except ye be converted, and become as little children, ye shall in no wise enter into the kingdom of heaven."

Oh! but it does not need a prophet's eye to see changes and trials before you all! The breaking up of family circles, the separation from those you love best, the loss of health, friends, earthly possessions :

who knows but they may be very near? and alas for
those among you who have got no sure resting-place
for your weary souls, who are building your happiness
on the frail and perishable things of earth, for when
ye look for solid consolations ye shall find none! O
man, the time is flying, death and judgment are at
hand; and what wilt thou do if thou hast to seek
thy spiritual comforts at the eleventh hour? Of all
thy riches thou canst carry nought away: naked thou
didst come into the world, and naked thou must
return; of all thy dear friends, who now weep when
thou dost weep and rejoice when thou dost rejoice,
not one can go with thee beyond the tomb; they may
sit beside thee in thy last hours, they may watch thy
spirit's flight, they may follow thy body to its long
home with measured pace and slow, but there earthly
friendship must stop,—it can go no farther than the
brink of thy narrow bed,—they will turn away each to
his own duties, and thou shalt be left alone.

O man, be wise in time; learn to lay up treasures
in heaven, think first of a house not made with hands,
look to that precious Friend who never faileth: away
with thy cold and sleeping shadow of religion; cease
to be a Christian in name and form only, become a
man of God in deed and in truth; come to thy eternal
Father as a little child, with confession and prayer;
take all thy sins to the Saviour who died upon the
cross; let nothing satisfy thee till thou art a living
member of Jesus Christ, one with Christ and Christ
with thee; in Him I can warrant thee a hope that
never changes, a title to happiness that shall never
be overthrown.

But are there any among you who have tasted of this
blessed change—who have put off the old man which is
corrupt, and put on the new man which after God is

created in righteousness and true holiness—who mourn
over your own daily shortcomings, and sigh after more
holiness, more self-denial, more mortification of the flesh
with all its lusts? We bid you take comfort, and
remember that Christ is still the same : He called you
and gave you the witness of the Spirit, and He will
not forsake you. You may waver and tremble : go
forward in faith, and He will still support you. There
is but one more change before you : the changing of this
vile body that it may be made a spiritual body, the
putting off the corruptible to put on the incorruptible,
the giving up what is mortal to receive what is immortal, the laying aside the earthly tabernacle, the
entering on a heavenly one. Watch, then, and pray, and
He that gave you the first change shall give you the
second also ; and then ye shall go no more out : no
more weariness, no more weakness, no more fainting ;
ye shall see your Saviour as He is and love Him as
ye ought, and like Him at last be unchanged and the
same for evermore.

XV

THE SECOND ADVENT (*THE TEN VIRGINS*)

"Then shall the kingdom of heaven be likened unto ten virgins, which took their lamps, and went forth to meet the bridegroom. And five of them were wise, and five were foolish. They that were foolish took their lamps, and took no oil with them : but the wise took oil in their vessels with their lamps. While the bridegroom tarried, they all slumbered and slept. And at midnight there was a cry made, Behold, the bridegroom cometh ; go ye out to meet him. Then all those virgins arose, and trimmed their lamps. And the foolish said unto the wise, Give us of your oil ; for our lamps are gone out. But the wise answered, saying, Not so ; lest there be not enough for us and you : but go ye rather to them that sell, and buy for yourselves. And while they went to buy, the bridegroom came ; and they that were ready went in with him to the marriage : and the door was shut. Afterward came also the other virgins, saying, Lord, Lord, open to us. But he answered and said, Verily I say unto you, I know you not. Watch therefore, for ye know neither the day nor the hour wherein the Son of man cometh."— MATT. xxv. 1-13.

THIS is one of the most solemn parables that the Lord Jesus ever spoke : partly because of the time at which it was spoken ; partly because of the matter which it contains.

As to the *time,* it was but a few days before our Lord's death. It was spoken within view of Gethsemane and Calvary, the cross and the grave.

As to the *matter,* it stands as a beacon to the Church in all ages. It is a witness against carelessness and slothfulness, against apathy and indifference, and a witness of no uncertain sound. It cries to sinners, "Awake," and it cries to saints " Watch."

Now, I must necessarily pass over many points that
might be spoken of in handling this parable. I have
no time to follow out many trains of thought which it
opens up. I stand here not to make a book, but to
preach a single sermon ; and, this being the case, I
shall keep to those points which it most concerns you
and me to know.

The marriage customs of the country where the
parable was spoken *call for a word of explanation.*
Marriages generally took place there in the evening.
The bridegroom and his friends came in procession
to the bride's house after nightfall. The young women
who were the bride's friends were assembled at the
bride's house to wait for them. As soon as the lamps
or torches of the bridegroom's party were seen in the
distance, these young women lighted their lamps and
went forth to meet him ; then, having formed one united
party, they all returned together to the bride's house.
As soon as they entered it, the door was shut, and
the marriage ceremony took place ; and after that
no one was admitted. All these were familiar things
to those who heard the Lord Jesus, and it is right
and proper that you should understand them.

The figures used in the parable also call for a word of
explanation. I give you my own view of their meaning.
I may be wrong : but you have a right to know what
I think, and I will tell you shortly, but decidedly—I
have no time to do more.

I believe the TIME spoken of in this parable means
the time when Christ shall return in person to the
world. The word "then" compared with the end of
the twenty-fourth chapter appears to me to settle the
question.

I believe the virgins carrying lamps represent professing Christians, the visible Church of Christ.

I believe the bridegroom represents the Lord Jesus Christ Himself.

I take the wise virgins to be the true believers, the converted part of the visible Church. I take the foolish to be the mere nominal Christians—the unconverted.

I take the oil, which some had and others had not, to be the grace of the Spirit, the unction of the Holy One.

I consider the midnight cry to mean the second coming or advent of Christ into the world.

I consider the going in to the marriage of the wise to mean the reward of the believers. I consider the shutting out of the foolish to mean the final exclusion from heaven of the unbelieving.

And now, without saying anything more of preface, let me go on to point out the great practical lessons which this parable is meant to teach.

I. Learn first that the visible Church of Christ will always be a mixed body till Christ comes again.

II. Learn secondly that this visible church is always in danger of neglecting the doctrine of Christ's second advent.

III. Learn thirdly that whenever Christ does come again, it will be a very sudden event.

IV. Learn fourthly that Christ's second advent will make an immense change to all members of Christ's Church, both good and bad.

Let me try to set each of these truths before you.

I. Learn firstly that the Church of Christ will always be a mixed body till Christ comes again.

I can gather no other meaning from the beginning of the parable. I see wise and foolish virgins mingled in one company—virgins with oil and virgins with no oil all side by side. And I see this state of things going on till the very moment the bridegroom appears. I see all this, and I cannot avoid the conclusion that the visible Church will always be a mixed body till Jesus comes again. Its members will never be all unbelievers; Christ will always have His witnesses. Its members will never be all believers; there will always be imperfection, hypocrisy, and false profession.

I frankly say that I can find no standing ground for the common notion that the Church will gradually advance towards perfection, and that it will become better and better, holier and holier up to the very end. I see no warrant of Scripture for believing that sin will gradually dwindle away in the earth, consume, melt and disappear by inches, like the last snowdrift in spring; nor yet for believing that holiness will gradually increase like the banyan tree, blossom, bloom, and fill the face of the world with fruit.

I have no doubt whatever that true gospel religion admits of ebbs and flows in its progress, of spring tides and of neaps; and that, like the moon, Christ's bride is sometimes full and walking in brightness, and like the same moon is sometimes under an eclipse and scarcely seen at all. That there will always be a vast amount of evil in the world until the second advent, I am fully persuaded. Evil men and seducers shall wax worse and worse, deceiving and being deceived. The tares and the wheat shall grow together till the harvest. I fully expect that the earth will one day be filled with the knowledge of the glory of the Lord, but I believe that day will be in an entirely new dispensation—will not be till after the Lord's return. Till the Bridegroom comes there will always be wise and foolish in the Church.

The wise are those who have that wisdom which the Holy Ghost alone can give. They know their

sins, they know Christ, they know how to walk and
please God, and they act upon their knowledge. They
look on life as a season of preparation for eternity,
not as an end but as a way, not as a harbour but a
voyage, not as a home but a journey, not as full age
but a school. Happy are those who know this!

The foolish are those who are without spiritual knowledge. They neither know God, nor Christ, nor their
own hearts, nor sin, nor the world, nor heaven, nor hell,
as they ought. There is no folly like soul-folly. To
expect wages after no work, or prosperity after no
pains, or learning after no diligent reading—all this is
folly. But to expect heaven without faith in Christ,
or the kingdom of God without being born again, or
the crown without the cross—all this is greater folly
and yet more common.

Till the Bridegroom comes there will always be some
who have grace and some who have not grace in the
visible Church. Some will have nothing but the name
of Christian, others will have the reality; some will
have the profession of religion, others will have the
possession also. Some will be content to belong to
the church, others will never be content unless they
also belong to Christ. Some will be satisfied if they
have only the baptism of water, others will never be
satisfied unless they also feel within the baptism of the
Spirit. Some will stop short in the form of Christianity,
others will never rest unless they have also the substance.

Brethren, the visible Church of Christ is made up
of these two classes. There always have been such;
there always will be such until the end. Borderers
and undecided ones, whom man's eyes cannot make
out, there must needs be. But gracious and graceless,
wise and foolish, make up the whole Church of Christ.
You are all written down in this parable yourselves.

You are all either wise virgins or foolish virgins ; you have all oil of grace, or you have none ; you are all either members of Christ, or not ; you are all either travelling towards heaven or towards hell.

See now how important it is that we ministers should divide our congregations in preaching to them. See how we ought to address you as an assembly in which some are converted and some unconverted, some are regenerate and some unregenerate, and some have grace and some have no grace at all. I know well that some do not like it ; I know that some fancy that we should address you all as good Christian people. I for one will never do so, and I know not how any one can do it with the Bible in his hands.

There is a notion abroad that all have grace who have been baptised, and that all congregations of baptised people should be addressed as regenerate. I protest against such a notion as a dangerous contradiction of Scripture ; I protest against it as calculated to confound the minds of people as to what real grace is. I protest against the idea of grace which nobody can see, of grace which a man may have in his heart and yet no one be aware of its existence. I know of no such grace in Scripture. Grace or no grace, oil or no oil, living or dead, having the Spirit or not having the Spirit,—these are the only distinctions that I can find. These are the old paths, and in them I advise you to walk. Beware of false prophets ! From ministers who do not draw a broad line between having the lamp of profession and having the oil of grace, may the good Lord ever deliver you !

II. Learn, secondly, that the Church of Christ is always in danger of neglecting the doctrine of Christ's second personal advent.

I draw that truth from the solemn words " While

the bridegroom tarried, they all slumbered and slept."
I am quite aware that men explain that verse in
different ways. I stand here to call no man master.
I am set for the proclamation of that which I believe
in my conscience to be true, and I cannot be bound
by the opinion of others.

I do not believe that the words "they all slumbered
and slept" mean the death of all ; though many think
so. To my mind such an interpretation involves a
simple untruth. All the professing Church will not be
dead when Christ comes. St. Paul says, "We which
are alive remain (not 'all sleep') unto the coming of
the Lord."

I do not believe that the words mean that all the
professing Church got into a slumbering and sleeping
state of soul, though many think so. Such a view
appears to me to wipe away the distinction between
believers and unbelievers far too much. Sleep is one
of the emblems which the Spirit has chosen to signify
unconversion. "Awake, thou that sleepest," etc.

I believe that the words are to be explained with a
special regard to the great event on which the whole
parable chiefly runs—the second advent of Christ ; and
I believe that our Lord's meaning in this verse of the
parable was simply this : that during the interval
between His first and second advent the whole Church,
both believers and unbelievers, would get into a dull
and dim-sighted state of soul about the blessed doctrine
of His own personal return.

And I say deliberately that, so far as my own judgment goes, there never was a saying of our Lord's more
thoroughly verified by the event. I say that, of all
doctrines of the gospel, the one in which we are most
unlike the first Christians in our sense of its true value
is the doctrine of Christ's second advent. In our view

of man's corruption, of justification by faith, of our need
of the sanctifying Spirit, upon these matters I believe
we should find that English Christians were much of
one mind with believers at Corinth, Ephesus, Philippi,
or Rome in olden times ; but in our view of the
second advent I believe we should find there was a
mighty difference if we could but compare our experience. We should find that we fell wofully short of
them in our estimate of its importance and realisation
of its nature. We should discover, in one word, that
we slumber and sleep about it.

I must speak my mind on this subject, now that I
am upon it. I do so at the risk of giving offence and
rubbing against prejudices. But speak I must.

I submit, then, that the Church of Christ has gone
too long not seeing that there are two personal advents
of Christ spoken of in the Old Testament—an advent
in humiliation and an advent in glory too, an advent
to suffer and an advent to reign. We have got into
a vicious way of taking all the promises spiritually
and all the curses and denunciations literally. The
curses on Jews and Babylon and Edom and Egypt
we have been content to take literally ; the blessings
on Zion, Jerusalem, Jacob, Israel, and so forth, we have
taken spiritually and comfortably applied to the Church
of Christ. No man can read sermons or commentaries
and not be aware of this. I believe it has been a wrong
system of interpreting Scripture. I believe that prophetical denunciations and prophetical promises in their
primary sense are always to be taken literally. That
primary sense we have sadly lost sight of, and by so
doing I think we have got into a slumbering and sleeping
state about the second advent of Christ.

But I say further, that the Church of Christ has
gone on too long putting a strange sense on the passage

which speaks of the coming of the Son of man in the
New Testament. Some tell us that this expression
always means death. No man can read the thousands
of epitaphs on tombstones in which the Son of man's
coming is thrust in, and not observe how widespread
this view is. Some tell us it means the conversion of
the world. Some tell us it means the destruction of
Jerusalem. That also is a very common way of interpreting the expression with many. They find Jerusalem
everywhere in the New Testament prophecies, and, like
Aaron's rod, they make it swallow up everything else.
Now, I have no desire to underrate the importance of
death, the conversion of the world, or the destruction
of Jerusalem ; but I must express my own firm belief
that the coming of the Son of man is an entirely
distinct subject from any of the three I have mentioned.
And the acceptance they have met with I hold to be
one more proof that in the matter of Christ's second
advent the Church has slumbered and slept.

The plain truth of Scripture, I believe, is as follows.
When the number of the elect is accomplished, Christ
shall come again to this world, with power and great
glory. As He came the first time in person, so He
shall come the second time in person ; as He went
away visibly, so He shall return visibly. Then shall
be fulfilled those words of Acts i. : " This same Jesus,
which is taken up from you into heaven, shall so come
in like manner as ye have seen Him go into heaven " ;
and the words of Zechariah xiv. : " The Lord my God
shall come, and all the saints with Thee " ; and the words
of Enoch in Jude : " Behold, the Lord cometh with
ten thousand of His saints." And the grand shortcoming of the Church in these days has been and is
this : that we ministers do not preach enough about
this second advent, and private believers do not think

enough about it. There are a few, but what are they?
Many do not. We none of us live on it, feed on it,
act on it, work from it, take comfort in it, as God
intended us to do. In short, the Bridegroom tarries,
and we all slumber and sleep.

It proves nothing against the true doctrine that
it has sometimes been fearfully abused. I should
like to know what doctrine has not. Salvation by
grace has been made a pretext for licentiousness;
election an excuse for all manner of unclean living;
and justification by faith a warrant for antinomianism.
But if men will draw wrong conclusions we are not
obliged to throw up good principles. We do not give
up the gospel because of the extravagancies of Saltmarsh
and William Huntington, of Jumpers and Shakers;
and we need not give up the second advent because
of the Fifth Monarchy men of the Commonwealth or
Irvingites of our own time.

Nor yet does it prove anything against the doctrine
that it is attended with many difficulties. I do not
think there are half so many difficulties as those
connected with the first coming, and yet those difficulties were all overcome. I am satisfied there are far
more difficulties upon any other system of interpretation,
whatever it may be. And after all, what have we to
do with the "how" and "in what manner" prophecies
are to be fulfilled? Our only question is, "Has
God said a thing?" If He has, no doubt it will be
done.

For myself, I can only give my individual testimony;
but the little I know experimentally of the doctrine
makes me regard it as most practical and precious,
and makes me long to see it more generally received.

I find it a powerful spring to holy living; a motive
for patience, for moderation, for spiritual-mindedness;

a test for employment of time—"would I like my Lord to find me so doing?"

I find it the strongest argument for missionary work. The time is short. The Lord is at hand. The gathering out from all nations of a witnessing people will soon be accomplished, and then the King shall come.

I find it the best answer to infidels. I tell them it proves nothing that all the world is not holy after eighteen hundred years; that it was never said it would be in the present order of things; that the King will come one day and then make all bow before Him.

I find it the best argument with the Jew. If I do not take all the prophecy of Isaiah literally, I know not how I can persuade him that the fifty-third chapter is fulfilled. But if I do, I have a resting-place for my lever which he cannot shake.

Who is there that cannot yet receive the doctrine of Christ's second personal advent? I invite you to consider the subject calmly. Dismiss from your mind traditional interpretation; separate the doctrine from the mistakes and blunders of many who have held it; do not reject the foundations because of the wood, hay and stubble; do not condemn it because of injudicious friends. Only examine the texts which speak of it in the same calm way that you weigh texts in the Romish and Socinian controversy, and I am hopeful as to the result on your mind.

Who is there here that receives the doctrine? Try to realise it more. Alas! how little do we feel it at the very best! Be gentle in argument with those that differ. Remember that a man may be mistaken on this subject and yet be a bright child of God. It is not the slumbering on this subject that ruins souls, but the want of grace. Above all avoid dogmatism and

positiveness, and specially about symbolical prophecy.
It is a sad truth, but a truth never to be forgotten, that
none have injured the doctrine of the second advent
so much as over-zealous friends

III. Learn, thirdly, that whenever Christ does come
again it will be a very sudden event. I draw that from
the verse in the parable : "At midnight there was a
cry made, Behold the Bridegroom cometh, go ye forth
to meet Him."

I do not know when Christ will come. I am no
prophet, though I love the subject of prophecy. I
dislike date-fixing, and I think it has done great harm.
I only assert positively that Christ will come again
one day in person to set up His kingdom, and that
whether the day be near, or whether it be far off, it
will take the Church and world exceedingly by surprise.

It will come on men suddenly. It will break on
the world all at once. It will not have been talked
over, prepared for and looked forward to by everybody.
It will awaken men's minds like a cry of fire at midnight.
It will startle men's hearts like a trumpet blown by
their bedsides in their first sleep. Like Pharaoh and
his host, men will know nothing till the very waters
are upon them. Before they can recover their breath
and know where they are, they shall find that the
Lord is come.

I suspect there is a vague notion floating in men's
minds that the present order of things will not end
quite so suddenly. I suspect men cling to the idea
that there will be a kind of Saturday night in the world
—a time when all will know the Lord's day is near, a
time when all will be able to cleanse their consciences,
look up their best garment, shake off their earthly
business, and prepare to meet the Lord. If any one
here has got such a notion I charge him to give it up

for ever. If anything is clear in unfulfilled prophecy,
this one fact seems clear, that the Lord's coming will
be sudden, and take men by surprise ; and any view
of prophecy which destroys the possibility of its being
a sudden event, appears to carry about with it a fatal
defect.

Everything which is written in Scripture on this point
confirms the truth that Christ's second coming will be
sudden. " As a snare shall it come on the face of all
them that dwell on the earth," says one place : " As
a thief in the night," says another ; " As the lightning,"
says a third ; " In an hour when no man thinketh," says
a fourth ; " At a time when they shall be saying Peace
and safety," says a fifth.

Our Lord Jesus Christ Himself uses two most striking
comparisons when dwelling on this point. He says in
one, that as it was in the days of Lot, so shall it be
in the days when the Son of man is revealed. Do
you remember how it was? In the days when Lot
went out of Sodom the men of Sodom were eating and
drinking, planting and building, marrying and giving
in marriage. The sun rose as usual. They thought
of nothing but worldly things ; they saw no sign of
danger. But all at once the fire of God fell upon them
and destroyed them.

He says in another place, " As it was in the days of
Noe, so shall it be also in the days of the Son of man."
Do you remember how it was in the days of Noah ?
Stay a little, and let me remind you.

When the flood came on the earth there was no
appearance beforehand of anything so awful being near.
The sun rose and set as usual ; the day and night
followed each other in regular succession. The grass
and trees and crops were growing ; the business of the
world was going on ; and though Noah preached con-

tinually and warned men of coming danger, no one
believed him.

But at last one day the rain began and did not cease ;
the waters ran and did not stop. The flood came and
the flood swelled ; the flood went on and covered one
thing after another, and all were drowned who were
not in the ark. Everything in which was the breath
of life perished.

Now, as the flood took the world by surprise, just
so will the coming of the Son of man. It will come
on men like a thunderclap. In the midst of the world's
business, when everything is going on just as usual,
in such an hour as this the Lord Jesus Christ will
return.

See here what solemn thoughts the Lord Jesus Christ's
return should raise in every mind. Think for a moment
how little prepared the world is for such an event.
Look at the towns and cities of the earth, and think
of them. Mark how absorbed are men in the business
of their callings. Banks, shops, law, medicine, commerce,
railways, banquets, balls, theatres,—all and each are
drinking up hearts and souls, and thrusting out the
things of God. Think what a fearful shock would be
the stoppage of all these things,—the sudden stoppage
which will be in the day of Christ's appearing. Yet one
day it shall be.

Look at the rural parishes of such a land as ours,
and think of them. See how the minds of the majority
are buried in farms and allotments, in cattle and corn,
in rent and wages, in digging and sowing, in buying
and selling ; and then fancy the awful effect of a sudden
cessation of all these things,—the final cessation which
must be when Christ comes again to finish all things.
Yet remember one day it shall be. Picture these things
to your mind's eye ; picture your own home, your own

family, your own fireside,—picture, above all, your own
feelings, your own state of mind.   And then remember
that this is the end to which the world is hastening ;
this is the way in which the world's affairs will be wound
up.   This is an event which might possibly happen in
your own time ; and surely you cannot avoid the conclusion that this second coming of Christ is no mere
curious speculation, but is of vast moment to your soul.

Ah ! some will say, I have no doubt : " This is all
mere cant and nonsense.   This is all extravagant
fanaticism.   Where is the likelihood, where is the
probability of all this ? "

Do not say so.   Men said the same in the day of
Noah and Lot ; but they found to their cost that Noah
and Lot were right.   Do not say so.   The apostle
Peter foretold that men would talk so in the latter
days.   Do not fulfil his prophecy by your unbelief.

Where is the cant and fanaticism of that which I
have been saying?   I calmly say the present state of
things will come to an end one day.   Will any one
deny that?   Will any one say we are to go on as we
do now for ever?   I calmly say that Christ's coming
will be the ending of the present state of things.   I
have said so because the Bible says it.   I have calmly
said that Christ's coming will be a sudden event,
whenever it may be, and might possibly be in our own
time.   I have said so because thus and thus I find it
written.   If you do not like it, I am sorry for it.   One
thing only you must remember : you are finding fault
with the Bible, not with me.

IV. Learn, in the last place, that Christ's coming
will make an immense change to all members of
Christ's Church, both good and bad.

I draw that from the concluding portion of the
parable, from the discovery of the foolish virgins that

their lamps were gone out, from their anxious address
to the wise, "Give us of your oil," from their vain
knocking at the door when shut, crying, "Lord, Lord,
open to us," from the happy admission of the wise who
were ready to the marriage supper, in company with
the bridegroom. All these points are food for thought.
But I have no time to dwell on them particularly. I
can only take one single broad view of all. To all
who have been baptised in the name of Christ,—converted or unconverted, believer or unbeliever, holy or
unholy, godly or ungodly, wise or foolish, gracious
or graceless,--to all, the second coming of Christ shall
be an immense change.

It shall be an *immense change to the ungodly*, to
the mere nominal Christian.

They will see the value of real heart-religion if they
never saw it before ;—"Give us of your oil," they will
cry to the godly, "for our lamps are gone out."

Who does not know that spiritual religion never
brings a man the world's praise? It never has done,
and it never does. It entails the world's disapprobation,
the world's persecution, the world's ridicule, the world's
sneers. The world will let a man go to hell quietly,
and never try to stop him. The world will never let a
man go to heaven quietly—they will do all they can
to turn him back. Who has not heard of nicknames in
plenty bestowed on all who faithfully follow Christ ?—
Pietist, Methodist, saint, fanatic, enthusiast, righteous
overmuch, and many more? Who does not know
the petty family persecution which often goes on in
private society in our own day. Let a young person
go to every ball and theatre and racecourse, and utterly
neglect his soul, and no one interferes ; no one says
"Spare thyself," no one says "Be moderate—remember
your soul." But let him begin to read his Bible and

be diligent in prayers, let him decline worldly amuse-
ment and be particular in his employment of time, let
him seek an evangelical ministry and live as if he had
an immortal soul,—let him do this, and the probability
is all his relations and friends will be up in arms.
"You are going too far," "You need not be so very
good," "You are taking up extreme lines,"—this is the
least that he will hear. Alas that it should be so, but
so it is. These are ancient things. As it was in the
days of Cain and Abel, as it was in the days of Isaac
and Ishmael, even so it is now. They that are born
after the flesh will persecute those that are born after
the Spirit. The cross of Christ will always bring
reproach with it. If a man will become a decided
evangelical Christian he must make up his mind
to lose the world's favours; he must be content to
be thought by many a perfect fool.

But, brethren, all this will be at an end when Christ
returns. The light of that day will show everything
in its true colours; the scales will fall from the poor
worldling's eyes. The value of the soul will flash on
his astonished mind; the utter uselessness of a mere
nominal Christianity will burst upon him like a thunder-
storm. The blessedness of regeneration and faith in
Christ and a holy walk will shine before him like
"Mene, Mene, Tekel, Peres" on the wall. The
veil will fall from his face; he will discover that the
godly have been the wise, and that he has played
the fool exceedingly; and just as Saul wanted Samuel
when it was too late, and Belshazzar sent for Daniel
when the kingdom was departing from him, so will
the ungodly turn to the very men they once mocked
and despised, and cry, "Give us of your oil, for our
lamps have gone out."

But again: the ungodly will seek salvation earnestly

when Christ returns, but not find it. They will find
that opportunities once let slip shall never be regained.
They will seek the oil of grace, they will knock at the
door for admission, they will cry, " Lord, Lord, open to
us," but all in vain.

Who does not know that thousands are urged to
pray now, who never attempt it ? They mean to do so
one day, perhaps ; they fancy it will never be too late
to seek the Lord.

But there is a time coming when prayer shall be
heard no longer. There is a time when the door
by which Saul of Tarsus and Magdalen entered in
shall be shut for ever. There is a time when men
shall know the folly of sin, but, like Judas, too late for
repentance ; when they shall desire to enter into the
promised land, but, like Israel at Kadesh, not be able ;
when they shall see the value of God's favour and
covenant blessing, but like Esau, when they can no
longer procure it ; when they shall believe every jot
and tittle of God's revealed word, but, like the miserable
devils, only to tremble. Yes ! beloved brethren, many
come to this, and many will come to this in the
day of Christ's reappearing. They will ask and not
receive, they will seek and not find, they will knock
and the door shall not be opened to them. Alas,
indeed, that it should be so ! Woe to the man who
puts off seeking his manna till the Lord's day of return !
Like Israel of old, he will find none. Woe to the man
who goes to buy oil when he ought to be burning it !
Like the foolish virgins, he will find himself shut out
from the marriage supper of the Lamb.

But as Christ's coming will be a mighty change to
the ungodly, so also will it be a *mighty change to the
godly*.

They shall be placed in a position of perfect safety.

"The door shall be shut." They shall no longer be
vexed by temptations, persecuted by the world, warred
against by the devil. Their conflicts shall all be over.
Their strife with the flesh shall for ever cease. They
shall be where there is no Satan, no world, and no sin.
Ah! brethren, the second Eden shall be better far than
the first. In the first Eden the door was not shut ;
but in the second the Lord shall shut us in.

Furthermore the godly shall be placed in a position
of perfect blessedness. They shall go in with the
Bridegroom to the marriage ; they shall be with Christ.
Faith shall be swallowed up in sight, hope shall become
certainty, knowledge shall at length be perfect, prayer
shall be turned into praise, desires shall receive their
full accomplishment, fears and doubtings shall not rise
to mar their comforts, the thought of parting shall not
spoil the pleasure of meeting ; the company of saints
shall be enjoyed without hurry and distraction, and
weariness shall be all unknown. Thus shall they
understand the meaning of the text, " In Thy presence
is fulness of joy, and at Thy right hand are pleasures
for evermore." Then shall they experience the truth
of that beautiful hymn which says :

> "Let me be with Thee where Thou art,
>   My Saviour, My eternal rest;
> Then only shall this longing heart
>   Be fully and for ever blest.
>
> "Let me be with Thee where Thou art,
>   Thy unveiled glory to behold;
> Then only will this wand'ring heart
>   Cease to be false to Thee and cold.
>
> "Let me be with Thee where Thou art,
>   Where none can die, where none remove,
> Then neither death nor life shall part
>   Me from Thy presence and Thy love."

Is there a single man or woman here that can laugh at true vital religion? Is there any one who persecutes and ridicules true godliness, and talks of people being over-particular and righteous overmuch? Beware what you are doing! Again I say beware. You may live to think differently; you may live to alter your opinion,—but perhaps too late. Ah! there is a day coming when there will be no infidels,—no, not one! "Before the name of Jesus every knee will bow, and every tongue confess that He is Lord." Remember that day, and beware.

Is there any dear child of God here who is mocked and despised for the gospel's sake, and feels as if he stood alone? Take comfort; be patient: wait a little— your turn shall come. When the spies returned from searching Canaan, men talked of stoning Caleb and Joshua. A few days passed away, and all the assembly confessed that they alone had been right. Strive to be like them. Follow the Lord fully, and sooner or later all men shall confess that you did well. Men seem to be afraid of going too far, men seem to be afraid of being too holy. Millions will lament in the day of Christ's return that they had not religion enough; not one will be heard to say that he had too much.

And now, brethren, it only remains for me to close this sermon by *three words of application*, which seem to me to arise naturally out of the parable of which I have been speaking. I heartily pray God to bless them to your souls, and to make them words in season at the beginning of a new year.

1. My first word of application shall be a *question*. I take the parable of the ten virgins in my hands, and I address that question to everybody here present. I ask, "Are you ready?" Remember the words of the Lord Jesus: "they that were ready went in with the

bridegroom to the marriage,"—they that were ready and
none else. Now here, in the sight of God, I ask you
every one, " Is this your case ? " " Are you ready ? "

I do not ask whether you are a Churchman and make
a profession of religion ; I do not ask whether you sit
under an evangelical ministry, and like evangelical people,
and can talk of evangelical things. All this is the surface
of Christianity, and may be easily attained. I want
to search your heart more deeply by far. I want to
know whether grace is in your heart, and the Holy
Ghost. I want to know whether you are ready to meet
the Bridegroom, ready for Christ's return. I want to
know, if the Lord should come this week, whether you
could lift up your head with joy, and say, " This is our
God ; we have waited for Him ; let us be glad and
rejoice in His salvation."

Ah! some will be saying, " This is far too high a
standard. This is requiring far too much. This is
extravagance. This is a hard saying : who can bear
it ? " I cannot help it. I believe it is the standard
of the Bible ; I believe it is the standard St. Peter
sets before us when he tells us to be " looking for and
hasting unto the coming of the day of God " ; I
believe it is the mark at which every believer should
be continually aiming, to be found ready to meet
Christ.

I want no man to become a hermit and cease to do
his duty in the world ; I call on no one to leave his
lawful calling or neglect his earthly affairs. But I do
call on every one to live like one who expects Christ
to return, to live like a pilgrim and stranger, to live ever
looking unto Jesus and leaning on Jesus, to live like
a good servant with his loins girded and his lamp
burning, to live like one whose treasure is in heaven
and best things yet to come, with his heart packed up

and ready to be gone. Now, is this too much to ask ?
I say decidedly that it is not.

Now, are you ready in this way ? If not, I would
like to know what good your religion does you. A
religion that does not make a man ready for anything
is a religion that may well be looked on with suspicion.
If your religion does not make you ready, its source is
not derived from the Bible.

2. My second word of application shall be an
invitation. I address it to every one who feels in his
conscience that he has no grace in his heart,—to every
one who feels that the character of the foolish virgin
is his own. To all such I give an invitation this day :
I invite you to " *awake.*"

You know, many of you, that your hearts are not
right in the sight of God. In the broadest, fullest sense
you are asleep—not merely asleep about the doctrine
of Christ's second advent, but asleep about everything
that concerns your souls. You are wide-awake perhaps
about temporal things ; you read the newspapers, it
may be, and have your head stored with earthly wisdom
and useful knowledge. But you have no heart-felt
sense of sin, no peace and friendship with God, no
experimental acquaintance with Christ, no delight in
the Bible and prayer ; and what is all this but being
asleep ?

How long is this to go on ? When do you mean
to arise and live as if you had a soul ? When will
you cease to hear as those who hear not ? When will
you give up running after shadows and seek something
substantial ? When will you throw up the mockery of
a religion that cannot satisfy, cannot comfort, cannot
sanctify, cannot save, and will not bear a calm examination ? When will you give up having a faith which
does not influence your practice—having a book which

you say is God's word, but do not use—having the name of Christian, but knowing nothing of Christ? Oh! when shall it once be?

Why not this very new year? Why not this very night? Why not awake and call upon your God, and resolve that you will sleep no longer? I set before you an open door. I set before you Jesus the Saviour who died for sinners on the cross, Jesus able to save to the uttermost, Jesus willing to receive. Go to Him first and foremost if you would know what step to take. Go to Him in prayer and cry, " Lord, save me or I perish ; I am weary of sleeping—I would fain sleep no longer." Oh! "awake thou that sleepest, and arise from the dead, and Christ shall give thee light."

Sun and moon and stars are all witnessing against you ; they fill their place in creation, and you do not. Sabbaths and ordinances are witnessing against'you: they are all proclaiming there is a God, there is a judgment, and you are living as if there were none. The tears and prayers of godly relations are witnessing against you : others are sorrowfully thinking you have a soul, though you seem to forget it. The very gravestones you walk past this night are witnessing against you ; they are silently whispering, " Life is short and death is near," all, all are saying, " Awake! awake! awake!" Oh, brethren, the time past may surely suffice you to have slept. Awake to be wise, awake to be safe, awake to be happy. Awake, and sleep no more.

3. My last word of application shall be an *exhortation* to all who have the oil of grace in their hearts. I draw it from the words of our Lord at the end of the parable. I exhort you to " watch."

I exhort you to watch against everything which might interfere with a readiness for Christ's appearing. Watch against inconsistencies of walk, watch against besetting sins, watch against the harm of false doctrine, watch against formality in the use of spiritual things, watch against slothfulness about the Bible and private prayer. Backsliding begins from within. Watch against bitterness and uncharitableness : a little love weighs more than many gifts. Watch against pride and self-conceit : Peter said, " Though all men deny Thee, yet will not I " ; and presently fell. Watch against the sin of Galatia, Ephesus, and Laodicea : believers may run well for a season, then lose their first love, and then become lukewarm. Watch against the sin of Jehu : a man may have great zeal from false motives. It is a much easier thing to oppose antichrist than to follow Christ.

Brethren, believers, let us all watch, and watch more every year we live.

Let us watch for the *world's sake*. We are the book they chiefly read ; they watch our ways. Oh ! let us strive to be plain epistles of Christ.

Let us watch for *our own sakes*. As our walk is, so will be our peace ; as our conformity to Christ's mind, so will be our sense of Christ's atoning blood. If a man will not walk in the full light of the sun, how can he expect to be warm?

And, not least, let us watch *for our Lord's sake*. Let us live as if His honour was concerned in our behaviour ; let us live as if every slip and fall was a wound to our Head. Oh ! let us exercise a godly jealousy for thought, word, and action—motive, manner, and walk. Never never let us fear being too strict. " Herein is my Father glorified, that ye bear much fruit ; so shall ye be my disciples."

XVII

PROFIT AND LOSS

"What shall it profit a man, if he gain the whole world, and lose his own soul?"—MARK viii. 36.

IT is a sad proof, beloved, of our evil and corrupt nature, that our Lord Jesus Christ should have thought it necessary to use such language and to ask such a question. He was preaching to His own people —to the children of Abraham, Isaac and Jacob, to the nation which for fifteen hundred years had alone enjoyed the privilege of knowing the true God ; He was not instructing ignorant heathen, but Israelites, to whom pertained the adoption and the glory and the covenant, and the giving of the law and the service of God and the promises ; and yet behold He deals with them as if they had still to learn the first principles of religious knowledge—" What shall it profit a man, if he gain the whole world, and lose his own soul ? " But it is far more sad, beloved, and far more deplorable, that at the present hour, eighteen hundred years after Jesus died for men, it should still be necessary for a minister of the gospel to urge upon you the very same words. Who, indeed, would have thought it possible that we should be obliged to remind you that the care of the soul is the one thing needful—needful for all : for the rich, because of their temptations ; for the poor, because of their trials ; for the old, because death is close at hand ; for the young,

219

because life with all its intoxicating follies is before
them, and they can never have a more convenient season?
—to remind you that, although men have different
abilities and fill different stations here on earth, they
have one thing at least in common, they have ALL
immortal souls, they must all give account of themselves
at the day of judgment. And yet, "hear, O heavens, and
give ear, O earth," we are obliged to tell you, professing
Christians, all this. I say *obliged*, and is there not a
cause? Mark now what I am about to say, and listen
to my proofs.

I appeal, then, to your consciences, whether I do not
say the truth in Christ, when I declare my belief that
the greater number of baptised persons are living just
as if this world was their abiding home and resting
place, and the things of this world their only object
—as if there was no such text as "It is appointed
unto men once to die, but after this the judgment."
As if Jesus had never come down on earth, preached,
suffered, died and risen again for human guilt; as if the
Bible was a beautiful book, but a thing to be admired
and respected more than studied; as if churches and
ministers were convenient enough for keeping people
in order, but not witnesses of truth and messengers
of glad tidings to a lost and ruined creation. I often
observe, when persons meet, they ask each other a great
deal about their bodily health (" Are you quite well?"
they say, " Have you got over that cold, or that fever, or
that rheumatism?") but I never yet met with any one
who made a point of inquiring about his friend's soul; and
yet we are told plainly in the Bible, that the body (comparatively speaking) is vile and perishable, but the soul
precious and eternal. Men seem to go blindly forward,
intent upon the earth they walk on, and confining all
their anxiety to the life that now is; one generation

after another is struggling to get on in this world, but
few indeed appear to care where they shall be found
in the next.

Seeing then, beloved, that these things cannot be
spoken against, for who shall gainsay them?—seeing that,
even in this ,parish, I have found already, to my deep
sorrow, there are some persons quite careless and indifferent about religion, some who drink, some who live
immoral lives, some who without good reasons attend
church only once a day, some who only attend now
and then when it is convenient, (think what a profanation
for a sinful creature to talk of honouring his Maker and
Redeemer and Judge when it is convenient), some who
never attend at all, and go nowhere, some who appear
to think it no sin to go to sleep and some to talk in
God's own house, before the very eyes of Christ who
is now in the midst of you,—seeing that these things
are so, I feel it my solemn duty, in love and charity towards you, to begin the year by laying open the first
foundations of religious belief. I shall place side by
side the world and the soul, and shortly compare their
respective value ; and if after that you choose to lose
your own souls (which God forbid), you shall not say
that I did not at least attempt to give you warning.
May the Holy Ghost convince you all of the importance
of the subject, and give you new hearts, for Christ's sake.

I. What then shall I say of the things of this world,
which men appear to think so valuable—money, houses,
land, clothes, food, drink, learning, honours, titles,
pleasures, and the like? Beloved, I shall say two things.
First, they are all really worthless : capable, no doubt,
of being turned to a good use (every creature of God,
says the Bible, is good if sanctified by the word of God
and prayer), but I mean this, that if you suppose they
are in themselves able to make you really happy, you

are wofully deceived. If any unconverted person in this parish could have just as much as he wished of every earthly good thing, he would still find in a very short time that he was not one whit happier than before. They are all comfortless without a new heart and a living faith in Christ Jesus. I dare say you think I am mistaken, but let me tell |you many a rich man has tried the experiment, and can bear witness that the case is so. Many a one could tell you that he seeks out everything which money can purchase, he passes his life in a constant round of amusement and excitement, going from one pleasure to another, and yet he must confess that peace of mind has been like a shadow or will-o'-the-wisp, always before his eyes but never within his grasp. And if this does not convince you, read the book of Ecclesiastes, and there you will find the deliberate opinion of the wisest man that ever lived—I mean Solomon—and you will see that he put the question to the proof in his own case ; and what was the result? " Vanity of vanities," saith the preacher, " all is vanity." " I was great," he says, " and increased more than all that were before me in Jerusalem : also my wisdom remained with me. And whatsoever my eyes desired I kept not from them, I withheld not my heart from any joy ; for my heart rejoiced in all my labour : and this was my portion of all my labour. Then I looked on all the works that my hands had wrought, and on the labour that I had laboured to do : and, behold, all was vanity and vexation of spirit, and there was no profit under the sun."

Secondly, I say that all the things of the world are perishable. Surely, dear friends, this cannot require any evidence. You must have seen with your own eyes that none of the things I have mentioned are sure, lasting, permanent, incorruptible, and to be depended on. Money and property may be lost ;

health may fail ; friends may be deceitful ; and unless
we can make a covenant with death and hell, we
ourselves may suddenly be cut off in the midst of our
days and hurried to our last account. Oh, remember
the parable in Luke xii. 16. We do not read that he
was immoral or an evil-liver in any way, yet see the
conclusion our Lord draws. There may be times when
everything looks bright and sunshiny, but let us not
forget the days of darkness, for they shall be many—
the days when you shall say in the morning " Would
God it were evening," and in the evening " Would God
it were morning," for the longer you live the more will
you feel the truth of Job's words, " Man that is born
of a woman is of few days, and full of trouble. He
cometh forth like a flower, and is cut down ; he fleeth
also as a shadow, and continueth not " (xiv. 1, 2).
There is hope of a tree, if it be cut down, that it will
sprout again ; but " man dieth and wasteth away, yea,
man giveth up the ghost, and where is he ? "

II. Such is the world ; and now what shall I say of
the soul, which people appear to hold so cheap?

First, then, let me tell you it is the most valuable
part of man, because it is the part in which we differ
from the brute creation. It is that wonderful principle
by which God made a distinction between ourselves
and the other works of His hand, for we read that
" God formed man of the dust of the ground, and
breathed into his nostrils the breath of life," and then
what was the grand conclusion ?—" man became a living
soul." It was the soul for which Christ was content
to take our nature on Him, and suffer death upon the
cross ; the soul, of whose interests you are so careless,
was the cause which brought Him down from the right
hand of God, to give His own blood as the price of
its redemption. Think, beloved, I beseech you, what a

privilege it must be to have a soul. I once heard an
anecdote of a gentleman who was visiting a large lunatic
asylum or madhouse near London, when he met with
a patient who was only out of his mind upon certain
subjects, as I daresay you know is sometimes the case ;
and this poor creature asked him a startling, a most
wonderful question. " Sir," he said, " did you say your
prayers this morning?" " Yes," was the answer.
" Then, sir, I trust you thanked God that you have
the use of your reason." Beloved, I wish you to apply
this to your own case. Have you ever thanked God
that you have got a soul capable of renewal, of regeneration, capable of eternal life? Oh, if you have not, go
down upon your knees this day, and acknowledge the
mercies you have received, and your own ingratitude
and unworthiness.

This leads me to the second thing I have to say
about the soul. It is eternal. This frail body of ours
shall one day perish ; the worm shall feed sweetly on
it ; " ashes to ashes, and dust to dust," will probably be
read over the fairest and strongest in this church ; but
the soul shall never perish, and when the earth and all
that it contains are burning up, the soul shall enter
upon a new state of existence, which shall never change,
and that state shall be everlasting life or everlasting fire.

Such is the soul, and such is the world ; and may
we not wonder, with such undeniable facts before us,
that any can be found so foolish as to think of the last
more than of the first, to cleave to earth and disregard
heaven? This is indeed to come down to the level of
the beasts that perish, to call the sword less valuable
than the sheath which contains it, and the jewel less
precious than the case in which it is enclosed. " Where-
fore," asks the prophet Isaiah, " do ye spend your
money for that which is not bread ? and your labour for

that which satisfieth not? Hearken diligently unto me, and eat ye that which is good, and let your soul delight itself in fatness."

Now, if the heart of man were less deceitful than it is, such general argument might be enough : but I dare not stop here, for it is no light matter—it is your life ; and therefore I will bring before your notice the testimony of two most unexceptionable witnesses, the dying and the dead. Ask them for an answer to the question "What shall it profit a man, if he gain the whole world, and lose his own soul?" and I would be content to leave the decision of our text in their hands.

Ask the dying sinner ; stand by his bedside, and inquire of him, whether it proves a comfortable and supporting thought that he has cared more for the world than for his soul. Perhaps you never saw the deathbed of one who had not got his feet upon the rock. Oh! it is a fearful, an instructive, a soul-moving sight! When the heart begins to beat faintly and the eyes to grow dim, when friends are weeping around and human medicines avail no longer, when all the intoxication of worldly pleasure or business is past and far away, when each lies in his own silent chamber, with nothing apparently between himself and God, when something whispers "Thou shalt not come down from that bed on which thou art gone up, but shalt surely die," in that solemn hour, beloved, we have little idea how small appears this earth and how broad eternity ; how much the memory of sin improves ; how deeply a guilty conscience darkens. You would then hear him acknowledge that his life had been a grand mistake ; you would hear him confess that the care of the soul was indeed the one thing needful, and bitterly repent the time he had lost, the opportunities he had neglected, and the instruction he had despised. God

grant I may be spared the pain of seeing any of you
in such a plight !

And then, beloved, turn to the bedside of one of
God's own children in his last moments : you might
perhaps observe some few doubts and fears, from a
strong sense of his own unworthiness, and a knowledge
of his own sinfulness—for Satan is strong and the flesh
weak—though it is far more probable you would hear
him say, " I know that my Redeemer liveth, and at
the latter day He shall stand upon the earth, and
though after my skin worms devour this body, yet in
my flesh shall I see God " ; " Though I walk through
the valley of the shadow of death, I will fear no evil,
for Thou art with me ; Thy rod and Thy staff they
comfort me." But this at least is most certain : you
never would hear one single member of Christ declare
that he only regretted he had not cared enough about
the world, that he had paid too much attention to the
welfare of his own soul.

Let us now examine the witness of the dead upon
this momentous question. Think not that I am going
to incur the charge of intruding into things which I
have not seen : I shall simply lay before you one of
the most remarkable passages in the New Testament,
the parable of the rich man and Lazarus. (Luke xvi.)
The words are so simple that I should only weaken
their force if I were to add any comment ; I only
ask you to remark that little is said about Lazarus,
excepting that he was poor, yet we see he was rich
in faith and had treasure in heaven. Nothing is said
against the rich man : we do not learn that he was
immoral or cruel, and yet it is clear he had laid up all
his treasure upon earth. " He that hath ears to hear,
let him hear."

Beloved, are not these things written for our learning ?

Are not these the words of Him who spake to the
world the things which He had heard of His Father?
Is it not then a wonderful and a horrible thing that
so many of you can live on in utter carelessness about
your soul, setting your affections upon things below,
giving God your spare time and the season when you
have nothing to do, but giving all your hearts to that
which cannot profit you in this life and will not deliver
you from condemnation in the life to come. "Oh that
mine head were water and mine eyes a fountain of
tears, that I might weep night and day for the slain
of the daughter of my people!" for unbelief such
as this is marvellous, inexplicable, unaccountable,
incomprehensible.

I trust, beloved, I have now proved to you how
false and unworthy is the estimate men usually place
upon the world and upon the soul. I have endeavoured
to show you a more excellent way; but I cannot
conclude without supplying a few hints, which may
assist each of you in finding out whether he is loving
his own soul at this minute or not.

Many a one, I daresay, is disposed to think that all
this may be very true—you knew it long ago—but it
does not apply to yourself: you wish your soul to be
saved.

You wish to be saved. There are few that do not;
but unfortunately men generally want to be saved in
their own way, and not according to the Bible; they love
the crown, although they will seldom take up the cross.
Friend, you need not be in any uncertainty about it;
you may soon know what your state is; it is all to be
found in this little Book; the marks, the signs, the
tokens, the evidences are so clearly recorded, that he
who runs may read. And what are they? Listen,
I beseech you.

It is written here, " All have sinned, and come short of the glory of God ; " " There is not a just man upon earth that doeth good and sinneth not." Do you know this ? Have you been brought to the wholesome conclusion that you are no better than a lost sinner by nature, wretched and miserable and poor and blind and naked, without one spark of natural goodness, deserving of nothing but God's wrath and condemnation ? Oh ! if you have not, tremble for yourself and repent : be very sure you are losing your own soul.

Again, it is written : "Except a man be born again, he cannot see the kingdom of God"; "Ye must be born again." Have you gone through that mighty change ? Do you feel an abhorrence of former carelessness and indifference, a desire to serve God from the heart, a putting away of old things and a putting on of new ? Has godly sorrow wrought in you repentance unto salvation not to be repented of ? Oh, if it has not, tremble for yourself : know for a certainty you are losing your own soul.

Again it is written, " He that believeth not shall be damned." " Without faith it is impossible to please Him." Have you any of this faith ? Have you been convinced of the utter insufficiency of your own righteousness, of the wretched poverty of your own best works ? Have you come in humility and lowly-mindedness, renouncing all confidence in yourself, to the Lamb of God which taketh away the sin of the world, trusting simply in His blood and righteousness, resting solely on His merits and intercession ? Oh ! if you have not, tremble for yourself and repent. Be not deceived : you are losing your own soul.

Lastly, it is written : " Be ye holy, for I am holy." " Without holiness no man shall see the Lord." What do you know of this holiness ? Can you say that God

the Holy Ghost has actually begun the blessed and
never-dying work of sanctification within you? Do
you feel any pure love towards God and your neighbours? Is it your supreme desire to advance God's
glory? Have you any zeal for the extension of His
kingdom? Do you strive not to be conformed to this
world? Do you profess to regulate every thought
and word and action by the Holy Scriptures? Do you
hunger and thirst after a complete mortification of sin,
and look forward with longing to the time when Satan
shall be bound, and there shall be no more struggle
between the flesh and the spirit? Are you meek and
gentle towards all men? Do you redeem the time
daily, looking on every minute as a talent for which
you are accountable, and aiming to be employed as
far as possible in the things which are just and honourable and lovely and of good report? Are the ordinances of Christ's Church sweet and precious to your
soul? Are prayer and praise a delight—in public, in
your family, in private? Is your Bible your daily
food, a light to your feet and a lantern to your path?
Are you above the fear of men, and can you think
lightly of their praise in comparison with that which
is of God? Do you count all things but loss if you
can but win Christ, and the life that now is as nothing
compared with that which is to come? Oh! if you
know not something, however little, of these things,
tremble for yourself and repent: rest assured you
are losing your own soul.

O beloved, be merciful to yourselves. Cease to think
so much about this vile body, this perishable world;
think more about those precious souls which Jesus
purchased with His own blood—about that eternal
resting-place where your Saviour sitteth at the right
hand of God. " Labour not for the meat that perisheth,

but for that meat which endureth unto everlasting life, which the Son of man shall give you."

True Christian, a word for you. You know these things ; you can say, " By the grace of God I have been brought to see the emptiness of this world, and the value of my soul ; by the grace of God I am what I am." Oh, remember then, to make full proof that you are one of Christ's flock, by your daily conduct, your habits, your temper.

Let your life throughout the coming year be a silent witness to the Gospel. Strive to assist Christ's ministers, in your families and among your friends and acquaintances, by speaking to them of the things pertaining to the kingdom of God, by showing them what great things your heavenly Father has done for you. Let all take knowledge that to have been with Jesus has made you happier, holier, better in every relation of life ; and so perchance it may please God to give some repentance to the acknowledging of the truth, and thus their souls may be delivered from the snare of the devil, and saved in the great day when the secrets of all hearts shall be revealed.

XVIII

ENOCH

"Enoch walked with God, and he was not : for God took him."
GEN. v. 24.

YOU all wish to go to heaven. I know it. I am
fully persuaded of it ; I am certain of it. There
is not one of you, however false may be his views of
what he must believe and what he must do, however
unscriptural the ground of his hope, however worldly-
minded he may be during the week, however careless
when he gets outside that door—there is not one of you,
I say, who does not wish to go to heaven. But I do
sadly fear that many of you, without a mighty change,
will never get there. You would like the crown, but
you do not like the cross ; you would like the glory,
but not the grace ; the happiness, but not the holiness ;
the peace, but not the truth ; the victory, but not the
fight ; the reward, but not the labour ; you would like
the harvest, but not the ploughing ; you would like
the reaping, but not the sowing ; and so I fear that
many of you will never get to heaven.

Well, you may say, these are sharp words, this is
hard measure ; but we should like to know what sort
of people they are who will be saved. I shall give
you a short and very general answer. They who have
the same faith as those holy men whose names are
recorded in the Bible—they who walk in that same

231

narrow path which all the saints of God have trodden
—such persons and such only shall have eternal life
and never enter into condemnation.

Indeed, beloved, there is but one way to heaven ;
and in this way every redeemed soul that is now in
Paradise has walked. This is the way you must yourselves be content to follow ; and if you are really
wise, if you really love life, as you profess to do, you
will take every opportunity of examining the characters
of those who have gone before you, you will mark
the principles on which they acted, you will note the
end they had in view, you will try to profit by their
experience, you will follow them so far as they followed
Christ.

Now, I purpose this morning to speak to you about
the history of Enoch, who was one of the first among
those who by faith and patience have inherited the
promises ; and I shall divide what I have to say upon
the subject into four parts.

I. What was the character of the age in which he
lived ?

II. What was his own character ?

III. What was the leading motive or principle which
influenced him ?

IV. What was his end ?

God grant that you may all be stirred up to a
diligent inquiry into your own state ; may many of you,
hearing how Enoch walked with God, be led to pray,
" Lord, I would walk with Thee (I have sinned, but I
repent in dust and ashes), Lord Jesus, I would be Thine,
create in me a clean heart, guide me with Thy counsel,
and afterward bring me unto glory."

I. Now, respecting the age when Enoch lived we
know little, but that little is very bad. He was the
seventh from Adam, and lived in the time before the

flood. In those days, we are told, the earth was
corrupt before God, and filled with violence. Every
sort of wickedness seems to have prevailed ; men walked
after the vile lusts of their hearts, and did that which
appeared good to them without fear and without shame.
The children of Cain, after he murdered Abel, as far
as we can learn, made no attempt whatever to keep
God in their thoughts,—like the prodigal son, they
went afar off from Him and gave themselves up to
worldly employments, as if they would keep the Lord
out of their minds as much as possible. They got a
name as founders of cities, like men who looked upon
this earth as their home, and set all their affection on
things below and had no desire after the new Jerusalem
above, the city of the Lord God and of the Lamb.
They became famous and skilful in all the works of
this life : one was called the father of shepherds, and
another the father of musicians ; but we read of none
that was a father of faithful lambs in Christ's flock,
of none that was a father of children who made God's
statutes their song in the house of their pilgrimage.
And another was a teacher of artificers in brass and
iron ; but we do not hear of any who taught the good
knowledge of the Lord. In short, they were all clever
in finding out how to be rich and how to be merry
and how to be powerful ; but they were not wise unto
salvation, there was nothing of God and His fear and
His service among them.

Such were the children of Cain ; and they seem to
have been such pleasant company, so little disposed to
trouble other people by talking about the soul and
heaven and hell, that nearly everybody took after them,
and the world was tainted and infected with their
manners ; insomuch that the few who still clung to the
true God became separated from the rest by a line of

distinction : they began to be called by the name of
the Lord.

But even this separation did not last long. We are
next told, that they who professed to be the sons of
God began to think there was no harm in marrying
persons who cared nothing about religion ; they chose
wives who were unbelievers,—beautiful and agreeable,
no doubt, but still enemies of God,—and (as it has almost
always proved when a Christian has been united to
one that is not a Christian), the bad soon corrupted the
good, or else the good did not convert the bad, and
the families that were born of these unions proved
earthly, sensual, and devilish, and in a short time the
whole world was full of sin.

Consider, beloved, what a fearful proof you have here
of the natural bent of man's heart towards wickedness !
They had the recollection of God's anger against transgression fresh upon their minds ; they had Paradise
before their eyes, they had the angels of God keeping
the way of the tree of life with flaming swords ; and
yet, in spite of all this, they sinned with a high hand.
They went on much as the world likes to do now :
they ate, they drank, they planted, they builded, they
bought, they sold, they made light of warnings. " What
have we do with the Lord ? " they thought ; " let us enjoy
ourselves while we can."   But God will not be mocked,
and though He bore with them long and exhorted them
by His servants, He dealt with them at last according
to their works ; and just as He will one day send the
fire upon this earth, so did He send the waters of
the deep : the flood came and cut them off in the
middle of their revellings, and drowned the whole world
excepting eight persons.

Such was the character of the men before the flood ;
and in the middle of this age of wickedness Enoch

lived, and Enoch walked with God. There were no
Bibles then, no prayer-books, no religious tracts, no
churches, no ministers, no sacraments : Christ had never
been seen ; the way of salvation had never been clearly
made known ; the gospel was only seen dimly in the
distance ; it was not fashionable to think about religion,
it was not fashionable to worship God at all, there
was nothing to encourage people to make a profession.
Yet in the middle of this wicked and adulterous generation this saint of the Most High did live; Enoch walked
with God. It is almost impossible to imagine a more
splendid proof of what grace can do for a weak, sinful
man than is to be found in these words ; in the world
before the flood " Enoch walked with God."

II. I promised in the second place to tell you something about Enoch's character. You have heard he
walked with God, and you know, perhaps, it is an
expression of great praise ; but I may not leave you
here without trying to give you a clear notion of its
meaning. People often get a habit of using words without exactly knowing what they mean, and a very bad
habit it is. Now, I say that this walking with God has
many different senses ; it is an expression full of matter.

A man that walks with God is one of *God's friends*
That unhappy enmity and dislike which men naturally
feel towards their Maker has been removed ; he feels
perfectly reconciled and at peace. How indeed can
two walk together except they be agreed ? He does
not hide himself from the Lord, like Adam in the
trees of the garden, but he seeks to be in constant
communion with Him ; he is not as many who are
uncomfortable at the idea of being alone with God
for he is never perfectly happy excepting in His company ; he feels that he cannot be too much with Him,
because he desires to be of the same mind, to think

like Him, to act like Him, to be conformed to His image. Such a one was Enoch.

Again, he that walks with God is one of *God's dear children*. He looks upon Him as his Father, and as such he loves Him, he reveres Him, he rejoices in Him, he trusts Him in everything. He makes it his constant study to please Him, and whenever he has offended, he sorrows over his offence with a true childlike sorrow. He thinks that God knows better than himself what is good for him, and so in everything that happens— sickness or health, sorrow or joy, riches or poverty—he says to himself, "It is well: my Father sends this." Such a one was Enoch.

Again, he that walks with God is one of *God's witnesses*. He never hesitates to stand forward on the Lord's side. He is not content with giving his own heart to God, but he is also ready and willing to bear his testimony in public on behalf of the cause of righteousness and truth. He is not ashamed to let men know whose servant he is; he will not be turned aside from raising his voice against sin for fear of giving offence. Such a one was Enoch. His lot was cast in evil days; but did he join the multitude? Did he walk in the way of sinners? Did he hold his peace and say, I can do nothing? Far from it! He thought not what his neighbours liked, but what his Lord required. He sought not to please the world, but to please God; and therefore, living in the midst of sin and corruption, he was separate from it. He was a witness against it; he was as the salt of the earth; he was as a light shining in a dark place.

Ay, and he was a plain speaker, too. He made no excuse about youth and temptation; he did not let men go to hell for fear of being thought unchari- table, but he told them openly of their danger; and

when they were living wickedly and carelessly, as if
there was no God and no devil, he said, as the apostle
Jude relates, "The Lord cometh with ten thousand
of His saints, to execute judgment upon all, and to
convince all that are ungodly of their ungodly deeds."
No doubt he was thought a troubler of the people,
and a disagreeable man ; but he was a witness, and
so he declared continually : "The Lord cometh";
whether ye will hear or whether ye will forbear, there
shall be a day of account, sin shall not always go
unpunished—repent, for the Lord cometh. This was
the burden of his testimony. He walked with God,
and so he was a faithful witness.

But I say further, to walk with God is to walk in
God's ways, to follow the laws He has given for our
guidance, to look on His precepts as our rule and
our counsellor, to esteem all His commandments concerning all things to be right ; to fear turning aside
from the narrow path He has set before us for one
single instant ; to go straightforward, though all things
seem against us, remembering the word on which He
has caused us to hope.

And to walk with God is to walk in the light of
God's countenance ; to live as men who remember
that all things are naked and opened unto the eyes
of Him with whom we have to do, that the darkness
is no darkness with Him, and remembering this, to
aim at never thinking or saying or doing anything
we should be ashamed of in the presence of the great
Searcher of hearts.

And to walk with God is to walk after the Spirit—
to look to the Holy Ghost as our Teacher, to lean on
Him for strength, to put no confidence in the flesh, to
set our affections on things above, to wean them from
things on earth, to be spiritually-minded.

But truly, beloved, I might keep you here all day, and yet the half would not be told of the things which are contained in walking with God. To walk with God is to walk humbly confessing ourselves unworthy of the least of all His mercies, acknowledging that we have no power of ourselves to help ourselves, that we are constantly coming short and backsliding, that we are unprofitable servants, and without His grace are sure to fall. It is to walk circumspectly, bearing in mind our besetting sins and temptations, and avoiding all places and companies and employments in which we are likely to be assailed by them. It is to walk in love towards all, both God and man, full of the mind that is in our heavenly Father, kind and affectionate and gentle to every one, yea, even to the unthankful and the evil. To walk with God is to serve Him as a habit, continually; we are not to walk with Him on a Sunday and forget Him on a weekday; we are not to walk with Him in public but not in private; we are not to walk with Him before ministers and good men only, but in our own families and before our own household.

And lastly, to walk with God is to be always going forward, always pressing on, never standing still and flattering ourselves that we are the men and have borne much fruit; but to grow in grace, to go on from strength to strength, to forget the things behind, and if by grace we have attained unto anything, to abound yet more and more.

Beloved, this is a very faint picture of a walk with God, but time will not allow me to draw another stroke. This was some part of Enoch's character; this was in some degree the meaning of the record God has given us about him.

Oh, it is a simple but a weighty record! No doubt

there were many great and many wise and many noble
in those days; but all we know of them is that they
lived and they died and they begat sons and daughters.
Of Enoch only is it written that he walked with God.
Oh, this walk with God, beloved! It is the only talent
which will never fail us, the only treasure which will
prove eternal, the only character which will serve us
beyond the grave; and in the day when names and
titles and honours shall sink to nothing, and all shall
stand upon a level, the poorest and the humblest in
the land shall be more highly honoured than the mighty
and the rich, if he has walked with God and they have
not; the first shall be last and the last first.

Comfort ye, comfort ye, all that belong to Christ's
little flock; comfort ye, all that are thinking first about
your souls; others may live in courts and palaces and
have the praise of this world, but of you it shall be
written in the books of heaven, "They walked with
God"; the King of kings and Lord of lords was their
Shepherd, their Guide, their Companion, their familiar
Friend, and your joy shall no man take away.

III. I must now say a few words about Enoch's
motive. He walked with God; and you will ask me,
"What was the secret cause of it, what was the hidden
spring and principle which influenced him, that we may
go forth and do likewise?" Beloved, God has told us
plainly in the Epistle to the Hebrews—it was faith.
Faith was the seed which bore such goodly fruit; faith
was the root of his holiness and decision on the Lord's
side—faith without which there has never been any
salvation, faith without which not one of you will ever
enter into the kinglom of heaven.

Now this faith is no mystery; it is neither more nor
less than a thorough belief of the heart.

Enoch believed that as a child of Adam he was

himself born a sinner and deserving of nothing but wrath and condemnation ; he believed that his first parents had forfeited all right to eternal life, and that he as one of their descendants had inherited a heart deceitful above all things and desperately wicked. He did not merely look upon himself as naturally very thoughtless and liable to be led away by bad company, and the like, as many of you are content to do, but he went further, he looked within and laid the blame on the old Adam, the corrupt fountain of his own heart ; he really believed himself to be a miserable sinner.

But Enoch believed that God had graciously provided a way of salvation, that He had appointed a great Redeemer to bear our sins and carry our transgressions and bruise the serpent's head. He saw clearly that without this he had not the slightest chance of being saved, whatever he might do ; he looked far forward, and in his mind's eye he saw a long way off the Messiah that was yet to come to pay the ransom of the world, and he built all his hopes on Him. Enoch believed in the Lord Jesus Christ.

And Enoch believed that God was a God of perfect holiness, "of purer eyes than to behold iniquity." He never held with those who said, "You are righteous overmuch, the Lord will not be so very particular, we need not be so very strict, men cannot be always keeping watch over themselves ;" for he trembled at the thought of allowing himself in any shadow of impurity or unrighteousness ; and though he never dreamed of setting up his own works as anything worth, though he rejoiced in the hope of salvation by free grace, still he believed that he who walks with God and would have eternal life must be holy even as He is holy.

And Enoch believed that God would one day come to judge the world and give to all men according to

their works. Though iniquity abounded and the love
of many waxed cold, and all things seemed to go on
as if God took no notice of this earth, he still believed
the Lord would come to take account in such an hour
as no one expected Him ; in faith he saw the judgment
close at hand, and he walked with God as one waiting
for it. He lived as if he felt this was not his rest ; he
looked beyond the things which are seen to that abiding
city which remaineth for the people of God ; by faith
he saw that heaven was his only home and in the
Lord's presence alone was fulness of joy. Such was
the ruling principle which possessed this holy man of
old. Oh that you would pray earnestly for a like
precious faith ! Without it you will never walk in
Enoch's way, and so you will never come to Enoch's
end.

IV. And this leads me, in the last place, to speak
about Enoch's end. We are simply informed in the
text that " He was not, for God took him." The interpretation of this is, that God was pleased to interfere
in a special manner on His servant's behalf, and so He
suddenly removed him from this world without the
pains of death, and took him to that blessed place
where all the saints are waiting in joyful expectation
for the end of all things, where sin and pain and sorrow
are no more.

And this, no doubt, was done for several reasons. It
was done to convince a hard-hearted, unbelieving world
that God does observe the lives of men and will honour
those who honour Him. It was done to show every
living soul that Satan had not won a complete victory
when he deceived Eve ; that men may yet get to heaven
by the way of faith, and although in Adam all die, still
in Christ all may be made alive. Yes, beloved, Enoch
walked with God, and so God took him. Here was a

splendid and a comforting assurance that the Lord's eye is upon all His children, that there is a heaven and a life to come, that there is a reward for the righteous, though men may laugh at them, and their walk is not fashionable, and their way is spoken against and their seriousness is despised. Oh, cast not away your confidence, ye that walk with God : it is but a little season and He that shall come will come and take you to an everlasting rest.

And now, beloved, I do beseech you all, if you care about your souls,—if you really desire to go to heaven, —if you really have the slightest wish to die in peace, and rise in glory, and join the company of the just,— I do beseech you ask yourselves the question, " Am I walking with God? am I in that way which Enoch and all the saints have walked in ? How many among you have one grain of that living faith which guided this holy man's feet into the way of peace?

Would you have me suppose they are walking with God who live in any known sin which the Bible condemns? Are they walking with God who regard Him and His service in the second place and the care of this world's matters in the first? Are they who never think, and say to each other " Never mind this anxiety—I dare say we shall be right at last " ? Are they who neglect any means of grace which God has placed within their reach, or let the most trifling excuse prevent their using it? Are they who profess to know the Lord and believe in Jesus, but do not make Jesus their example? Oh! no, no! It is impossible ; all such must be walking away from God ; day after day they get farther from Him, and at last, unless they turn, they will walk into hell.

And when I see men going towards this place of torment—for all must be who are not walking with

God—when I see the loving and tender-hearted Lord
Jesus holding out His hands and saying, " Come unto
me : why will ye die ? I can and will cleanse you from
all sin ! "—when I see all this, and find you cold and
undecided, and flattering yourselves you are in a middle
path and tolerably safe, I must cry aloud and spare
not, and run the risk of being thought uncharitable, if
by any means I may awaken you and deliver you from
the power of Satan and guide you unto Christ. Oh
that your hearts may be stirred within you, that you
may never rest till you are in Enoch's way and have
some portion of Enoch's faith !

Think not to put off the question by saying these
things cannot be true. Go to your Bibles and see what
they testify. They that are utterly deceived and blind
may tell you that punishment is not eternal, and hell
is a delusion, and the devil a lie ; but they will find to
their cost they are all true, most fearfully true, and so
long as you attend the worship of the Church of
England, which only appeals to Scripture, you must
not expect to hear of any other way than that which
Enoch took.

Think not to say, " We cannot walk with God : we
mean well in church, but when we get outside the
world lays hold upon us, and acquaintances and evil
company turn us aside." Oh, be honest with yourselves !
This is as much as saying " If all the world be religious
we will be religious too, and not till then " ; in the meanwhile you do not like to be singular, you cannot make
up your minds to be in earnest, you think I may be
mistaken, you will go with the stream, you will walk
according to the course of this world. But look at
Enoch : his heart was naturally like yours ; the same
grace which strengthened him can strengthen you,—the
Lord's hand is not shortened ; by grace he walked with

God three hundred years, and surely you may trust the power of God will keep you also through faith unto salvation for threescore years and ten. But know that if you cannot be saints on earth you never can be saints in heaven.

Think not I am shutting you up without hope. What though it be true that few are saved and the way is narrow?—there is nothing to prevent any of you entering it, except your own unwillingness, your own unbelieving hearts, your own indifference. Oh, begin to walk as Enoch did! Come to the Lord Jesus Christ! He that cometh to Him shall never hunger, he that believeth on Him shall never thirst : though your past life may have been that of Esau or Manasseh or Judas or Mary Magdalen, come to Him repenting of everything, and He will never cast you out. Take with you words ; and say, " Lord Jesus, I have sinned ; I do repent, I put all my trust in thee : Lord receive me, Lord increase my faith," and then the word of God is my warrant for saying He shall give you His Holy Spirit, and you shall walk with Him and before Him and after Him, and rest with Him.

Are you old!—then walk with God ; and be in haste : your next step may be in hell ; thank the Lord you are not there yet. You have but a short time ; you hang by a slender thread ; Jordan is before you, and you will never cross in safety unless the ark is with you, and the ark is only with those who walk with God.

Are you young?—then walk with God, and be in haste. Do not put it off a single day. Young people die as well as old. Young people have precious souls to save as well as others. The devil, who rejoices to see so many of you neglecting private prayers and private reading of the Bible, has an especial eye to you: he knows if he can only prevent you thinking while you are young, he has a better chance of making you his own forever.

O let it not be written of you in the books of God that on this Sabbath day you came together not for the better but for the worse; you were invited to walk with God, and would not: let it not be in vain you have heard this history of one of the Lord's elect; but cast aside your old habits, arise to newness of life, even as the face of the fair country around you is renewed at this season of the year; and be ye followers of Enoch even as he followed God.

Remember, all of you, the prophecy he spake: "the Lord cometh, to execute judgment." This earth, lovely and fair and shining as it seems, shall be burned up; but your soul shall live for ever, either in heaven or in hell: this very Church shall crumble into dust, but they that sleep around it shall rise again, bone shall come together unto bone, and all stand before the throne and be judged according to their lives. The Lord grant you may all find mercy in that day; but if you would find it, you must walk with God, and then indeed you shall live by faith and sleep in Jesus and have your portion with the spirits of just men made perfect.

XIX

DANIEL

"Then said these men, We shall not find any occasion against this Daniel except we find it against him concerning the law of his God."—
DANIEL vi. 5.

IT would be impossible, I think, to imagine a higher testimony to a man's character than you have heard in these words. You know how ready the world is to find fault with a Christian—how closely his conduct is watched, how eagerly his shortcomings are proclaimed—and happy indeed are those who by grace are so enabled to live, that the godless and profane can find no occasion against them.

In order, however, that you may fully understand the peculiar value of the testimony in my text, you ought to know something of the time and circumstances in which it was given.

Daniel, who was a prince of the royal family of Judah, and descended directly from David, had been carried to Babylon as a prisoner, with many other Jews, when Jerusalem was destroyed. While there, it pleased God to bring him into favour with the heathen kings of Babylon, and he was advanced to great dignity and honour. Nor was his honour ever taken from him; for when Belshazzar was overthrown, and the kingdom of Babylon was taken by the Medes and Persians, the Lord inclined the heart of Darius the Mede to make Daniel the first among his counsellors, who ordered all things under the king. But the wicked followers of Darius became jealous of Daniel. They made a conspiracy against him, and for a while they succeeded ; for they obtained a decree that Daniel should be cast into the den of lions. But God, whom he served, here came to his assistance : he was miraculously preserved ; his enemies were condemned, and perished in his stead ; and King Darius gave glory to God.

Such is a short account of the interesting history which you will find in the chapter from which my text is taken—a chapter which I take occasion to recommend to your particular attention.

I purpose this afternoon to speak on two points only in this history. One is the character of Daniel, which here came out like gold from the fire, as an example for your imitation. The other is the mysterious dealings of God with him, as a ground for our instruction and comfort. May God the Holy Spirit apply the subject to all your consciences ; may none of you be content with admiring the faith and patience of the saints, but may you he led to pray for the grace of God, that you may follow in their steps.

I. First, then, with respect to Daniel's character, I would observe there are *three points* to be especially noticed.

(*a*) There is his steady walk with God. He was now ninety years of age ; he had spent more than the ordinary life of man in the very heart of a wicked city and a corrupt court. He had riches and honours and everything to make this world enjoyable ; but he never turned aside from the narrow way, either to the right hand or the left. The eyes of all were fixed upon him ; many envied and hated him. They examined his public conduct ; they inquired into his private character ; they sifted his words and actions ; but they

sought in vain for any ground of accusation. He was
so steady, so upright, so conscientious, that they could
find no occasion or fault in him—they could not touch
him except as concerning the law of his God. Oh,
what an unanswerable argument is a believer's life!
Oh, what an epistle of Christ is the daily conduct
of a child of God! Men cannot see your hearts, nor
understand your principles, but they can see your lives;
and if they find that pious masters, servants, brothers,
friends, sisters, husbands, wives, do far exceed all others
in their several positions, then you are bringing glory
to God and honour to your Redeemer. Think not
that your profession is worth anything, if it is not
known of others by its fruit; without this it is little
better than sounding brass and a tinkling cymbal.
We do not find that Daniel blew his trumpet before
him, and talked everywhere about his own experience;
but he walked close to God, and his life spoke for
him, and his character became known in Babylon, and
even his enemies were obliged to confess, The hand
of God is here, the Lord is with this man of a truth.

   (b) Another point which I would have you notice is
Daniel's habit of private prayer. This was the hidden
cause of all his steadiness, and it was discovered acci-
dentally on this occasion. It seems that his enemies
had obtained a decree of the king, that whosoever
should ask a petition of any God or man for thirty
days should be cast into the den of lions. And having
laid this snare for this holy man, we read that they
assembled and found Daniel praying and making
supplication before God.
   We are also told that he was in the habit of kneeling
upon his knees and praying three times a day; this
was the practice of holy David, as we read in the
Psalms, and this was the spirit of the centurion in the

Acts, who prayed to God alway. So Paul exhorts
the Ephesians to pray always with all prayer and
supplications, and the Thessalonians to pray without
ceasing ; and such has been the habit of all the most
eminent saints of God : they have not been content
with a few cold heartless words every morning and
every night, they have lived in the spirit of prayer,
and sent up many a short earnest petition throughout
the day.

Moreover, we are told that Daniel prayed with his
windows open towards Jerusalem, and this is a most
important circumstance. He did this, and so did every
pious Jew, not only because it was the land of his
fathers and the land of promise, not simply because
God would be worshipped there and there only, but
chiefly because all the types and emblems of the
Messiah, the one way of salvation, the altar, the
sacrifice, and the high priest, were to be found there.
And so also we, if we would have our prayers heard,
must pray towards the Lord Jesus Christ, the true
Temple, our Altar, our High Priest and our Sacrifice.
These are the prayers which God will answer ; this is
the only way by which we can draw near with confidence, and find grace to help in time of need. Mark
well, beloved, the habit of private prayer : here is the
secret of that steadiness which Daniel showed in
Babylon—here was the staff which preserved him upright in the middle of temptations.

We know that he had all the cares of government
upon his shoulders ; he must have been surrounded
with the business and affairs of nations,—but none of
these things prevented him from drawing near to God.

Nor was he a man to say " I am a chosen servant
of God, I need not be so anxious about means " ; he
knew that God would keep him, but not unless he

showed anxiety to have protection, not without diligence in using all the means of grace. Oh, he will rise in judgment and condemn many a one, who dares to think that he will find mercy while he lives in the neglect of regular heartfelt private devotion!

(c) The last point to be observed in Daniel's character is his faith, his confidence in God. The decree appeared, forbidding all sorts of worship for thirty days on pain of death; and oh, how many professors of our generation would have held their peace! how many would have said, " It is but a short time, we need not give offence; the Lord doth not require us to lose our lives in His service"? But look at Daniel: he knew that the writing was signed,—he knew that he was watched,—he knew that his life was at stake,—and yet he went to his house and kneeled on his knees and prayed as he did aforetime. He did not on the one hand run into danger, nor did he on the other flinch from it: here was no carnal policy, no time-serving, no crooked contrivance, no love of expediency. He made a straight path for his feet; he did as usual, neither more nor less; and why? Look at the twenty-third verse: he believed in his God. Mark here the fruits of daily communion with God; see how a habit of prayer will produce quietness and assurance in the hour of trial and difficulty.

There never have been wanting lewd men of the baser sort, who say, Where is the use of your praying? what good will it do you? But wait till the days of affliction come upon you, and the Lord will provide you with an answer. A habit of prayer will impart special reliance upon God in time of danger; it will give a special boldness; it will secure a special deliverance, for them that honour God He will honour. Happy indeed are those who, like Daniel, pray without ceasing : they will find within them the same spirit of faith, they never need fear being surprised, they are like him, always the same and always ready.

II. Let us now consider the other branch of our subject : I mean the mysterious dealings of God with His faithful and holy servant.

(a) Observe, then, there was first a season of darkness. Who would have supposed that God would have allowed iniquity so far to triumph as to leave Daniel in the hands of enemies ! Who would have thought that this pious old man would be cast into the den of lions. But God's ways are not as our ways ; and wonderful as it may appear, the wicked were permitted to work their will for a season : he was accused of breaking the laws ; he was pronounced guilty ; he was condemned to death ; the king laboured to deliver him, but he could not ; the decree could not be altered—Daniel must die. He was let down into this pit—the den of savage beasts, and a stone was laid upon the mouth of the den. And then, no doubt, he was looked upon as one dead ; sin appeared to have prevailed, the wicked rejoiced at their success, and the righteous, the little flock at Babylon, wept and mourned to think that a brother, a faithful witness, had been taken from the earth.

Pause here, beloved, for an instant. This hour of darkness seems to you a mystery. But is it not agreeable to all the dealings of God with man ? Do you not often see things hard to be understood in the world around you ? How often the wicked prosper, and have all that man could desire ; how often iniquity abounds and the love of God waxes cold—and the righteous are oppressed and silenced and afraid ; how often it seems as if the Lord has forgotten this earth, and cares not though His servants are persecuted and His name blasphemed ; how often we feel disposed to cry, how long, O Lord, holy and true, dost Thou not judge and avenge Thyself on the ungodly!

And does not the Christian often see things hard to be explained in his own heart? Is he not often tried with seasons of darkness and sorrow? Yes: many a believer can testify that sometimes he has felt like Paul before his shipwreck; neither sun nor stars have appeared for many days, and almost every hope of being saved has been taken away,—many a one could tell you that the enemy has sometimes come in upon him like a flood, he has been overwhelmed with afflictions and temptations, he has been ready to cry out of the deep, as it were, "Lord I am sinking,--my soul is among lions, I am destitute, afflicted, tormented, deserted, forlorn, forsaken."

Yes: God's ways are often difficult and mysterious to His people; we cannot see the meaning of many things which happen around us, we think them hard, we almost quarrel with the Lord's arrangements; but they that are really wise will be patient, they will wait to see the end, and lay to heart the words of the Lord Jesus. "What I do thou knowest not now; but thou shalt know hereafter."

(b) Come now and hear how the darkness was scattered and the light returned. Heaviness may endure for a night, but joy cometh in the morning. Daniel, you have seen, was allowed to go through the furnace of tribulation, but the time came at last when God interfered on his servant's behalf, and made his dealings clear and plain. Daniel was cast into the lions' den, but the Lord was with him and therefore he was safe. We read that the king, Darius, came very early in the morning to the mouth of the cave, and cried with an anxious and lamentable voice, "O Daniel . . . is thy God . . . able to deliver thee." And oh, how joyful must his

feelings have been when he heard the holy man's
reply : " O King, live for ever ; my God hath sent His
angel and shut the lions' mouths, that they have not hurt
me : forasmuch as before him innocency was found in
me ! "

And need I tell you that Daniel was brought forth,
and honoured and exalted ; while his enemies, in their
turn, were cast into the den and the lions destroyed
them all ? So true it is that light is sown for the
righteous, that God will keep them in perfect peace
whose minds are stayed on Him. So true are the
words of Psalm xci." " He that dwelleth in the secret
place of the Most High shall abide under the shadow
of the Almighty, He shall cover thee with His
feathers, and under His wings shalt thou trust. . . . His
truth shall be thy shield and buckler. . . . There shall no
evil befall thee, neither shall any plague come nigh thy
dwelling. For He shall give His angels charge over
thee, to keep thee in all thy ways. . . . Because he hath
set his love upon Me, therefore will I deliver him : I will
set him on high, because he hath known My Name."

(c) Consider now, beloved, what showers of good
descended from this dark cloud which at one time
seemed so threatening. Think what a blessed effect
this deliverance would have on Daniel ! What deep
views of God's love and power and goodness and wisdom
he would obtain ! What strength it would add to his
faith, what warmth to his prayers ! How every grace
within his bosom would shoot forth with renewed
vigour. Think, too, what an impression would be made
upon the godless and profane ; what shame would cover
the faces of those who had thought Daniel went too
far and was righteous overmuch ; how many would
be brought to tremble and fear before a God who
could deliver after such a fashion.

(*d*) Think, lastly, what mighty good would come to the people and cause of God, how much they would be comforted by such a miracle, how much they would be encouraged to go forward : the very thing which once appeared so untoward, which threatened the destruction of Israel and the dishonour of God, would bring glory to the Lord, and set forward the kingdom of heaven.

And so, beloved, it has always been. God's dealings may seem mysterious ; but wait awhile, and the darkness shall disappear and the light shall shine and the crooked shall appear straight, and the rough places shall become smooth.

Satan doth often seem to have his own way in the world, but still there are many proofs that the prosperity of the wicked is short, and the lying lips are but for a moment, and there are seasons when many a hardened sinner is forced to confess, " Verily there is a God that judgeth the earth." Many a Christian would tell you that the trials and chastisements which appeared so bitter have borne most blessed fruit to his soul ; he has sown in tears, but he has reaped in joy ; and there are few who shall not find in the world to come that afflictions which bowed them to the dust, and were grievous at the time, were nothing less than mercies ; they were the very medicines which healed their sin-diseased souls, and purified their hearts for heaven.

Who is there among you that is timid and undecided and inconsistent—afraid to do anything to displease men and yet not satisfied if he does not give his heart to God—conscious that he ought to bear the cross and follow Christ, but fearful of giving offence to the world ? Go, study the character of Daniel, and make it your example. Behold a child of Adam like yourself following the Lord fully, not only when all were with him, but when all were against him ; ready to lose his life in

this world if so he might attain to life eternal. Are
you flesh and blood? so was he; are you by nature
sinful? so was he. The grace of God did make him what
he was, and the grace of God can make you like him,
if you are only willing. But go, confess your faith as
he did: if you are ashamed of Christ, most surely Christ
will be ashamed of you. The double-minded and the
unstable shall never gain the heavenly crown.

Where are the men who say "We cannot do the things
which you require; we cannot come to Christ upon
your terms? There would be no living in the world,
no caring for our families, if we took your advice. We
have no time for such religion; we cannot altogether
give up the world." Oh, look at holy Daniel! He
had the charge of millions upon his hands, he was the
chief among the presidents of an empire, he had the
management of kingdoms and their affairs; and yet—
mark this, O ye despisers and lazy ones—and yet he
found time to be a faithful servant of God, he found
time to cultivate the vineyard of his soul most closely,
he contrived to walk with God as few have ever walked.
Are you wiser than he? Are your leisure hours more
entirely taken up? Oh, be ashamed of vain excuses,
and take this man of business for your pattern, and
do not tell us you cannot come to Christ, until you have
followed Daniel's steps and prayed without ceasing.

Is there an humble-minded follower of Jesus among
you? Set Daniel before your eyes. Be bold, be
faithful, be meek, be persevering; endeavour to walk
so uprightly that all may glorify God on your behalf,
that none may find occasion against you except as
concerning the law of your God.

Fear not because you sometimes walk in darkness
and have no light. Remember that you cannot understand the mind of the Lord nor the meaning of His

dealings. But when the clouds do compass you about, believe in God as Daniel did ; trust in the Lord Jesus at all times ; sing to Him in the dungeon, as Paul and Silas ; sing to Him even in the fire, as the three children did ; be sure, be very sure, he who believeth shall never be ashamed.

I will add for your comfort the words of a very Christian poet, a sweet singer in Israel :—

"God moves in a mysterious way,
    His wonders to perform ;
He plants His footsteps in the sea,
    And rides upon the storm.

Deep in unfathomable mines
    Of never-failing skill,
He treasures up His bright designs,
    And works His sovereign will.

Ye fearful saints, fresh courage take,
    The clouds ye so much dread
Are big with mercy, and shall break
    In blessings on your head.

Judge not the Lord by feeble sense,
    But trust Him for His grace ;
Behind a frowning Providence
    He hides a smiling face.

His purposes will ripen fast,
    Unfolding every hour ;
The bud may have a bitter taste,
    But sweet will be the flower.

Blind unbelief is sure to err,
    And scan His work in vain.
God is His own interpreter,
    And He will make it plain."

XXII

THE BLOOD OF THE LAMB

" These are they which came out of great tribulation, and have washed their robes, and made them white in the blood of the Lamb. Therefore are they before the throne of God, and serve Him day and night in His temple : and He that sitteth on the throne shall dwell among them. They shall hunger no more, neither thirst any more ; neither shall the sun light on them, nor any heat. For the Lamb which is in the midst of the throne shall feed them, and shall lead them unto living fountains of waters : and God shall wipe away all tears from their eyes."—REV. vii. 14, 15, 16, 17.

THIS is a very glorious account, and yet we need not wonder, for it was a vision of heavenly things : you may call it a short glimpse within the vail which separated this world from the world to come. We read in the verses before our text, that the apostle John saw in the spirit a great multitude which no man could number, clothed with white robes, and bearing palms in their hands, standing before the throne and before the Lamb : and not knowing himself who or what these might be, he received information from one of the elders or chief angels, and was told in the words you have heard, that these were the blessed company of all faithful people, the redeemed out of every nation and kindred and tongue, the true children of God, the heirs of everlasting salvation.

I propose this morning to consider fully the account which this elder gave. I counsel you, beloved, to search and see what you know of it in your own selves. The

day shall come when the sun shall become black as
sackcloth of hair, and the moon shall become as blood,
and the stars of heaven shall fall unto the earth, and
they who are strangers to the character described in our
text shall find it had been better for them if they had
never been born. Blessed are they who are not
ashamed to confess that they seek a more abiding city
than this world, even a heavenly one, and count all
things loss if they can only win Christ and be found
in Him.

Now there are three points to be examined in our
text.

I. First, where did these saints come from whom
St. John saw.

II. Second, how they had been able to reach the
place where he saw them.

III. Third and last, what was their reward.

I. First, then, we learn that God's saints have come
out of great tribulation—that is, they have come out
of a world full of sin and danger, a world in which they
have so much to encounter which is hurtful to their
souls that you may truly call it a place of great tribulation. How strange that seems! this earth so fair and
lovely as it appears, so full of everything to make life
enjoyable, this earth on which millions do set all their
affections and have not a thought beyond it, is a
wilderness beset with trials and difficulties to every
true believer. Write this down on the tablet of your
memory, that if you make up your mind to follow
Christ and have your soul saved, you will sooner or
later have to go through great tribulation.

Brethren, why are these things so? Because the
world you live in is a fallen world, the devil is the prince
of it, and by far the greater part of the men and women
on it have shut their eyes and given themselves up to

his service. Once become a follower of Christ, you
will see iniquity abounding on every side, you will see
your blessed Saviour's laws trampled under foot, you
will find the immense majority of those around you to
be spiritually dark, sleeping and dead—some altogether
thoughtless, some resting on a form of godliness without
the power ; and if you love the Lord Jesus in sincerity,
to see your Redeemer thus despised will make the world
a place of tribulation.

But this is not all. The earthly-minded, the thoughtless, will never let you hold on your way in peace. Oh
no ! you are condemning their practices and fashions,
you are a witness against their deadness and neglect of
religion ; and so if you set your face towards Zion they
will try to turn you back. Perhaps it will be laughter,
perhaps it will be hard words ; one day they will accuse
you of pride, another of self-conceit ; sometimes they
will annoy you with arguments, sometimes they will
avoid your company ; but, one way or another, you will
soon discover that the worldly-minded will never let
you go quietly to heaven. You cannot please them.
You may exercise yourself like Paul to have a conscience
void of offence towards all men ; it matters not, you
cannot serve the Lord and Mammon, and if you walk
with God, you will find your way is spoken against by
nearly all.

And then there is your own heart—deceitful, treacherous, and cold—the flesh lusting against the spirit
and the spirit warring with the flesh ; your readiness
to make excuses, your deadness in the use of means,
your wandering thought in prayer, your lack of faith
in sorrow, your presumptuous self-confidence in joy.
O Christian, you have an enemy within which needs
your constant watchfulness ; you have a fountain
of trials in your own breast ; you will have daily

occasion to crucify the flesh with its affections and
lusts. And add to this those cares which you have
in common with all children of Adam—sickness, disease
and pain, the loss of property, the unkindness of friends,
the daily toil for a livelihood, the fear of want, the
many nameless causes of anxiety which every week
almost brings round, and say whether it be not true
that all God's people come out of great tribulation.
They must deny themselves, they must take up the
cross, they must reckon on many a trial, if they would
enter into the kingdom of heaven.

Mark well, beloved, this truth—the path to glory
has been always filled with thorns ; it is the experience
of all those holy men who have left us an example
that we should walk in their steps : Abraham, and
Jacob, and Moses, and David, and Job, and Daniel, there
was not one of them who was not perfected through
sufferings.

We are all too much disposed to think a time may
come when we shall have a season of repose and not
be harassed with these vexations and disappointments.
Almost every one supposes he is tried more than his
neighbours ; but let us not be deceived—this earth is
not our rest ; it is a place for working, not for sleeping.
Here is the reason that so many run well for a time,
and seem to have the love of Christ in their hearts,
and yet, when persecution or affliction ariseth for the
word's sake, they are offended. They had not counted
the cost ; they had reckoned on the reward without
the labour ; they had forgotten this most important
point in the character of God's saints—" they are men
who have come out of great tribulation."

This seems a hard saying, but I would have you
know these trials are laid on us for the most wise and
merciful purposes. We live in such a fair and pleasant

world, we are so surrounded with so much that is smiling and gay, that if we were not often obliged to taste of sickness and trial or disappointments, we should forget our heavenly home, and pitch our tents over against this Sodom. Therefore it is that God's people pass through great tribulations ; therefore it is they are often called upon to suffer the sting of affliction and anxiety, or weep over the grave of those whom they have loved as their own soul. It is their Father's hand which chastens them ; it is thus He weans their affection from things below and fixes them on Himself ; it is thus He trains them for eternity, and cuts the threads one by one which bind their wavering hearts to earth. No doubt such chastening is grievous for the time, but still it brings many a hidden grace to light, and cuts down many a secret seed of evil ; and we shall see those who have suffered most shining among the brightest stars in the assembly of heaven. The purest gold is that which has been longest in the refiner's furnace. The brightest diamond is often that which has required the most grinding and polishing. But our light affliction endureth but for a moment, and it worketh for us a far more exceeding and eternal weight of glory ; the saints are men who have *come out* of great tribulation, they are never left to perish in it ; the last night of weeping will soon be spent, the last wave of trouble will have rolled over us, and then we shall have a peace which passeth all understanding ; we shall be at home for ever with the Lord.

I repeat, this seems at first sight a hard saying ; and yet it is a true one. Count‚ up the enemies which encompass the children of God,—the world with its unkindnesses or its snares and seductions, the flesh with its unceasing backwardness and indifference to the Lord's service, the devil with his arts and devices,—

and see whether you could give a more correct picture
of the saints' experience than may be found in the
words, "these are they which came out of great tribulation." An unconverted man may not understand
this, and a thoughtless man may not consider it; they
neither know nor care about this spiritual conflict ;
it is foolishness to them ; but they that are born again,
and have learned the value of their own souls, can
set to their seals that it is all true.

II. The second question rising out of the text is
this: "How did these shining ones reach that blessed
place where John saw them ? " Think not it was their
own righteousness which brought salvation, and their
own strength which upheld them : the cross will surely
lead to the crown, but the cross will never deserve
it ; not all the tears which they have shed, not all the
patience they have shown in tribulation, could ever
avail to make atonement for transgression, or wash
away one single sin. What says the apostle ? " They
have washed their robes, and made them white in the
blood of the Lamb." They have not been ashamed
to acknowledge their iniquities, and they have laid
them all before the Lord Jesus Christ, and for His
cross and passion, and for His righteousness' sake they
have sought a free forgiveness, and they have found
it. Lay this to heart, all ye that are wise in your
own eyes and holy in your own sight. No doubt
there were prophets and righteous men of old, men
who had wrought miracles and given their bodies to
be burned, men who had been valiant for the truth
even unto death, in that great multitude which John
beheld ; but none came boasting of his own attainments
and clothed in his own apparel,—they were all washed
and made white in the blood of the Lamb.

And lay this well to heart, all ye that are pressed

down with the burden of your sins, if any such there be, and dare not lift up your eyes to heaven. No doubt there were sinners before God exceedingly in that company, many who had been publicans and harlots, the very filth of the earth and offscouring of all things, and yet they found a place of forgiveness and, behold, they are washed, and white as the driven snow. They were in a world of tribulation like yourselves, but they found time to listen to the report of God's ministers, and when they listened they believed ; they did not think scorn of the goodly land before them ; they did not make light of their Master's invitations, but they loathed themselves for their past transgressions and forgetfulness, and with earnest supplication and prayer sought to the Lamb of God which taketh away the sins of the world, and no sooner did they knock than the door was opened. They were not content with hearing of this fountain for sin and uncleanness, like many of yourselves, and talking of it as a thing to be admired, and very useful for others ; they did not sit beside the pool of Bethesda without endeavouring to step in, but they cried, " Lord, have mercy, wash *me*, even *me* also," and so they were washed they were sanctified, they were justified, in the name of the Lord Jesus and by the Spirit of our God ; they obtained a free pardon, and their iniquities were all taken out of the way. By nature they were as weak and timid and sinful and shortcoming as any among yourselves,—there is not a danger or an obstacle or a doubt or a discouragement in any of your minds with which they were not familiar,—and yet they were all saved by the free grace of God, they were washed and made white in the blood of the Lamb, they were more than conquerors through Him that loved them. Around that throne you would find many who used to be the

vilest of the vile. Go up, and ask them, every one,
" How did you come hither? whence got you that white
robe?" They will answer you, "We were once a
generation without God in the world, without light and
without hope, we cared for nothing but fulfilling the
desires of the flesh and the mind, we were known as
drunkards and revilers and fornicators; many a time
we hardened our hearts against advice; many a careless
neighbour did we follow to the grave, and tempted God
to cut us off by continued impenitence; but at last
our conscience spoke so loudly that we dared no longer
delay; we tried to keep God's law, but we could not
answer it one in a thousand, it brought us to flat
despair; we made a great profession, and men said we
were converted; but it would not do—sin lay upon us
like a mountain, all unatoned for, and we were miserable.
But we heard a voice, saying, ' If any man thirst, let him
come unto Me and drink,'—He that believeth on Me,
though he were dead yet shall he live,' ' Come unto
Me and I will give you rest,' and when we heard it,
we went at once to the Lord Jesus Christ, we waited
for nothing, we laid all our sorrows and all our
wickedness before Him, and, behold, that very day we
were healed and made whole, not having spot or
wrinkle or any such thing." Such is the answer you
would get from many in that company which the
apostle saw.

This is the way you must walk in, if you would ever
stand with them in glory. You must lay aside all
pride and self-dependence, you must use the publican's
prayer, you must believe yourself a miserable unde-
serving sinner, you must lay hold on the cross of Christ
with a simple childlike faith, and pray that you may be
washed in His blood and pardoned for His name's sake.
Show me another way of salvation which will bring

you peace at the last ; I cannot find one in the Bible.
I hear of men who live on many a long year without a
thought about this precious washing in Christ's blood,
this precious garment of Christ's righteousness, and yet
can tell us they trust it will be all right with them at
last ; but I never hear that it is right, and if the Bible
be true it is impossible. I see many who profess a
belief in their need of this fountain for sin and uncleanness, but I fear they do no more than talk about it,
they do not count all things loss until they are
forgiven. But whether men will receive the doctrine
or not, the foundation of God standeth sure, and though
the saints of God do form a multitude which none can
number, I cannot read of one who had not washed his
robes and made them white in the blood of the Lamb.

III. The third and last part of my text is that
which describes the reward of the redeemed : "they
are before the throne of God, and serve Him day and
night in His temple : and He that sitteth on the throne
shall dwell among them. They shall hunger no more,
neither thirst any more, neither shall the sun light on
them, nor any heat. For the Lamb which is in the
midst of the throne shall feed them, and shall lead them
unto living fountains of waters, and God shall wipe
away all tears from their eyes." Here is a list of
privileges ; you have heard of tribulation, but it leads,
you see, to comfort ; you have heard of the cross, but
the end is indeed a crown.

Now we can tell you something of the affliction of
God's children, for we are able to speak that we know ;
but when we have to treat of the glory which shall be
revealed, we are on ground which human eye hath not
seen, and we must be careful not to go beyond what
is written.

The saints "shall serve God day and night." There

shall be no weariness in heaven; there shall be no
earthly labours to distract our attention.   Here, alas !
the cares of the world are continually breaking in,
and these poor frail bodies of ours do often tie us
down to the earth by their weakness, even when the
spirit is willing. We may be on the mount for a short
season sometimes, but our powers are soon exhausted ;
but *there* we shall have no wandering thoughts, no
distractions, no bodily wants, we shall never faint.
How little indeed do we worship God in spirit and
in truth ; at our very best moments, how cold and dull
we feel towards our blessed Redeemer, how willing to
allow any excuse for shortening our prayers and
diminishing our communion with our Father which is
in heaven ; but they that stand before the throne of
God shall feel no fatigue, they will require no repose,
they will count it their highest privilege to be continually singing the song of Moses and the Lamb,
and saying, " Blessing, and honour, and glory, and
power, be unto Him that sitteth on the throne, and
unto the Lamb for ever and ever."

But let us read on. " He that sitteth on the throne
shall dwell among them." They shall no longer walk
by faith, and see through a glass darkly, they shall
see face to face the God in whom they have believed,
and behold His countenance as that of a familiar friend.
They shall have no more dark seasons, they shall
never feel that their beloved Lord is at a distance,
they shall never tremble lest they compel Him to
withdraw Himself by their lack of service, but they
shall see Him as He is, and be for ever at His side.
And if, while groaning in their body of sin, the Christian
finds such peace and comfort in drawing nigh to God
in prayer—if even in the flesh he has tasted that
it is a joyful thing to pour out his heart before the

throne of mercy—oh ! who shall describe his blessedness when he shall find himself for ever in his Redeemer's presence, and shall be told, It is finished, thou shalt no more go out? It is a pleasant thing to have the company of those we love : our very earthly happiness is incomplete while those who have the keys of our affection, the husband, the wife, the brother, the sister, the friends who are as our own souls, are far away ; but there shall be no such incompleteness in heaven ; there we shall have the presence of our glorious Lord before our eyes, who loved us and gave Himself for us, and paid the price of our salvation, even His own blood, and the Scripture shall be fulfilled which saith, " In Thy presence there is fulness of joy, and at Thy right hand there are pleasures for evermore."

But we may not linger here. We read, "They shall hunger no more, neither thirst any more." They shall have no more wants and necessities ; they shall no longer stand in need of daily application for the bread of life, and find their souls starving in the wilderness of this world ; they shall not walk as pilgrims trembling lest their spiritual food should not support them, and thirsting after a fuller draught of the water of life ; but they shall find that prophecy made good, "When I awake up after Thy likeness, I shall be satisfied." But again, " the sun shall not light on them, nor any heat." There shall be no more trial and persecution. There shall not be one reviling tongue nor one ensnaring temptation. The mockers and the flatterers and the scoffers shall be silent for ever, the fiery darts of the wicked will all be quenched ; there will be nothing to mar and disturb the Christian's peace. The time will have come at last when he may rest ; he will be far above the scene of his old conflicts, and the strife shall never be renewed.

But what is the crowning privilege? "The Lamb, which is in the midst of the throne, shall feed them, and shall lead them unto living fountains of water: and God shall wipe away all tears from their eyes." The Lord Jesus Christ Himself shall minister to their comforts; the same kind hand which raised them from the death of sin to the life of righteousness, which healed their spiritual diseases, and brought them health and peace, and made them new creatures upon earth, the same hand shall welcome them in heaven, and conduct them as highly favoured guests to a banquet of happiness, such as eye hath not seen, neither can it enter into the heart of man to conceive. Time was when He sought them out as wandering sheep in the wilderness of this world, and made them members of His little flock by the renewing of the Holy Ghost, and refreshed their weary, heavy laden souls with the water of life. And the same Jesus who began the good work in the days of their tribulation upon earth, the same Good Shepherd shall complete the work in heaven. Here they have tasted something of the streams, a little trembling company, from north and south, east and west, but there they will be gathered round the fountain itself, and there will be one fold and one shepherd, one heart and one mind, and none shall make them afraid. And then there shall be no more weeping, for " God Himself shall wipe away all tears." A dwelling-place in which there shall be no weeping! I know no part of heaven more difficult to imagine. We live in a world of sorrow, a very vale of tears; tears for ourselves and tears for others, tears over our own shortcomings, tears over the unbelief of those we love, tears over disappointed hopes, tears over the graves of those on whom our affections are set, and all because of sin: there would have been no sorrow if Adam had never fallen, but our very weeping is a proof of sin.

Yet it shall not always be so : a day is still to come when sadness shall flee away, and God Himself shall say, Refrain thy voice from weeping, for the former things are passed away. There shall be no sadness in heaven, for there shall be no sin ; the days of our tribulation shall be forgotten ; we shall be able at last to love our God without coldness, to reverence His holiness without torment, to trust Him without despair, to serve Him without weariness, without interruption, without distraction ; the days of weakness and corruption will be past, and we shall be like unto our Lord in holiness as well as happiness, in purity as well as immortality.

And now, beloved, let me ask you what is the purpose for which the Church of God has been established upon earth, and ministers have been appointed to watch for your souls ? What is the object of Bibles and Sacraments, and prayer and preaching? Is it not simply this, that you may be numbered with the saints in glory everlasting, that you may enjoy those blessings you have heard described ?

Then search and see what solemn questions spring out of my text. Have you taken up the cross ? are you denying yourself? do you know anything of this spiritual tribulation ? Be very sure except you will declare yourself decidedly on the Lord's side, and fight His battle with the fashion of the world, and the lusts of the flesh, and the wiles of the devil ; you will never stand before the throne in robes of white and carry the palm of victory in your hand.

That carelessness about sin, that trifling with temptation, that earnestness about the things of time, that forgetfulness about eternity, that readiness to swim with the tide about religion, that unwillingness to become more serious than your neighbours, that fear of being thought righteous overmuch, that love of the world's good opinion,—is this what you call coming out of great tribulation? Is this sowing to the Spirit? Is this striving and labouring after eternal life? Oh, look to your foundations, set your house in order. No empty trust in God's mercy will ever save you. You were not baptised unto idleness and indifference. Without a real hatred of sin, and a real forsaking of sin, Christ can profit you nothing. You never can be made white with the blood of the Lamb, except you desire to have this earth's defilements really washed away.

And then consider, lastly, O unhappy children of this world, could you be happy in the heaven you have heard described? Know ye not all, that sickness and death do seldom work a change of heart, they seldom plant in man new taste and new desires?—and do you think that men who count it a great matter to come to church, and find the services a weariness and rejoice when they are over, will such be ready to serve God day and night in His temple? Will those who take no pleasure in drawing nigh to Jesus in prayer, delight to be for ever in His presence and dwell with Him? Are you who never hunger and thirst after righteousness, are you to be satisfied with the living fountains of water? Are you who never know what it is to weep over sin and corruption, who never grieve over the wickedness of this world, are you likely to understand the privilege of that rest when God shall wipe away all tears? Oh, no, it cannot be, it cannot be! Whatever a man sows he shall also reap; whatever we love in time we shall love in eternity; whatever we think wearisome now we shall think wearisome then. Ye must be born again, or heaven itself would be a miserable abode; there is no place there for the worldly-minded and profane. Ye must be renewed in the spirit of your minds, or ye will hear that dreadful voice, Friend, how camest thou in hither without a wedding-garment? Ye must become new creatures; and how long will you insult your Redeemer by putting it off? Oh! pray ye to the Lord Jesus Christ, while it is called to-day, to send His Holy Spirit on you; go to the fountain while the door of mercy is yet open, wash and be clean.

But blessed are all ye that mourn, for ye shall be comforted; blessed are ye that are persecuted for righteousness' sake, for great is your reward in heaven. Ye have wept with them that weep, but ye shall soon rejoice with them that rejoice, and your joy shall no man take away. It is but a single step, and you shall be for ever with the Lord, where the wicked cease from troubling, and the weary are at rest. The worm may destroy these bodies, and yet in the flesh ye shall see God, and your own eyes shall behold Him, and your own ears shall hear Him say, "Come, ye blessed of my Father, inherit the kingdom prepared for you from the foundation of the world." The saints whose faith and patience you have so often admired; the holy men and women of whom you have so often said, "Oh, that I were like them"; the ministers who have shown you the way of life, and implored you to be steadfast and unmoveable; the friends who advised you to come out of the world, and took sweet counsel with you about the kingdom of God; the beloved ones of your own house, who slept in Jesus and went home before you: all are there, all waiting to receive you, and there shall be no more parting, no more weeping, no more separation; and you, even you, this vile body being changed, shall sing the song of the redeemed: "Unto Him that loved us, and washed us from our sins in His own blood, and hath made us kings and priests unto God and His Father, to Him be glory and dominion for ever and ever."

In this world ye may have tribulation, but be of good cheer : your Lord and Saviour hath overcome the world.

XXIII

HEAVEN

"There shall in no wise enter into it any thing that defileth, neither whatsoever worketh abomination, or maketh a lie : but they which are written in the Lamb's book of life."—REV. xxi. 27.

BRETHREN, there can be no question about the place described in our text : it is heaven itself, that holy city, the new Jerusalem, which is yet to be revealed.

I would fain begin this my last Sunday among you by speaking of heaven. Before I depart and leave you in the wilderness of this world, I would dwell a little on that Canaan God has promised to them that love Him ; *there* it is the last and best wish of my heart you may all go ; *there* it is my consolation to believe I shall at all events meet some of you again.

Brethren, you all hope to go to heaven yourselves. There is not one of you but wishes to be in happiness after death. But on what are your hopes founded ? Heaven is a prepared place ; they that shall dwell there are all of one character, the entrance into it is only by one door. Brethren, remember that. And then, too, I read of two sorts of hope : a good hope and a bad hope ; a true hope and a false hope ; a lively hope and a dead hope ; the hope of the righteous and the hope of the wicked, of the believer and of the hypocrite. I read of some who have hope through grace, a hope that maketh not ashamed, and of

273

others who have no hope and are without God in the
world. Brethren, remember that. Surely it were wise
and prudent and safe to find out what the Bible tells
you on the subject, to discover whether your confidence
is indeed well founded ; and to this end I call your
attention to the doctrine of my text. There you will
find three things :

I. There is mention of the place itself.

II. We are told the character of those who will
certainly not be there ; and

III. Who alone will.

The Lord grant you may consider well your own fitness
for heaven. There must be a certain meetness for that
blessed place in our minds and characters. It is sense-
less, vain, and absurd to suppose that all shall go there,
whatever their lives have been. May God the Holy
Ghost incline you to examine yourselves faithfully while
you have time, before that great day cometh when the
unconverted shall be past all hope and the saints past
all fear.

I. First of the place itself. There is such a place
as heaven. No truth is more certain in the whole of
Scripture than this, there remaineth a rest for the people
of God. This earth is not our rest ; it cannot be ; there
breathes not man or woman who ever found it so. Go,
build your happiness on earth, if you are so disposed ;
choose everything you can fancy would make life enjoyable,—take money, house, and lands ; take learning,
health, and beauty ; take honour, rank, obedience, troops
of friends ; take everything your mind can picture to
itself or your eye desire,—take all, and yet I dare to
tell you even then you would not find rest. I know
well that a few short years, and your heart's confession
would be, it is all hollow, empty, and unsatisfying ; it
is all weariness and disappointment ; it is all vanity

and vexation of spirit. I know well you would feel
within a hungering and famine, a leanness and barren-
ness of soul ; and ready indeed would you be to bear
your testimony to the mighty truth, " This earth is
not our rest."

O brethren, how faithful is that saying, " If in this
life only we have hope, we are indeed most miserable."
This life, so full of trouble and sorrow and care, of
anxiety and labour and toil ; this life of losses and
bereavements, of partings and separations, of mourning
and woe, of sickness and pain ; this life of which even
Elijah got so tired that he requested he might die ;
truly I should be crushed to the very earth with misery,
if I felt this life were all.   If I thought there was
nothing for me beyond the dark, cold, silent, lonely
grave, I should indeed say, Better never have been
born. Thanks be to God this life is not all. I know
and am persuaded there is a glorious rest beyond the
tomb ; this earth is only the training-school for eternity,
these graves are but the stepping-stone and half-way
house to heaven. I feel assured this my poor body
shall rise again ; this corruptible shall yet put on in-
corruption, and this mortal immortality, and be with
Christ for ever. Yes, heaven is truth and no lie. I
will not doubt it. I am not more certain of my own
existence than I am of this, there does remain a rest
for the people of God.

And, brethren, what sort of a place shall heaven be ?
Before we pass on and consider its inhabitants, let us
just pause an instant and think on this. What sort of
a place shall heaven be ?   Heaven shall be a place
of perfect rest and peace. They that dwell *there* have
no more conflict with the world, the flesh, and the
devil ; their warfare is accomplished, and their fight is
fought ; at length they may lay aside the armour of

God, at last they may say to the sword of the Spirit,
Rest and be still. They watch no longer, for they have
no spiritual enemies to fear ; they fast and mortify the
flesh no longer, for they have no vile earthy body to
keep under ; they pray no more, for they have no evil
to pray against. *There* the wicked must cease from
troubling ; *there* sin and temptation are for ever shut
out; the gates are better barred than those of Eden,
and the devil shall enter in no more. O Christian
brethren, rouse ye and take comfort; surely this shall
be indeed a blessed rest. *There* shall be no need of
means of grace, for we shall have the end to which
they are meant to lead ; *there* shall be no need of
sacraments, we shall have the substance they are
appointed to keep in mind ; *there* faith shall be
swallowed up in sight, and hope in certainty, and
prayer in praise, and sorrow in joy. Now is the
school-time, the season of the lesson and the rod, then
will be the eternal holiday. Now we must endure
hardness and press on faint yet pursuing, then we
shall sit down at ease, for the Canaanite shall be
expelled for ever from the land. Now we are tossed
upon a stormy sea, then we shall be safe in harbour.
Now we have to plough and sow, there we shall reap
the harvest ; now we have the labour, but then the
wages ; now we have the battle, but then the victory
and reward. Now we must needs bear the cross, but
then we shall receive the crown. Now we are journeying through the wilderness, but then we shall be at
home. O Christian brethren, well may the Bible
tell you, "Blessed are the dead that die in the Lord,
for they rest from their labour." Surely you must feel
that witness is true.

But again. Heaven shall be a place of perfect and
unbroken happiness. Mark what your Bible tells you

in the very chapter which contains my text, "God
shall wipe away all tears from the eyes of His people ;
and there shall be no more death, neither sorrow, nor
crying, neither shall there be any more pain : for the
former things are passed away." Hear what the prophet
Isaiah says in the twenty-fifth chapter : " The Lord God
will wipe away tears from off all faces ; and the rebuke
of His people shall He take away from off all the
earth.   And it shall be said in that day, Lo, this is
our God ; we have waited for Him and He will save
us : this is the Lord ; we have waited for Him, we will
be glad and rejoice in His salvation." Brethren, think
of an eternal habitation in which there is no sorrow.
Who is there here below that is not acquainted with
sorrow ? it came in with thorns and thistles at Adam's
fall, it is the bitter cup that all must drink, it is before
us and behind us, it is on the right hand and the left,
it is mingled with the very air we breathe.   Our bodies
are racked with pain, and we have sorrow ; our worldly
goods are taken from us, and we have sorrow ; we are
encompassed with difficulties and troubles, and we
have sorrow ; our friends forsake us and look coldly
on us, and we have sorrow ; we are separated from
those we love, and we have sorrow ; those on whom
our hearts' affections are set go down to the grave and
leave us alone, and we have sorrow.   And then, too,
we find our own hearts frail and full of corruption, and
that brings sorrow ; We are persecuted and opposed
for the Gospel's sake, and that brings sorrow ; we see
those who are near and dear to us refusing to walk
with God, and that brings sorrow.   Oh, what a
sorrowing, grieving world we live in !

Blessed be God ! there shall be no sorrow in heaven.
There shall not be one single tear shed within the
courts above.   There shall be no more disease and

weakness and decay ; the coffin, and the funeral, and
the grave, and the dark-black mourning shall be things
unknown. Our faces shall no more be pale and sad ;
no more shall we go out from the company of those
we love and be parted asunder—that word, farewell, shall
never be heard again. There shall be no anxious
thought about to-morrow to mar and spoil our enjoyment, no sharp and cutting words to wound our souls ;
our wants will have come to a perpetual end, and all
around us shall be harmony and love. O Christian
brethren, what is our light affliction when compared
to such an eternity as this ? shame on us if we murmur
and complain and turn back, with such a heaven before
our eyes ! What can this vain and passing world give
us better than this? this is the city of our God Himself,
when He will dwell among us Himself. The glory of
God shall lighten it, and the Lamb is the light thereof.
Truly we may say, as Mephibosheth did to David,
" Let the world take all, forasmuch as our Lord will
come in peace." Such is the Bible heaven, there is none
other ; these sayings are faithful and true, not any of
them shall fail. Surely, brethren it is worth a little
pain, a little labouring, a little toil, if only we may have
the lowest place in the kingdom of God.

II. Let us now pass on and see that great thing
which is revealed in the second part of our text. You
have heard of heaven ; but all shall not enter it: and
who are the persons who shall not enter in ?

Brethren, this is a sad and painful inquiry, and yet
it is one that must be made. I can do no more than
declare to you Scripture truth : it is not my fault
if it is cutting and gives offence. I must deliver my
Master's message and diminish nothing ; the line I have
to draw is not mine, but God's : the blame, if you will
lay it, falls on the Bible not on me. " There shall in

no wise enter into heaven any thing that defileth, neither
whatsoever worketh abomination, or maketh a lie."
Verily these are solemn words; they ought to make you
think.

" Nothing that defileth." This touches the case of
all who are defiled with sins of heart, and yet feel it not,
and refuse to be made clean. These may be decent
persons outwardly, but they are vile and polluted within.
These are the worldly-minded. They live to this
world only, and they have no thought of anything
beyond it. The care of this world, the money, the
politics of this world, the business of this world, the
pleasures of this world, these things swallow up their
whole attention and as for St. James' advice to keep
ourselves unspotted from the world, they know not
what it means.

These are the men who set their affections on earthly
things ; they have each their idol in the chamber of their
imagination, and they worship and serve it more than
God. These are the proud and self-righteous, the self-
honouring and the self-conceited ; they love the praise
of men, they like the good opinion of this world, and
as for the glorious Lord who made them, His honour,
His glory, His house, His word, His service—these
are all things which in their judgment must go
down, and take the second place. These know not what
sorrow for sin means. They are strangers to spiritual
anxiety ; they are self-satisfied and content with their
condition, and if you attempt to stir them up to zeal
and repentance it is more than probable they are
offended. Brethren, you know well there are such
people ; they are not uncommon ; they may be honourable in the eyes of men, they may be wise and knowing
in this generation, admirable men of business, they
may be first and foremost in their respective callings,

but still there is but one account of them ; they bring
no glory to their Maker, they are lovers of themselves
more than of God, and therefore they are counted as
defiled in His sight and nothing that is defiled shall
enter heaven.

But again : "Nothing that worketh abomination."
This touches the case of all who practise those sins of
life which God has pronounced abominable, and take
pleasure in them, and countenance those who practise
them. These are the men who work the works of the
flesh, each as his heart inclines him. These are the
adulterers, fornicators, and unclean livers ; these are
the drunkards, revellers, and gluttons ; these are the
blasphemers, swearers, and liars. These are the men
who count it no shame to live in hatred, variance,
wrath, strife, envyings, quarrellings and the like. They
throw the reins on the neck of their lusts ; they follow
their passions wherever they may lead them ; their
only object is to please themselves.

Brethren, you know well there are such people. The
world may give smooth names to their conduct, the world
may talk of them as light and gay, and loose and wild,
but it will not do. They are all abominable in the
sight of God, and except they be converted and born
again, they shall in no wise enter heaven.

Once more : "Nothing that maketh a lie." This
touches the case of hypocrites. These are the false
professors ; the lip-servants ; they say that they know
God, but in works they deny Him ; they are like barren
fig-trees, all leaves and no fruit ; they are like tinkling
cymbals, all sound, but hollow, empty and without
substance ; these have a name to live while they are
dead, and a form of godliness without the power.
They profess what they do not practise, they speak
what they do not think, they say much and do little,

their words are most amazing, their actions are most
poor. These men can talk most bravely of themselves;
no better Christians than they are, if you will take
them at their own valuation. They can talk to you of
grace, and yet they show none of it in their lives; they
can talk to you of saving faith, and yet they possess
not that charity which is faith's companion. They can
declaim against forms most strongly, and yet their own
Christianity is a form and no more; they can cry out
loudly against Pharisees, and yet no greater Pharisees
than they are themselves.

Oh, no; this religion is of a sort that is public, and
not private; plenty abroad, but none at home; plenty
without, but none within; plenty in the tongue, but none
in the heart. They are altogether unprofitable, good
for nothing, they bear no fruit.

Brethren, you must know well there are such miserable persons; alas! the world is full of them in these
latter days. They may deceive ministers, they may
deceive their neighbours, they may even deceive their
friends and family, they may try hard to deceive
themselves; but they are no better than liars in God's
sight, and except they repent, they shall in no wise
enter heaven.

Brethren, consider well these things: " the sin-defiled,
the abominable, the hypocrite, shall in no wise enter
into heaven." Look well to your own souls; judge
yourselves that ye be not judged of the Lord; I call
heaven and earth to witness this day, they that will
live these bad lives, whether they be Churchmen or
dissenters, old or young, rich or poor, *they shall* in no
wise enter in. Go, cleave to the ways of the world if
you are so determined, stick to your sins if you must
needs keep them, but I warn you solemnly this hour,
they that will have these things shall in no wise enter

in. Go, blame me now for speaking sharply to you—
think I am too particular if you like it—but, oh!
remember if you ever stand without the gates, crying,
" Lord, open to us," in vain, remember there was a time
when I told you, the worldly-minded and the evil livers
shall in no wise enter in. Brethren, I have told you
before, and I tell you now again for the last time, if
you will cling to the things that God hates, you shall
in no wise enter into heaven.

III. Brethren, we must pass on. The text has told
you who shall not enter heaven. Oh! what a mighty
crowd those words shut out! But it tells you something
more: who are they that shall. Short is the account and
simple: " They only that are written in the Lamb's
book of life." What is this book of life? There is a
book, a little book, a book prepared from all eternity,
which God the Father keeps sealed—the book of His
election ; of that book man knows nothing, excepting
this blessed truth that there is such a book. With that
book man has little or nothing to do. But there is
another book, a little book, a book belonging specially
to the Lord Jesus Christ, a book still unfinished, though
year after year there are more names written in it; a
book still open, still ready to receive the names of
believing penitents : there are still some blank pages left
for you ; and this is the Lamb's book of life. And who
are written in this precious book ? I do not know their
names, but I do know their characters, and what those
characters are I will endeavour to tell you shortly, for

the last time.

They are all true penitents. They have been convinced of their own unworthiness in God's sight ; they
have felt themselves to be sinners in deed and in truth ;
they have mourned over their sins, hated their sins,
forsaken their sins ; the remembrance of them is grievous,

the burden of them intolerable ; they have ceased to
think well of their own condition and count themselves
fit to be saved ; they have confessed with their whole
heart : " Lord, we are really chief of sinners—Lord, we
are indeed unclean."

Again : they are all believers in Christ Jesus. They
have found out the excellency of the work He did to
save them, and cast on Him the burden of their souls.
They have taken Christ for their all in all : their wisdom,
their righteousness, their justification, their forgiveness,
their redemption. Other payment of their spiritual debts
they have seen none ; other deliverances from the devil
they have not been able to find. But they have believed
on Christ, and come to Christ for salvation ; they are
confident that what they cannot do Christ can do for
them, and having Jesus Christ to lean on, they feel
perfect peace.

Once more : they are all born of the Spirit and
sanctified. They have all put off the old man with his
deeds, and put on the new man which is after God.
They have all been renewed in the spirit of their minds ;
a new heart and a new nature has been given to them.
They have brought forth those fruits which only are the
proof of the Spirit being in them. They may have
slipped and come short in many things ; they may have
mourned over their own deficiencies full often ; but still,
the general bent and bias of their lives has always been
towards holiness,—more holiness, more holiness, has
always been their hearts' desire. They love God, and
they must live to Him. Such is the character of them
that are written in heaven. These, then, are the men
whose names are to be found in the Lamb's book of life.

Once they may have been as bad as the very worst—
defiled, abominable, liars : what matter ? they have repented and believed, and now they are written in the

book of life. They may have been despised and rejected
of this world, poor and mean and lowly in the judgment
of their neighbours : what matter ? they had repentance
and faith and new hearts, and now they are written
in the glorious book of life. They may have been of
different ranks and nations ; they may have lived at
different ages, and never seen each other's faces : what
matter ? they have one thing at least in common, they
have repented and believed, and been born again, and
therefore they stand all together in the Lamb's book
of life.

Yes, brethren, these are the men and women that
enter heaven ; nothing can keep them out. Tell me
not of deathbed evidences, and visions and dreams of
dying people ; there is no evidence like that of Christ's
followers—repentance, faith, and holiness ; this is a
character against which the gates shall never be closed.
Repent and believe in Christ and be converted, and
then, whatever happens to others, you, at least, shall
enter heaven ; you shall in no wise be cast out.

And now, men and brethren, in conclusion, let me
press upon you my old question. How is it with yourselves ? What, no answer ! Are you ready to depart ?
Again, no answer ! Is your name written in the book
of life ? Once more, have you no answer ?

Oh, think, think, unhappy man or woman, whoever
thou art, think what a miserable thing it is to be
uncertain about eternity. And then consider, if thou
canst not give thy heart to God now, how is it possible
thou couldest enjoy God's heaven hereafter. Heaven
is unceasing godliness ; it is to be in the presence of
God and His Christ for evermore. God is the light,
the food, the air of heaven. It is an eternal sabbath.
To serve God is heaven's employment, to talk with
God is heaven's occupation.

O sinners, sinners, could ye be happy there? to which of all the saints would ye join yourselves, by whose side would ye go and sit down, with whom of all the prophets and apostles would ye love to converse? Surely it would be a wearisome thing to you ; surely you would soon want to go forth and join your friends outside. Oh, turn ye, turn ye while it is called to-day! God will not alter heaven merely to please you ; better a thousand times to conform to His ways while ye can. Ye must love the things of heaven before your death, or else ye cannot enter heaven when ye die.

Christian, look up and take comfort. Jesus has prepared a place for you, and they that follow Him shall never perish, neither shall any man pluck them out of His hands. Look forward to that glorious abode He has provided ; look forward in faith, for it is thine. O Christian brethren, think what a glorious meeting that shall be. There we shall see the saints of old, of whom we have so often read ; there we shall see those holy ministers whose faith and patience we have admired ; there we shall see one another round the throne of our common Saviour, and be parted and separated no more. There we shall labour and toil no more, for the days of mourning shall be ended. Oh, but my heart will leap within me, if I see there faces I have known among you ; if I hear the names of any of yourselves! The Lord grant it, the Lord bring it to pass. The Lord grant we may some of us, at least, come together in that day, when there shall be one fold and one Shepherd, and with one heart and voice join that glorious song, "Worthy is the Lamb that was slain ; blessing and honour and glory and power be unto the Lamb for ever and ever."

XXIV

"READY TO BE OFFERED"

" For I am now ready to be offered, and the time of my departure is at hand.   I have fought a good fight, I have finished my course, I have kept the faith : henceforth there is laid up for me a crown of righteousness, which the Lord, the righteous judge, shall give me at that day : and not to me only, but unto all them also that love His appearing."— 2 TIM. iv. 6-8.

IN these words you see the apostle Paul looking three ways,—*downwards, backwards, forward;* downwards to the grave, backwards to his own ministry, forward to that great day, the day of judgment.   Let us stand by his side a few minutes, and mark the words he uses.   Happy is that soul among us who can look where Paul looked, and then speak as Paul spoke.   He looks downwards to the grave, and he does it *without fear.*   Hear what he says.

" I am ready to be offered."   I am like an animal brought to the place of sacrifice, and bound with cords to the horns of the altar.   The wine and oil have been poured on my head.   The last ceremonies have been gone through.   Every preparation has been made.   It only remains to receive the death-blow, and then all is over.

" The time of my departure is at hand."   I am like a ship about to unmoor and put to sea.   All on board is ready.   I only wait to have the moorings cast off that fasten me to the shore, and I shall begin my voyage.

Brethren, these are glorious words to come from the lips of a child of Adam like ourselves. Death is a solemn thing, and never so much so as when we draw near to it ourselves. The grave is a chilling, heart-sickening idea, and it is vain to pretend it is not ; yet here is a mortal man, who can look calmly into the narrow house appointed for all living, and say, while he stands upon the brink, " I see it all, and am not afraid."

Let us listen to him again. He looks *backwards*, to his ministerial life, and he does it without shame. Hear what he says.

" I have fought a good fight." There he speaks as a soldier. I have fought that good battle with the world, the flesh, and the devil, from which so many shrink and draw back.

" I have finished my course." There he speaks as one who has run for a prize. I have run the race marked out for me. I have gone over the ground staked out for me, however rough and steep. I have not turned aside because of difficulties, and have at length reached the goal.

" I have kept the faith." There he speaks as a steward. I have held fast that glorious gospel which was committed to my trust. I have not mingled it with man's traditions, nor spoiled its simplicity by adding my own notions, nor allowed others to adulterate it without withstanding them to the face. As a soldier, a runner, a steward, he seems to say, I am not ashamed.

Brethren, that Christian is happy who, as he quits this world, can leave such testimony behind him. A good conscience will save no man, wash away no sin, lift us not one inch towards heaven. Yet a good conscience will be found a pleasant visitor at our bedsides in a dying hour. Do you remember that place in Pilgrim's

Progress, which describes old Honest's passage over the river of death? "The river," says Bunyan, "at that time overflowed its banks in some places; but Mr. Honest in his lifetime had spoken to one, Good Conscience, to meet him there, the which he also did, and lent him his hand, and so helped him over." Believe me, there is a mine of truth in that passage.

Let us hear the apostle once more. He looks forward to the great day of reckoning, and he does it without doubt. Mark his words: "Henceforth there is laid up for me a crown of righteousness, which the Lord, the righteous judge, shall give me at that day: and not to me only, but unto all them also that love His appearing." A glorious reward, he seems to say, is ready and laid up in store for me, even that crown which is only given to the righteous. In the great day of judgment the Lord shall give this crown to me, and to all besides me who have loved Him as an unseen Saviour, and longed to see Him face to face. My work is over. This one thing now remains for me to look forward to, and nothing more.

You see, brethren, he speaks without any hesitation or distrust. He regards the crown as a sure thing, as his own already. He declares his belief that the righteous Judge will give it to him, with an unfaltering confidence. Paul was no stranger to all the circumstances and accompaniments of that great day to which he referred. The great white throne, the assembled world, the opened books, the revealing of all secrets, the listening angels, the awful sentence, the eternal separation, all these were things with which he was well acquainted. But none of these things moved him. His faith overleaped them all, and only saw Christ, his all-prevailing Advocate, and the blood of sprinkling, and sin washed away. "A crown," says he, "IS laid

up for me. The Lord Himself SHALL give it me."
He speaks as if he saw it all with his own eyes.

Such are the main things which these verses contain.
Of most of them I cannot pretend to speak. I shall
therefore only try to set before you one point in the
passage, and that is the "*assured hope*" with which
the apostle looks forward to his own prospects in the
day of judgment. I shall do this the more readily
because of the great importance which, I feel, attaches
to the subject, and the great neglect with which, I
humbly conceive, it is often treated in this day. But
I shall do it at the same time with fear and trembling.
I feel that I am treading on very delicate ground,
and that it is easy to speak rashly and unscripturally
in this matter. The road between truth and error
is here especially a narrow pass, and if I shall be
enabled to do good to some, without doing harm to
others, I shall be very thankful.

Now, there are just four things which I wish to bring
before you, and it may perhaps clear our way if I name
them to you at once:

I. First, then, I will try to show you that an assured
hope, such as Paul here expresses, is a true and
Scriptural thing.

II. Secondly, I will make this broad concession, that
a man may never arrive at this assured hope, and yet
be saved.

III. Thirdly, I will give you some reasons why an
assured hope is exceedingly to be desired.

IV. Lastly, I will try to point out some causes why
an assured hope is so seldom attained.

I. First, then, I said, an assured hope is a true and
Scriptural thing.

Assurance, such as Paul here expresses, is not a
mere fancy or feeling. It is not the result of high

animal spirits or a lively temperament of body. It is
a positive gift of the Holy Ghost, bestowed without
reference to men's bodily frames or constitutions, and
a gift which every believer in Christ should aim at and
seek after.

The word of God appears to me to teach, that a
believer may arrive at an assured confidence with regard
to his own salvation.

I lay it down deliberately that a true Christian or
converted man may reach that comfortable degree of
faith, that in general he shall feel confident as to the
safety and forgiveness of his own soul, shall seldom
be troubled with doubts, seldom be distracted with
hesitations, seldom be distressed with anxious questionings, seldom be alarmed about his own state ; he may
have many an inward conflict with sin, but he shall
look forward to death, like Paul, without trembling, and
to judgment without dismay.

Such is my account of assurance. Mark it well. I
say neither less nor more.

Now such a statement as this is often disputed and
denied. Many cannot see it at all.

The Church of Rome denounces assurance in the
most unmeasured tones. The Council of Trent declares
roundly that " a believer's assurance of the pardon of
his sin is a vain and ungodly confidence " ; and Cardinal
Bellarmine, their well-known champion, calls it a " prime
error of heretics."

The great majority of the worldly among ourselves
oppose the doctrine of assurance. It offends and
annoys them. They do not like others to feel comfortable and sure, because they never feel so themselves.
That *they* cannot receive it is certainly no marvel.

But there are also some true believers who reject
assurance. They shrink from it as a notion fraught

with danger. They consider it borders on presumption. They seem to think it a proper humility to live in a certain degree of doubt. This is to be regretted, and does much harm.

I frankly allow there are some presumptuous fools who profess to feel !a confidence for which they have no Scripture warrant. There always are some who think well of themselves when God thinks ill, just as there are some who think ill of their own case when God thinks well. There always will be such. There never yet was a Scriptural truth without abuses, impositions and counterfeits. Weeds will grow as well as wheat in rich ground. There will be fanatics as long as the world stands. But for all this, an assured hope is a real and true thing. My answer to all who deny the existence of real well-grounded assurance is simply this, " Look at Scripture." If assurance be not there I have not another word to say.

But does not Job say, " I KNOW that my Redeemer liveth, and that He shall stand at the latter day upon the earth : and though after my skin worms destroy this body, yet in my flesh shall I see God " (Job xix. 25, 26)?

Does not David say, " Though I walk through the valley of the shadow of death, I will fear no evil : for Thou art with me ; Thy rod and Thy staff they comfort me " (Psalm xxiii. 4)?

Does not Isaiah say, " Thou wilt keep him in perfect peace whose mind is stayed on Thee, because he trusteth in Thee " (Isaiah xxvi. 3)? and again, " The work of righteousness shall be peace ; and the effect of righteousness quietness and assurance for ever " (xxxii. 17)?

Does not Paul say to the Romans, " The Spirit beareth witness with our spirit, that we are the children of God " (Romans viii. 16)? and to the Corinthians, " We *know* that if our earthly house of this tabernacle were dissolved we have a building of God " (2 Cor. v. 1)? and to Timothy, " I know whom I have believed, and am persuaded that He is able to keep that which I have committed to Him" (2 Tim. i. 12)? And does He not speak to the Colossians of the " full assurance of understanding " (Col. ii. 2), and to the Hebrews of the " full assurance of faith and of hope " (Heb. vi. 11, x. 22)?

Does not Peter expressly say, " Give diligence to make your calling and election sure " (2 Peter i. 10)?

Does not John say, " We *know* that we have passed from death unto life " (1 John iii. 14)? and " These things have I written unto you that believe on the name of the Son of God : that ye may *know* that ye *have* eternal life" (1 John v. 13), " We know that we are of God, and the whole world lieth in wickedness " (1 John v. 19)?

Brethren, I desire to speak with all humility on every controverted point. I feel that I am only a poor fallible child of Adam myself. But I must say that in the passages I have quoted I see something far higher than the mere " hopes," and " trusts," where so many appear content to stop. I see the language of persuasion, confidence, knowledge, nay, I might almost say of certainty—and I feel for my own part, if I may take the Scriptures in their plain obvious meaning, assurance is true.

But my answer furthermore to all who dislike the doctrine of assurance, as bordering on presumption, is this. It cannot be presumption to tread in the steps of Peter and Paul, of John and of Job. They were all eminently humble and lowly-minded men, if ever any were, and yet they all speak of their own state with an assured hope. Surely this should teach us that deep humility and strong assurance are by no means incompatible, and for this simple reason, if for no other, the charge of presumption falls to the ground.

My answer furthermore is, that many have attained to such an assured hope as our text expresses, even in modern days. Many have appeared to walk in almost uninterrupted fellowship with the Father and the Son, have seemed to enjoy an almost unceasing sense of the light of God's reconciled countenance shining down upon them, and have left on record their experience. I could mention well-known names in proof of this, if time permitted. The thing has been, and is, and that is enough.

My answer lastly is, it cannot be wrong to *feel* confident in a matter where God speaks unconditionally, to believe decidedly when God speaks decidedly, to have a sure persuasion of pardon and peace when one rests on the word and oath of Him that never changes. It is an utter mistake to suppose that the believer who feels assurance is resting on anything he sees in himself. He simply leans on the Scriptures of truth, and on the Mediator of the new covenant. He believes the Lord Jesus means what He says, and takes Him at His word. Assurance is, after all, no more than a full-grown faith ; a masculine faith that grasps Christ's promise with both hands ; a faith that argues like the good centurion, If the Lord speak the word only, I am healed.

Depend on it, Paul was the last man in the world to build his assured hope on anything of his own. He, who wrote himself down chief of sinners, had a deep sense of his own guilt and corruption, but then he had a still deeper sense of the length and breadth of Christ's righteousness. He had a clear view of the fountain of evil within him, but then he had a still clearer view of that other fountain which removes all uncleanness. He had a lively feeling of his own weakness, but he had a still livelier feeling that Christ's promise, "They shall never perish," would never be broken. He knew, if ever man did, that he was a poor frail bark traversing a stormy ocean. He saw, if any did, the rolling waves and roaring tempest by which he was surrounded ; but then he looked away from self to Jesus, and so had hope. He remembered that anchor within the veil, sure and steadfast. He remembered the word and work and intercession of Him that loved him and gave Himself for him. And this it was that enabled him to say so boldly, "A crown is laid up for me ; the Lord shall give it to me ; the Lord will preserve me ; I shall never be confounded."

II. I pass on to the second thing I spoke of. I said a believer may never arrive at this assured hope, which Paul expresses, and yet be saved.

I grant this most fully. I do not dispute it for a moment. I would not desire to make one contrite heart sad that God has not made sad, or to discourage one fainting child of God, or to leave the impression that you have no part or lot in Christ except you feel assurance. To have saving faith is one thing : to have an assured hope like the apostle Paul's is quite another. I think this ought never to be forgotten.

I know some great and good men have held a different view. I believe that excellent man, Henry, of Weston Favel, the author of *Theron and Aspasia*, was one who did not allow the distinction I have stated. But I desire to call no man master. For my own part, I should think any other view than that I have given, a most uncomfortable gospel to preach, and one very likely to keep men back a long time from the gate of life.

I shrink not from saying, that by grace a man may have sufficient faith to flee to Christ, really to lay hold on Him, really to trust in Him, really to be a child of God, really to be saved ; and yet never, to his last day, be free from much anxiety, doubt, and fear.

"A letter," says old Watson, "may be written, which is not sealed ; so grace may be written in the heart, yet the Spirit may not set the seal of assurance to it."

A child may be born heir to a great fortune, and yet never be aware of his riches,—live childish, die childish, and never know the fulness of his possession. And so also a man may be a babe in Christ's family, think as a babe, speak as a babe, and though saved never enjoy a lively hope, never know the real privilege of his inheritance.

Do not therefore, my brethren, mistake my meaning. Do not do me the injustice to say I told you none were saved except such as could say, like Paul, "I know and I am persuaded, there is a crown laid up for me."

I do not say so. I tell you nothing of the kind. Faith in Christ a man must have. This is the one door. Without faith no man can be saved—that is certain. A man *must* feel his sins and lost estate, *must* come to Christ for salvation, *must* rest his hope on this alone. But if he have only faith to do this, however weak that faith may be, I will engage he will not miss heaven. Yes! though his faith be no bigger than a grain of mustard-seed, if it only bring him to Christ and enable him to touch the hem of His garment, he shall be saved, saved as surely as the oldest saint in Paradise, saved as completely and eternally as Peter or John or Paul. There are degrees in our sanctification. In justification there are none.

But all this time, I would have you take notice, the poor soul may have no assurance of his acceptance with

God. He may have fear upon fear, and doubt upon doubt, many a question and many an anxiety, many a struggle and many a misgiving, clouds and darkness, storm and tempest to the very end.

I will engage, I repeat, that bare, simple faith in Christ shall save a man, though he never attain to assurance ; but I will not engage it shall bring him to heaven with strong and abounding consolations. I will engage it shall land him safe in harbour, but I will not engage he does not reach the shore weather-beaten and tempest-tossed, scarce knowing himself that he is safe.

Brethren, I believe it is of great importance to keep in view this distinction between faith and assurance. It explains things which an inquirer in religion sometimes finds it hard to understand. Faith, let us remember, is the root, and assurance is the flower. Doubtless you can never have the flower without the root ; but it is no less certain you may have the root and never have the flower. Faith is that poor trembling woman, who came behind Jesus in the press, and touched the hem of His garment ; assurance is Stephen standing calmly in the midst of his murderers, and saying, " I see the heavens opened, and the Son of man standing on the right hand of God." Faith is the penitent thief crying, " Lord, remember me " ; assurance is Job, sitting in the dust, covered with sores, and saying, " I know that my Redeemer liveth." Faith is Peter's drowning cry, as he began to sink, " Lord, save me " ; assurance is that same Peter declaring before the council in after time, " There is none other name given under heaven whereby we can be saved ; we cannot but speak the things we have seen and heard." Faith is the still small voice, " Lord, I believe, help Thou mine un-belief " ; assurance is the confident challenge, " Who shall lay anything to the charge of God's elect? who is he that condemneth?" Faith is Saul praying in the house of Judas at Damascus, sorrowful, blind, and alone ; assurance is Paul the aged prisoner looking calmly into the grave, and saying, " I know whom I have believed ; there is a crown laid up for me."

Faith is life. How great the blessing ! Who can tell the gulf between life and death? Yet life may be weak, sickly, unhealthy, painful, trying, anxious, worn, burdensome, joyless, smileless, to the last. Assurance is more than life. It is health, strength, power, vigour, activity, energy, manliness, beauty.

Brethren, it is not a question of saved or not saved, but of privilege or no privilege ; it is not a question of peace or no peace, but of great peace or little peace ; it is not a question between the wanderers of this world and the school of Christ, it is one that belongs only to the school, it is between the first form and the last. He that has faith does well. Happy should I feel, if I thought you all had it. Blessed, thrice blessed, are they that believe : they are safe ; they are washed ; they are justified ; they are beyond the power of hell. But he that has assurance does far better, sees more, feels more, knows more, enjoys more, has more days like those spoken of in Deuteronomy, the days of heaven upon earth.'

III. I pass on to the third thing of which I spoke. I will give you some reasons why an assured hope is exceedingly to be desired.

I ask your attention to this point especially. I heartily wish that assurance was more sought after than it is. Too many among us begin doubting and go on doubting, live doubting, die doubting, and go to heaven in a kind of mist. It would ill become me ¡to speak slightingly of " hopes " and " trusts," but I fear many

of us sit down content with them and go no further.
I would like to see fewer "peradventures" in the Lord's
family, and more who could say "I know, and am
persuaded." Oh! that you would all covet the best
gifts, and not be content with less. You miss the full
tide of blessedness the gospel was meant to convey.
You keep yourselves in a low and starved condition
of soul, while your Lord is saying, "Eat and drink,
O beloved, that your joy may be full."

1. Know then, for one thing, that assurance is a thing
to be desired, because of the present joy and peace it
affords. Doubts and fears have great power to mar the
comfort of a true believer. Uncertainty and suspense
are bad enough in any condition—in the matter of our
health, our property, our families, our affections, our
earthly callings—but never so bad as in the affairs of our
souls. Now so long as a believer cannot get beyond "I
hope and I trust," he manifestly feels a certain degree
of uncertainty about his spiritual state. The very words
imply as much: he says "I hope" because he dare not
say "I know."

Assurance, my brethren, goes far to set a child of
God free from this painful kind of bondage, and mightily
ministers to comfort. It gives him joy and peace in
believing. It makes him patient in tribulation, contented
in trial, calm in affliction, unmoved in sorrow, not
afraid of evil tidings. It sweetens his bitter cups, it
lessens the burden of his crosses, it smooths the rough
places on which he travels, it lightens the valley of
the shadow of death. It makes him feel as if he had
something solid beneath his feet and something firm
under his hand, a sure Friend by the way and a sure
home in the end. He feels that the great business of
life is a settled business—debt, disaster, work, and all
other business is by comparison small. Assurance

will help a man to bear poverty and loss, it will teach him
to say, " I know that I have in heaven a better and more
enduring substance. Silver and gold have I none, but
grace and glory are mine and can never be taken away."
Assurance will support a man in sickness, make all his
bed, smooth his pillow. It will enable him to say, " If
my earthly house of this tabernacle fail, I have a building of God, an house not made with hands, eternal in
the heaven. . . . I desire to depart and be with Christ.
My flesh and my heart may fail, but God is the strength
of my heart and my portion for ever."

He that has assured hope can sing in prison, like
Paul and Silas at Philippi. Assurance can give songs
in the night. He can sleep with the full prospect of
execution on the morrow, like Peter in Herod's dungeon.
Assurance says, " I will lay me down and take my rest,
for thou, Lord, makest me dwell in safety." He can
rejoice to suffer shame for Christ's sake, as the apostles
did. Assurance says, " Rejoice and be exceeding glad
—there is a far more exceeding and eternal weight of
glory." He can meet a violent and painful death without fear, as Stephen did in olden time, and Cranmer,
Ridley, Latimer and Taylor in our own land. Assurance
says—" Fear not them which kill the body, and after that
have no more they can do. Lord Jesus, into Thy hand
I commend my spirit."

Ah, brethren, the comfort assurance can give in the
hour of death is a great point, depend upon it, and never
will you think it so great as when your turn comes to
die. In that awful hour there are few believers who
do not find out the value and privilege of assurance,
whatever they may have thought about it in their lives ;
general hopes and trusts are all very well to live upon,
but when you come to die you will want to be able to
say, " I *know* and I *feel*." Believe me, Jordan is a cold

stream to cross alone. The last enemy, even death, is a strong foe. When our souls are in departing, there is no cordial like the strong wine of assurance.

There is a beautiful expression in the Prayer-book's Visitation of the Sick. "The Almighty Lord, who is a most strong tower to all them that put their trust in Him, be now and evermore thy defence, and make thee *know* and *feel* that there is none other name under heaven through whom thou mayest receive health and salvation, but only the name of our Lord Jesus Christ." The compilers of that Service showed great wisdom there : they saw that when the eyes grow dim and the heart grows faint, there must be *knowing* and *feeling* what Christ has done for us if there is to be perfect peace.

2. Let me name another thing. Assurance is to be desired, because it tends to make a Christian an active, useful Christian. None, generally speaking, do so much for Christ on earth as those who enjoy the fullest confidence of a free entrance into heaven. That sounds wonderful, I daresay, but it is true.

A believer who lacks an assured hope will spend much of his time in inward searchings of heart about his own state. He will be full of his own doubtings and questionings, his own conflicts and corruptions. In short, you will often find that he is so taken up with this internal warfare that he has little leisure for other things, little time to work for God.

Now a believer who has, like Paul, an assured hope is free from these harassing distractions. He does not vex his soul with doubts about his own pardon and acceptance. He looks at the covenant sealed with blood, at the finished work and never-broken word of his Lord and Saviour, and therefore counts his salvation a *settled thing*. And thus he is able to give an undivided attention to the Lord's work, and so in the long run to do more.

Take, for an illustration of this, two English emigrants, and suppose them set down side by side in Australia or New Zealand. Give each of them a piece of land to clear and cultivate. Secure that land to them by every needful legal instrument, let it be conveyed as freehold to them and theirs for ever, let the conveyance be publicly registered, and the property made sure to them by every deed and security that man's ingenuity can devise. Suppose, then, that one of them shall set to work to bring his land into cultivation, and labour at it day after day without intermission or cessation. Suppose, in the meanwhile, that the other shall be continually leaving his work, and repeatedly going to the public registry to ask whether the land really is his own—whether there is not some mistake—whether after all there is not some flaw in the legal instruments which conveyed it to him. The one shall never doubt his title, but just diligently work on ; the other shall never feel sure of his title, and spend half his time in going to Sydney or Auckland with needless inquiries about it. Which, now, of these two men will have made most progress in a year's time ? Who will have done the most for his land, got the greatest breadth under tillage, have the best crops to show ? You all know as well as I do—I need not supply an answer. There can only be one reply.

Brethren, so will it be in the matter of our title to " mansions in the skies." None will do so much for the Lord who bought them as the believer who sees that title clear. The joy of the Lord will be that man's strength. " Restore unto me," says David, " the joy of Thy salvation ; . . . then will I teach transgressors Thy

ways." Never were there such working Christians as
the apostles. They seemed to live to labour: Christ's
work was their meat and drink. They counted not
their lives dear; they spent and were spent; they
laid down health, ease, worldly comfort at the foot of
the cross. And one cause of this, I believe, was their
assured hope. They were men that said, " We know
that we are of God."

3. Let me name another thing. Assurance is to be
desired, because it tends to make a Christian a decided
Christian. Indecision and doubt about our own state
in God's sight is a grievous disease, and the mother
of many evils. It often produces a wavering and an
unstable walk in following the Lord. Assurance helps
to cut many a knot, and to make the path of Christian
duty clear and plain. Many, of whom we feel a hope
that they are God's children, and have grace, however
weak, are continually perplexed with doubts on points
of practice. " Should we do such and such a thing?
Shall we give up this family custom? Ought we to
go to that place? How shall we draw the line about
visiting? What is to be the measure of our dressing
and entertainments? Are we never to dance, never
to play at cards, never to attend pleasure parties?"
These are questions which seem to give them constant
trouble. And often, very often, the simple root of
this perplexity is that they do not feel assured that
they themselves are children of God. They have not
yet settled the point which side of the gate they are
on. They do not know whether they are inside the
ark or not.

That a child of God ought to act in a certain decided
way they quite feel, but the grand question is, " Are
they children of God themselves?" If they only felt
they were so, they would go straightforward and take

a decided line ; but not feeling sure about it, their
conscience is for ever coming to a dead-lock. The devil
whispers, " Perhaps, after all, you are only a hypocrite ;
what right have you to take a decided course ? wait till
you are really a Christian." And this whisper too often
just turns the scale, and leads on to some wretched
conformity to the world.

Brethren, I verily believe you have here one reason
why so many are inconsistent, unsatisfactory, and half-
hearted in their conduct about the world. They feel
no assurance that they are Christ's, and so they feel
a hesitancy about breaking with the world. They
shrink from laying aside all the ways of the old man,
because they are not confident they have put on the
new. Depend upon it, one secret of halting between
two opinions is want of assurance.

4. Let me name one thing more. Assurance is to be
desired because it tends to make the holiest Christians.

This, too, sounds wonderful and strange, and yet it
is true. It is one of the paradoxes of the Gospel, contrary, at first sight, to reason and common-sense, and
yet it is a fact. Bellarmine was seldom more wide of
the truth than when he said, " Assurance tends to carelessness and sloth." He that is freely forgiven by
Christ will always do much for Christ's glory, and he
that has the fullest assurance of this forgiveness will
ordinarily keep up the closest walk with God. It is
a faithful saying in the first Epistle of John, " Every
man that hath this hope in him purifieth himself, even
as He is pure."

None are so likely to maintain a watchful guard over
their heart and life, as those who know the comfort of
living in near communion with God. They feel their
privilege, and will fear losing it. They will dread
falling from their high estate and marring their own

comforts by inconsistencies. He that goes a journey
and has little money to lose, takes little thought of
danger, and cares not how late he travels in a dangerous
country. He that carries gold and jewels, on the contrary, will be a cautious traveller : he will look well
to his road, his house, and his company, and run no
risks. The fixed stars are those that tremble most.
The man that most fully enjoys the light of God's
reconciled countenance will be a man tremblingly afraid
of losing its blessed comfort, and jealously fearful of
doing anything to grieve the Holy Ghost.

Beloved brethren, would you have great peace ?
Would you like to feel the everlasting arms around you,
and to hear the voice of Jesus drawing nigh to your
soul, and saying, " I am thy salvation "? Would you
be useful in your day and generation ? Would you be
known of all as bold, firm, decided, single-eyed followers
of Christ ? Would you be eminently spiritually-minded
and holy ? " Ah ! " you will some of you say, " these
are the very things we desire : we long for them, we
pant after them, but they seem far from us."

Then take my advice this day. Seek an assured hope,
like Paul's. Seek to obtain a simple, childlike confidence
in God's promises. Seek to be able to say with the
apostle, " I know whom I have believed ; I am persuaded
that He is mine and I am His."

You have many of you tried the ways and methods,
and completely failed. Change your plan. Go upon
another tack. Begin with assurance. Lay aside your
doubts. Cast aside your faithless backwardness to take
the Lord at His word. Come and roll yourself, your
soul and your sins upon your gracious Saviour. Begin
with simple believing, and all other things shall soon
be added to you.

IV. I come to the last thing of which I spoke. I

promised to point out some probable causes why an assured hope is so seldom attained. I will do so very shortly.

This, brethren, is a very serious question, and ought to raise in us all great searchings of heart. Few certainly of all the sheep of Christ ever seem to reach this blessed spirit of assurance. Many, comparatively, believe, but few are persuaded. Many, comparatively, have saving faith, but few that glorious confidence which shines forth in our text.

Now, why is this so? Why is a thing which Peter enjoins as a positive duty a thing of which few believers have an experimental knowledge? Why is an assured hope so rare?

I desire to offer a few suggestions on this point with all humility. I know that many have never attained assurance, at whose feet I would gladly sit both in earth and heaven. *Perhaps* the Lord sees something in some men's natural temperament which makes assurance not good for them. Perhaps to be kept in spiritual health they need to be kept very low. God only knows. Still, after every allowance, I fear there are many believers without an assured hope, whose case may too often be explained by causes such as these.

1. One common cause, I suspect, is a defective view of the doctrine of justification. I am inclined to think that justification and sanctification are in many minds insensibly confused together. They receive the gospel truth that there must be something done *in us*, as well as something done *for us*, if we are true believers ; and so far they are right. But then, without being aware of it perhaps, they seem to imbibe the idea, that this justification is in some degree affected by something within themselves. They do not clearly see that

Christ's work and not their own work, either in whole
or in part, either directly or indirectly, alone is the
ground of our acceptance with God ; that justification
is a thing entirely without us, and nothing is needful
on our part but simple faith, and that the weakest
believer is as fully justified as the strongest. They
appear to forget sometimes that we are saved and
justified as sinners, and only as sinners, and that we
never can attain to anything higher if we live to the
age of Methuselah.   Redeemed sinners, justified sinners,
and renewed sinners doubtless we must be, but sinners,
sinners always to the very last.   They seem, too, to
expect that a believer may some time in his life be in a
measure free from corruption, and attain to a kind of
inward perfection.   And not finding this angelical state
of things in their own hearts, they at once conclude
there must be something wrong, go mourning all their
days, and are oppressed with fears that they have no
part or lot in Christ.

My dear brethren, if you or any believing soul here
desires assurance and has not got it, go and ask yourself
first of all if you are sound in the faith, if your loins
are thoroughly girt about with truth and your eyes
thoroughly clear in the matter of justification.

2. Another common cause, I am afraid, is slothfulness
about growth in grace.   I suspect many believers hold
dangerous and unscriptural views on this point.   Many
appear to me to think that, once converted, they have
little more to attend to—that a state of salvation is a
kind of easy-chair, in which they may just sit still, lie
back, and be happy.   They seem to fancy that grace
is given them that they may enjoy it, and they forget
that it is given to be used and employed, like a talent.
Such persons lose sight of the many direct injunctions
to increase, to grow, to abound more and more, to add

to our faith and the like ; and in this do-little condition
of mind I never marvel that they miss assurance.

Brethren, you must always remember there is an
inseparable connection between assurance and diligence.
" Give diligence," says Peter, "to make your calling
and election sure." " I desire," says Paul, "that every
one of you do show the same diligence to the full
assurance of hope unto the end." " It is the diligent
soul," says the Proverb, " that shall be made fat."
There is much truth in the maxim of the Puritans,
" Faith of adherence comes by hearing, but faith of
assurance comes not without doing."

3. Another common cause is an inconsistent walk in
life. With grief and sorrow I feel constrained to say,
I fear nothing in this day more frequently prevents
men attaining an assured hope than this. Inconsistency of life is utterly destructive of great peace of
heart. The two things are incompatible. They cannot
go together. If you will have your besetting sins, and
cannot make up your minds to give them up, if you
shrink from cutting off the right hand and plucking
out the right eye when required, I will engage you
shall have no assurance. A vacillating walk, a backwardness to take a bold and decided line, a readiness to
conform to the world, a hesitating witness for Christ, a
lingering tone of profession, all these make up a sure
recipe for bringing a blight upon the garden of your
soul. It is vain to suppose you will feel assured and
persuaded of your pardon and peace, unless you count
all God's commandments concerning all things to be
right, and hate every sin whether great or small. One
Achan allowed in the camp of your heart will poison
all your springs of comfort.

I bless God our salvation in no sense depends on our
own works. " By grace are we saved ; " not by works

of righteousness that we have done, through faith, without the deed of the law. But I never would have any believer for a moment forget that our *sense* of salvation depends much on the manner of our living. Inconsistency will dim your eyes and bring clouds between you and the sun. The sun is the same, but you will not be able to see its brightness and enjoy its warmth. It is in the path of well-doing that assurance will come down and meet you. "The secret of the Lord," says David, "is with them that fear Him." "Great peace have they that love thy law : and nothing shall offend them." "To him that ordereth his conversation aright will I show the salvation of God." Paul was a man who exercised himself to have a conscience void of offence toward God and toward man ; he could say boldly, "I have fought a good fight, ... I have kept the faith." I do not wonder that the Lord enabled him to add confidently, " Henceforth there is laid up for me a crown of righteousness, which the Lord, the righteous judge, shall give me at that day."

Brethren, I commend the three points I have just named to your own private consideration. I am sure they are worth thinking over, and I advise every believer present who lacks assurance to do it. And may the Lord give him understanding in this and all things.

And now, brethren, in closing this sermon, let me speak first to those among you who have not yet believed, have not yet come out from the world, chosen the good part and followed Christ. See, then, my dear friends, from this subject the real privilege of a true Christian. Judge not the Lord Jesus Christ by His people. Judge not the comforts of His kingdom by the measure to which many of His subjects attain.

Alas! we are many of us poor creatures. We come
short, very short of the blessedness we might enjoy.
But depend upon it there are glorious things in the
city of our God, which they who have an assured
hope taste even in their lifetime. There is bread
enough and to spare in our Father's house, though
many of us, alas! eat but little of it, and continue
weak.

And why should not you enter in and share our
privileges? Why should not you come with us and
sit down by our side? What can the world give you,
after all, which will bear comparison with the hope of
the least member of the family of Christ? Verily the
weakest child of God has got more durable riches in
his hand than the wealthiest man of the world that ever
breathed. Oh! but I feel deeply for you in these days,
if ever I did. I feel deeply for those whose treasure
is all on earth and whose hopes are this side the grave.
Yes! when I see old kingdoms and dynasties shaking
to the very foundations; when I see property dependent
on public confidence melting like snow in spring, when
I see stocks and shares and funds losing their value, I
do feel deeply for those who have no better portion, no
place in a kingdom that cannot be removed.

Take the advice of a minister of Christ. Seek a
treasure that cannot be taken from you; seek a city
which hath lasting foundations. Do as the apostle
Paul did. Give yourself to Christ, and seek an incorruptible crown that fadeth not away. Come to
the Lord Jesus Christ as lowly sinners, and He will
receive you, pardon you, give you His renewing Spirit,
fill you with peace. This shall give you more real
comfort than this world has ever done. There is a
gulf in your heart which nothing but Christ can fill.

Lastly, let me turn to all believers here present and

speak to them a few words of brotherly counsel. For one thing, resolve this day to seek after an assured hope, if you do not feel you have got it. Believe, me, believe me, it is worth the seeking. If it is good to be sure in earthly things, how much better is it to be sure in heavenly things! Seek to know that you have a title, good and solid and not to be overthrown. Your salvation is a fixed and certain thing. God knows it. Why should not you seek to know it too? Paul never saw the book of life ; and yet Paul says "I know and am persuaded." Go home and pray for an increase of faith. Cultivate that blessed root more, and then by God's blessing you shall have the flower.

For another thing, be not surprised if you do not attain assurance all at once. It is good sometimes to be kept waiting. We do not value things which we get without trouble. Joseph waited long for deliverance from prison, but it came at length. For another thing, be not surprised at occasional doubts after you have got assurance. No morning sun lasts all the day. There is a devil, and a strong devil too, and he will take care you know it. You must not forget you are on earth and not in heaven. Some doubt there always will be. He that never doubts has nothing to lose. He that never fears possesses nothing truly valuable. He that is never jealous knows little of deep love.

And finally do not forget that assurance is a thing that may be lost. Oh! it is a most delicate plant. It needs daily, hourly watching, watering, tending, cherishing. So take care. David lost it. Peter lost it. Each found it again, but not till after bitter tears. Quench not the Spirit; grieve Him not; vex Him not. Drive Him not to a distance by tampering with small bad habits and little sins. Little jarrings make unhappy homes, and petty inconsistencies will bring in a strangeness between you and the Spirit.

Hear the conclusion of the whole matter. The nearest walker with God will generally be kept in the greatest peace. The believer who follows the Lord most fully will ordinarily enjoy the most assured hope.